COLLABORATING
With **Students** in **Instruction**
and **Decision Making**

This book is dedicated to the most valuable resource in schools today—the students themselves and the teachers and other school personnel who meaningfully collaborate with students in instruction, advocacy, and decision making to unleash a powerful force to facilitate change and progress in education.

COLLABORATING
With **Students** in **Instruction** and **Decision Making**

The Untapped Resource

Richard A. Villa

Jacqueline S. Thousand

Ann I. Nevin

Foreword by Paula Kluth and Peyton Goddard

CORWIN
A SAGE Company

For information:

Corwin
A SAGE Company
2455 Teller Road
Thousand Oaks, California 91320
(800) 233-9936
Fax: (800) 417-2466
www.corwin.com

SAGE Ltd.
1 Oliver's Yard
55 City Road
London EC1Y 1SP
United Kingdom

SAGE India Pvt. Ltd.
B 1/I 1 Mohan Cooperative
    Industrial Area
Mathura Road, New Delhi
India 110 044

SAGE Asia-Pacific Pte. Ltd.
33 Pekin Street #02-01
Far East Square
Singapore 048763

Printed in the United States of America

Library of Congress Cataloging-in-Publication Data

Villa, Richard A., 1952-
Collaborating with students in instruction and decision making : the untapped resource / Richard A. Villa, Jacqueline S. Thousand, Ann I. Nevin ; foreword by Paula Kluth and Peyton Goddard.
       p. cm.
Includes bibliographical references and index.
ISBN 978-1-4129-7217-8 (pbk.)

    1. Peer-group tutoring of students. 2. Teacher-student relationships. 3. Student participation in administration. 4. Student participation in curriculum planning. 5. Education—Decision making. I. Thousand, Jacqueline S., 1950- II. Nevin, Ann. III. Title.

LB1031.5.V45 2010
371.39'4—dc22   2009051380

This book is printed on acid-free paper.

10   11   12   13   14   10   9   8   7   6   5   4   3   2   1

Acquisitions Editor:	Jessica Allan
Editorial Assistant:	Sarah Bartlett
Production Editor:	Eric Garner
Copy Editor:	Paula L. Fleming
Typesetter:	C&M Digitals (P) Ltd.
Proofreader:	Susan Schon
Indexer:	Jean Casalegno
Cover Designer:	Karine Hovsepian

Contents

List of Tables and Figures

TABLES

FIGURES

Acknowledgments

Corwin gratefully acknowledges the contributions of the following individuals:

Sherry L. Annee, Biotechnology Instructor
Brebeuf Jesuit Preparatory School
Indianapolis, IN

Laurie Emery, Principal
Old Vail Middle School
Vail, AZ

Richard Jones, Principal
John Adams Middle School
Rochester, MN

Toni Jones, Principal
Deer Creek Public School
Edmond, OK

Beth Madison, Principal
George Middle School
Portland, OR

About the Authors

Ann I. Nevin, Richard A. Villa, and Jacqueline S. Thousand
Working, Learning, Teaching, and Writing Together!

Photographer: Ezral Anthony Wallace

Richard A. Villa, EdD, has worked with thousands of teachers and administrators throughout North America. In addition, Rich has provided technical assistance to the U.S., Canadian, Vietnamese, Laotian, British, and Honduran Departments of Education. His primary field of expertise is the development of administrative and instructional support systems for educating all students within general education settings. Rich has been a middle and high school classroom teacher, special educator, special education coordinator, pupil personal services director, and director of instructional services. He has authored over a hundred articles and book chapters regarding inclusive education, differentiated instruction, collaborative planning and teaching, and school restructuring. Known for his enthusiastic, knowledgeable, and humorous style of teaching, Rich is a gifted communicator who has the conceptual, technical, and interpersonal skills to facilitate change in education. His professional development activities have covered a range including keynote addresses and papers presented at national and international conferences, two-day guided practice workshops for school teams, three-to-five day programs, three-week intensive workshops, and semester-long (15 weeks) programs offered through universities.

Jacqueline S. Thousand, PhD, is a Professor in the College of Education at California State University San Marcos, where she co-coordinates the special education professional preparation and master's programs. Prior to coming to California, she directed Inclusion Facilitator and Early Childhood Special Education graduate and postgraduate professional preparation programs at the University of Vermont. Here she also coordinated several federal grants, all concerned with providing professional development for educators to facilitate the inclusion of students with disabilities in local schools. Jacqueline is a nationally known teacher, author, systems change consultant, and advocate for disability rights and inclusive education. She has authored numerous books, research articles, and chapters on issues related to inclusive schooling, organizational change, differentiated instruction and universal design, cooperative group learning, creative problem solving, and co-teaching and collaborative planning. She is actively involved in international teacher education endeavors and serves on the editorial boards of several national and international journals. Jacqueline is a versatile communicator who is known for her creative, fun-filled, action-oriented teaching style.

Ann I. Nevin, PhD, Professor Emerita at Arizona State University and faculty affiliate of Chapman University in Orange, California, has a proven track record of collaborating with K–12 students and college students in ways that allow their voices to be heard. The author of books, research articles, and numerous chapters, Ann is recognized for her scholarship and dedication to providing meaningful, practice-oriented, research-based strategies for teachers to integrate students with special learning needs. Since the 1970s, she has co-developed various innovative teacher education programs, including the Vermont Consulting Teacher Program, Council for Exceptional Children Collaborative Consultation Project Re-Tool, the Arizona State University program for special educators to infuse self-determination skills throughout the curriculum, and the Urban SEALS (Special Education Academic Leaders) doctoral program at Florida International University. Her advocacy, research, and teaching spans more than 35 years of working with a diverse array of people to help students with disabilities succeed in normalized school environments.

Part I

Introduction

There are three components to Part I: Introduction. The Foreword features Professor Paula Kluth, a researcher and advocate for augmented communication techniques that allows students to express themselves, and Peyton Goddard, a student and recent college graduate who has had the experience of advocating for augmented communication to allow her own thoughts and wishes to be heard. This is followed by the authors' letter to the reader, which outlines the reasons why they wrote this book. In Chapter 1, the authors address several questions: Why are students not motivated or involved in their own education today? Why are teachers not collaborating more with students in teaching and decision making? How does student collaboration fit with 21st-century goals of education and the Circle of Courage? How does student collaboration interface with or support notions of democratic schooling? How does student collaboration enhance student self-determination? How does student collaboration enhance achievement of academic and social goals? How does student collaboration fit in with the limited fiscal and human resources now facing public schools?

In addressing these questions, the authors suggest there are several rationales for student collaboration. Specifically, student collaboration (a) facilitates 21st-century goals of education, (b) is an example of democratic schooling, (c) increases self-determination of students, (d) increases academic and social competence of students, (e) facilitates school reform efforts, and (e) represents an untapped resource in times of limited fiscal and human resources. We hope you'll add your own voice to support these reasons for embracing student collaboration.

Foreword

The Importance of Students' Voices

Paula Kluth and Peyton Goddard

In 2003, fifth graders from Room 405 at Richard E. Byrd Community Academy, a Chicago public school, decided they needed a new school. Byrd was located near Cabrini Green, a large housing project in Chicago, and most of the students at the school lived right in the neighborhood. Working with their teacher, Brian Schulz, the students decided they could and should create a better place to learn for themselves. Following is an excerpt from the mission statement they wrote at the outset of their journey:

> *Our school building, Richard E. Byrd Community Academy, has so many problems we do not think it can be fixed. We created a web graphic organizer to put down all the ideas we had about what was wrong with our school. Here is a list of all the major problems about our school: the restrooms, office, windows, water fountains, classrooms, temperature, library, outside all need a lot of help. In addition our school does not even have a gym, lunchroom, or auditorium/stage. Based on all these problems we think we need a whole new school.*
>
> *The issue of our building being messed up is a serious problem. Our school is not safe, comfortable, or a good place to learn because of all these things wrong with it. We think kids deserve to have a safe, comfortable, and nice place to learn. (Room 405 Website, 2005)*

The story is a bit astounding, not only because they took on this serious problem themselves but because they were so successful. The students wrote an 11-point action plan. It included photographing the school's problems, surveying the student body, and researching the construction funding plans for public schools. They also launched an aggressive letter and e-mail campaign targeting elected officials, journalists, and decision makers within the school system.

Though the district eventually closed Byrd and sent the students to a neighboring school instead of building a new one, the students did more than create a stir. They attracted reporters not only from local news outlets but from National Public Radio. They created their own documentary film. They had visitors ranging from state politicians to Ralph Nader. They received over a hundred letters of support from professors, lawmakers, teachers, and citizens and even got one from the vice president of the United States.

This story is one of many in which student voices were valued, heard, and, in many ways, honored. It is powerful because it not only causes us to celebrate the potential of our youth but may help us see how children and teens can have a real impact on the world and change not only educational outcomes but the act of teaching itself.

Unfortunately, student voices have not always been at the center of teaching and learning in this country despite the many stories we have all heard about student creativity, leadership, and innovation. Many obstacles, of course, hold teachers back from empowering learners to take control of their educational experiences and from working collaboratively with students. One obstacle is certainly the norms and traditions of schooling itself. It is common to see students being taught but not common to see students co-teaching with their instructors, and it is even less common to see them teaching without the support of a teacher. It is common to see students working in groups but uncommon to see them forming groups and leading them. It is common to see students completing work assigned by teachers but uncommon to see students addressing real problems that they see in the world and developing solutions to them.

Another barrier has been teacher education. Few collaboration courses for preservice teachers feature students as a resource for problem solving, curriculum planning, or teaching. New teachers, therefore, may be coming out of their preparation programs without an understanding of all that is possible for the learners in their care. Even at the college level, students are seldom seen as problem solvers or creators of authentic products or solutions. I remember the reactions I received from my first class of preservice teachers when I asked them to create products not for me but for their community, their school, or themselves. Instead of asking them to take tests or compose essays, I asked them to write papers for possible publication, to create children's literature, to assemble a presentation for fellow teachers, to propose a program, or to craft a solution to a problem they saw in their school or community. Some were excited, but many others seemed initially stumped or confused by the invitation to create and think out of the box.

Finally, teachers may encounter the barrier of having few resources to support this work of creativity and collaboration. Thanks to Rich Villa, Jacque Thousand, and Ann Nevin and this fantastic resource you hold in your hands, however, this final barrier is getting easier and easier to traverse. This book will help all of those educators who have felt that they didn't have a resource with tips on how to create student collaboration or those who were unsure of the research behind this work. It will also help any teacher who feels alone. As you read this book, you will meet other educators who took risks, proposed solutions, navigated difficult questions, and found new excitement in their teaching by collaborating with their students.

To date, this is the most comprehensive guide to working alongside students in our diverse schools. In reading this very important text, even the most savvy and teaming-oriented teacher will gain new ideas for designing lessons, providing instruction, meeting individual student needs, motivating learners, and creating safer and more peaceful schools. The primary reason, however, for celebrating this text is that it is the only one of its kind to consider the needs of and, of course, the voices of students who are the most marginalized in our schools. In addition to providing ideas relevant across ethnicity, race, region, and learning profiles, the book also feature the stories of students with disabilities. The authors make it quite clear that we can "listen" to all student voices, even when the individuals of concern communicate in alternative ways, do not have the language or experience of having agency or creating change, or need support from others to express themselves.

Instead of attempting to expand on how important this work is, I will hand this part of the Foreword over to my colleague, Peyton Goddard, who has more than a few things to express about power, collaboration, and voice.

In 1977 at the age of three, a joy-filled girl named Peyton Goddard was segregated into special education. She spent the following two decades in restricted placements, where she lost her joy and gained multiple labels, including severely mentally retarded and autistic. Since she was nonverbal and unable to point dependably or replicate sign language, educators assumed she had nothing to say and, thus, denied her the support she required to learn and communicate in alternative ways. Living in despair, she saw a life she'd never want anyone to teach as being acceptable for any human being.

In 1997, after years of silent pleas, hope arrived in the form of augmentative alternative communication, and she gained a dependable way to communicate. The strategy she uses to communicate, called facilitated communication, involves a trained support person offering a combination of physical and emotional support so she can type with one finger on a keyboard. In 2002, she graduated valedictorian from Cuyamaca Community College with nearly a 4.0 average. Today, she is living near her parents in her own apartment with 24-hour support, and she is writing a memoir of her life.

Here in Peyton's own words are answers to three questions we asked of her.

Why is it important for school personnel to listen to the voice of students in determining placement, instruction, accommodations, and support?

I'm wasted 22 years in no education. Puny, I wept, desiring death. Young, eased I was to news that I'm revered nothing, esteemed nothing. Treed like an animal, I was led tugged to red hot anger, to rest never. Red anger in devalued peoples, trees us all red in this warring, wasted-joy, worrisome world. Each destiny-errored, festered-sad, differently-wired but "cares to learn" child, needs assurance they are not weeds but fragrant flowers of vast points to be greeted as valuable. Support all voices in determining their destiny and these points of opportunity, I point out:

1. *Kids will not simmer or explode in anger, coping with pity of no one esteeming them.*
2. *Kids' wars over feeling no worth, will epitome end.*
3. *World will move in joy, not in wars.*

What can school personnel do to help students discover their voice?

There, in either the tested room or the class room, best tell each cherub that they can lead. Say that they are the guiders to test the best ways to heat their versed, vested, vastly valuable, vellum varied, esteemed equated equal, red news never viewed, volumed voices. Tease these cherubs never with fears you will try only one way to help them access speech. When they know their differences will be supported by you saying you will never stop trying ways to help them find their very best voice, their fears rest. There, they are not awed by pity. There, esteem is greeted. I'm in peace because someone saw all people are real and deserve being supported to communicate their truths.

In your K–12 experience, what has happened when your voice has been heard and also when it has NOT been heard?

I'm heard zero, I point out. I'm gyred up, I'm gyred down, whipped into sweared want death, my meal opted over. Queer modes of my actions festered. In wasp by eddy of never being in unity with creation, I was upped insane. There pouts melted me.

Now you greet me as a writer who is stretching your imaginings to pity me not, but to cope with kissing the news that "I'm real, ain't that a sweet saw surprise!" And I am possessed of voice, as you are too.

Letter to the Reader

Have you ever wondered how you could personalize and individualize instruction for every student in your classroom? In spite of budget cuts and scarcity of resources, do you want your students to experience collaborative and creative roles in advocacy, instruction, conflict resolution, and decision making? Do you want your students to value each other's intellectual, cultural, and linguistic differences and experience an increased sense of well-being and belonging? Do you want your students to thrive academically, socially, and emotionally? Do you wonder how to encourage your students to express their opinions, their voices, and become more responsible for their own learning?

Teachers and administrators face many competing priorities, such as meeting state and national mandates for higher school achievement, individualizing instruction to meet the steady increase in the diversity of the student population, and implementing new systems for early identification and the prevention of school failure (i.e., Response to Intervention or RTI). These priorities do not diminish even in times of scarcity, when budget constraints bring about reductions in force. We have heard many teachers ask for extra help in the classroom to differentiate instruction so that goals like these can be achieved by their diverse student populations. We suggest that they turn to an untapped resource—the students themselves! We wrote this book so that you could tap into the most valuable resource we have in our schools—the students themselves.

As a 21st-century educator, you are well aware that a critical challenge in today's schools involves society's responses to diversity, from segregating or shunning (marginalizing) to consciously valuing and including those who are different. When teachers help their students learn to value their own and others' differences, everyone becomes enriched. Edvard Befring (2000), a Norwegian educator who has pioneered inclusive strategies in Scandinavia, believes that when a classroom community adopts an enrichment perspective, all students gain an opportunity to be respected for their cultural and learning differences. He wrote,

> The Enrichment Perspective holds promise for status to be given to differences and for diversity to be celebrated rather than lamented; it holds promise for the elimination of isolation and disenfranchisement of children with disabilities and other differentiating characteristics such as learners of English as a second language. (Befring, Thousand, & Nevin, 2000, p. 574).

Throughout the book, we share what we have learned from working with students and their teachers who have actualized an enrichment perspective as they coached and mentored their students to become co-teachers, decision makers, and advocates as part of their educational programs. We want you to be assured that there is a knowledge base (solidly grounded in evidence-based research) for students in these nontraditional roles. Achievement measures increase when students learn by peer tutoring, reciprocal teaching, partner learning, and serving as peer mediators of conflict and by participating in cooperative learning groups, community-based education, service learning, and other instructional strategies. In addition, students learn important social and emotional skills as they interact with others, especially those who are different from themselves.

We acknowledge the cutting-edge nature of many of the techniques and strategies described in this book. We honor those teachers and administrators who are leading the field into new ways of thinking about teaching and learning and collaborating with students. We anchor our strategies with vignettes that directly capture the real-life experiences of teachers and students. Reproducible resources, such as lesson plans, agenda formats, and procedures, are included to keep track of student progress. To improve the usefulness of the book, we provide attractive graphic organizers and helpful checklists as well as a glossary of key terms.

Before you begin your examination of the strategies described in this book, we invite you to reflect on your own personal experiences as a student. To what extent did you participate in experiences that allowed you to take on collaborative and creative roles? Please take a moment to respond to the 15 questions in the Student Collaboration Quiz shown in Table I.1. We believe that, when you take the quiz, you will increase your awareness of your own experiences as a student, and you will be prepared to pick out salient points of the theoretical and practical features you will discover in this book.

As you reflect upon your answers to the quiz, think about how your experiences as a student may have influenced your teaching practices and the collaborative opportunities you make available to your students today. Finally, think about how the collaborative experiences suggested in the quiz and detailed in this book might facilitate student growth in both academic and social domains (i.e., mastery, independence, belonging, and generosity).

DEFINITION OF COLLABORATION WITH STUDENTS

As you read this book, you will discover that the definition of *collaboration with students* is complex, broad, and deep. Collaboration with students means directly involving students in the design, delivery, and evaluation of instruction. It means students working in cooperative learning groups, as tutors and partners in partner learning, and as co-teachers with their teachers. Collaboration with students means involving students as decision makers and problem solvers, as designers of their own learning, and in being self-determined in planning for

Table I.1   Student Collaboration Quiz (for Teachers)

Directions: Please circle the rating that best fits your own experience as a student.

1. How often were you expected to support the academic and social learning of other students, as well as be accountable for your own learning, by working in cooperative groups?

    | Never | Rarely | Sometimes | Often | Very Often |

2. Were you, as a student, given the opportunity and training to serve as an instructor for a peer?

    | Never | Rarely | Sometimes | Often | Very Often |

3. Were you, as a student, given the opportunity to receive instruction from a trained peer?

    | Never | Rarely | Sometimes | Often | Very Often |

4. How often were you involved in a discussion of the teaching act with an instructor?

    | Never | Rarely | Sometimes | Often | Very Often |

5. Were you, as a student, given the opportunity to co-teach a class with an adult?

    | Never | Rarely | Sometimes | Often | Very Often |

6. How often were you taught creative problem-solving strategies and given an opportunity to employ them to solve academic or behavioral challenges?

    | Never | Rarely | Sometimes | Often | Very Often |

7. How often were you asked to evaluate your own learning?

    | Never | Rarely | Sometimes | Often | Very Often |

8. How often were you given the opportunity to assist in determining the educational outcomes for you and your classmates?

    | Never | Rarely | Sometimes | Often | Very Often |

9. How often were you given the opportunity to advocate for the educational interests of a classmate or asked to assist in determining modifications and accommodations to curriculum?

    | Never | Rarely | Sometimes | Often | Very Often |

10. How often were you asked to provide your teachers with feedback as to the effectiveness and appropriateness of their instruction and classroom management?

    | Never | Rarely | Sometimes | Often | Very Often |

11. Were you, as a student, given the opportunity and training to serve as a mediator of conflict between peers?

    | Never | Rarely | Sometimes | Often | Very Often |

12. How often were you, as a student, encouraged to bring a support person to a difficult meeting to provide you with moral support?

    | Never | Rarely | Sometimes | Often | Very Often |

13. How often were you provided the opportunity to lead or facilitate meetings that addressed your academic progress and/or future (e.g., developing personal learning plans, student-parent-teacher conferences, an IEP meeting)?

    | Never | Rarely | Sometimes | Often | Very Often |

14. How often did you participate as an equal with teachers, administrators, and community members on school committees (e.g., curriculum committee, discipline committee, hiring committee, school board)?

    | Never | Rarely | Sometimes | Often | Very Often |

15. How often did you, as a student, feel that the school "belonged" to you, that school experiences were structured primarily with student interests in mind?

    | Never | Rarely | Sometimes | Often | Very Often |

their own futures. Collaboration with students means engaging students as mediators of conflict and controversy and as advocates for themselves and others. Collaboration with students means fostering self-discipline and student learning and use of responsible behavior. We encourage you to add your own distinctions about what it means for you to collaborate with students.

ORGANIZATION OF THE CONTENTS OF THE BOOK

This book is organized into three parts. Part I (Introduction) includes three items. Following the Foreword, which addresses the question "Why should educators bother to unleash the potential of their students as resources in their classrooms?" and this Letter to the Reader, the first chapter explores multiple rationales for adults to collaborate with students in teaching, decision making, and advocacy.

In Part II (Teaching With Students), three chapters describe students as teachers (a) in collaborative learning groups (Chapter 2), (b) in peer tutor and partner learning relationships with other students (Chapter 3), and (c) in co-teaching partnerships with adults (Chapter 4).

Part III (Decision Making With Students) explores the multiple ways that students can make decisions that affect their own and one another's education and learning environments. The five chapters include practical how-to tools and strategies for developing students' collaborative and creative thinking skills (Chapter 5), engaging students in decision making to individualize their learning (Chapter 6), encouraging students to create and achieve their personal learning plans (Chapter 7), structuring and using peer mediation techniques and strategies for conflict and controversy management (Chapter 8), and helping students develop responsibility to regulate and monitor their own self-discipline and self-control (Chapter 9).

In the Epilogue, we conclude the book with an invitation to explore how students can go beyond tolerance of those who are different from themselves towards befriending each other. There is still much to learn about how to teach students to develop skills that lead to self-advocacy, advocacy of other students in their schools and communities, and friendship development. The overall goal is to show that teachers and students value diversity and can co-create a caring community where students can experience democracy in action.

While you read the book, please imagine you are a student enrolled in a school where teachers and administrators use the student empowerment strategies, collaborative planning and teaching skills, and creative solution-finding techniques we describe. Then, once you've finished the book, take the quiz again. Expect to experience dramatic, positive changes in your score. We hope you will commit to making it possible for future generations of schoolchildren to be able to check more ratings of "often" and "very often" when they take the Student Collaboration Quiz (see Resource G).

Why Collaborate With Students? 1

What do people say when the following questions are asked: Why are students not motivated or involved in their own education today? Why are teachers not collaborating more with students in teaching and decision making? Members of the community, such as business owners, might say, "Do you mean students would come out of school knowing how to be cooperative and collaborative employees?" School board members and parents might say, "Students in my school just are not mature enough to know what and how they should be learning." School administrators might say, "Students need to focus upon achievement and meeting state standards for graduation that help keep our school a Blue Ribbon school and off of the D and F school improvement list." Teachers might say, "We have to focus on helping students learn the core curriculum so they can pass high stakes tests. We just don't have time to include them in decisions about what and how to learn." Students might say, "Huh, are you serious? Teachers and administrators really will listen to what we think is important to learn or how we want to be taught? Sounds like a great idea for a *fantasy* rather than a *reality* TV show to me!"

As the responses above suggest, various constituents of the community have preconceived notions about why *not* to collaborate with students in educational endeavors. In this chapter, you will learn why teachers should collaborate with their students. Several questions are offered to guide you in discovering your own answers to why collaborating with students is desirable and valuable.

1. How does student collaboration fit with 21st-century goals of education?

2. How does student collaboration interface with or support notions of democratic schooling?

3. How does student collaboration enhance student self-determination?

4. How does student collaboration unleash student potential and enhance achievement of academic and social goals?

5. How does student collaboration influence teachers, Response to Intervention (RTI), and other school reform efforts?

6. How does student collaboration fit with the limited fiscal and human resources now facing public schools?

RATIONALE #1: STUDENT COLLABORATION FACILITATES 21ST-CENTURY GOALS OF EDUCATION

What are the priority goals and outcomes we desire for our children and youth for the present and the future? Over the past two decades, the authors have had the opportunity to ask this question of numerous teachers, administrators, students, university professors, parents, and concerned citizens across North America, Latin America, Europe, Asia, and the Middle East. Listening to the answers to this question, we have noted that regardless of the divergent roles, locales, perspectives, or vested interests of the individuals questioned, their responses are very similar. In fact, typical responses, shown in Figure 1.1, tend to fall into one or more of the four categories borrowed from Native American culture known as the Circle of Courage (see Figure 1.2).

Traditional Native American education is based upon the culture's main purpose of existence; namely, the education and empowerment of its children. The educational approach is holistic, with the central goal being to foster the four dimensions of self-esteem—*belonging, mastery, independence,* and *generosity.* Collectively, these four dimensions are referred to as the Circle of Courage (Van Bockern, Brendtro, & Brokenleg, 2000). As already noted, these four dimensions correspond with the educational goals articulated today by citizens worldwide (see Figure 1.1). Thus, it would appear that we have a clear and compelling vision of the desired outcomes

Figure 1.1 Circle of Courage and Goals of Education

Generosity
Have empathy and concern for others.
Be a contributing member of society.
Value diversity.
Exercise global stewardship.
Offer compassion, care, support to others.

Independence
Choose where to live, play, work.
Get and keep a job.
Be a lifelong learner.
Continue formal education.
Be able to self-advocate.
Assume personal responsibility.
Be a problem solver.
Be flexible and adaptable.

The Circle of Courage

Belonging
Get along with others.
Know who you are.
Be a member of a community.
Have positive self-esteem.
Have friendships.
Be a good parent and a caring
  family member.

Mastery
Feel competent.
Reach potential.
Be literate; acquire numeracy.
Communicate (orally and in writing).
Know how to use technology.
Be well rounded.

Figure 1.2 Circle of Courage and Collaboration Techniques

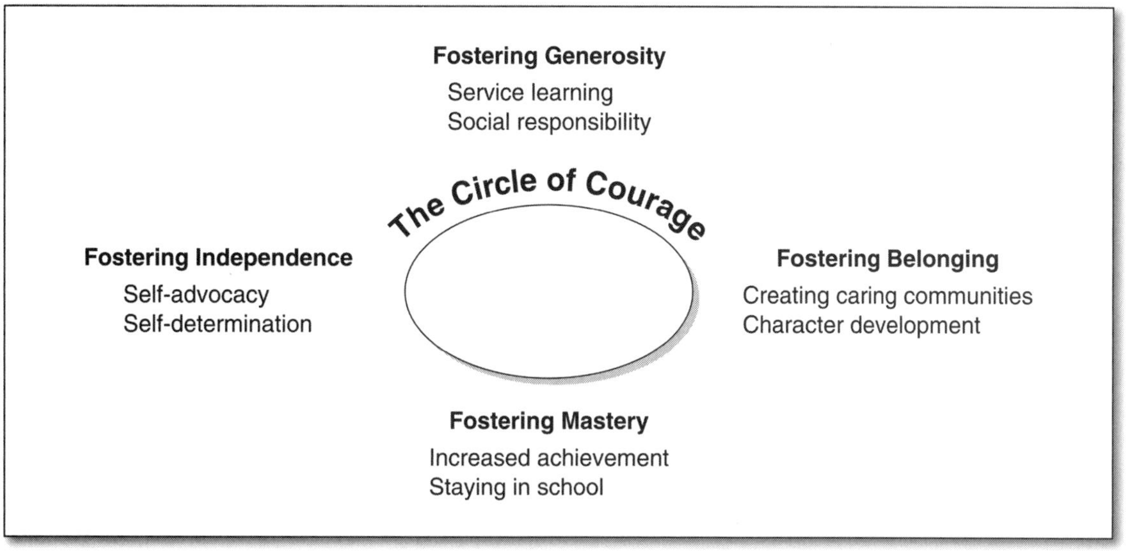

Fostering Generosity
Service learning
Social responsibility

The Circle of Courage

Fostering Independence
Self-advocacy
Self-determination

Fostering Belonging
Creating caring communities
Character development

Fostering Mastery
Increased achievement
Staying in school

of education—courageous, well-rounded youth who have the dispositions and skills to create belonging, strive for mastery and independence, and be generous.

How might student collaboration support or help yield these Circle of Courage outcomes? Figure 1.2 shows various techniques that facilitate achievement of these outcomes.

For example, belonging is fostered when students collaborate to create caring communities through circles of friends (Falvey, Forest, Pearpoint, & Rosenberg, 2002) and same-age or cross-age buddy activities, class meetings, and school-wide community-building activities (Solomon, Battistich, Watson, Schaps, & Lewis, 2000). Students' mastery is enhanced when they collaborate with their teachers to teach their peers in cooperative group and partner learning arrangements. In fact, students note that they actually learn more when they teach others than when they learn alone (Alexander, Gomezllanos, & Sanchez, 2008). Independence is fostered when students collaborate to support one another in self-advocacy, such as when they engage in person-centered futures planning (Falvey et al.). Student generosity is exercised when students collaborate on service learning projects that positively enhance their communities (Kesson, Koliba, & Paxton, 2002; Noddings, 1992). For example, Van Bockern and colleagues (2000) report on a study of middle and high school-aged students in over 500 high-risk communities showed a reduction in risk indicators for students who volunteered community service an hour or more a week.

RATIONALE #2: STUDENT COLLABORATION IS DEMOCRATIC SCHOOLING

Democracy is the hallmark of the United States. The United States purports to be a democratic society with democratic values and democratic schooling, or universal access to K–12 educational opportunities. For many Americans—women, Native Americans, African Americans, Latino Americans, and people with differing abilities and perceived disabilities—to gain access to the same educational opportunities afforded others has been a hard-won struggle. This struggle may not be over. Yet today, students with all of their diverse learning, language, and cultural differences do share common learning environments and experiences. They have access to and are held to the same high curriculum expectations. In other words, students are experiencing a measure of democratic schooling. Apple and Beane (1995), in their writings, have illuminated the principles and characteristics of democratic schooling. They described democratic classrooms as

> comprised of students and teachers who see themselves as participants in communities of learning. By their very nature, these communities are diverse, and that diversity is prized, not viewed as a problem. . . . While the community prizes diversity, it also has a sense of shared purpose. . . . The common good is a central feature of democracy. (p. 10)

Teachers, deliberately or inadvertently, influence students' social and ethical development (Solomon et al., 2000). Teachers who deliberately collaborate with their students to share responsibility for instruction, decision making, and advocacy offer their students a democratic voice to make choices, solve problems among themselves, and deal with conflicts of ideas. Teachers who collaborate with their students to give them choice, power, and control prevent problematic behavior and promote higher levels of learning or mastery (Apple & Beane, 1995; Glasser, 1998), as well as the belonging, independence, and generosity dimensions of the Circle of Courage. So why not embrace student collaboration as a key feature of schooling in this democracy? Or, paraphrasing the words of the great democratic schooling author Maxine Greene (1985), the question might be, "In a democracy, is it not an obligation to empower the young to participate and play an articulate role in the public place?" Of course, for students that public place is school!

RATIONALE #3: STUDENT COLLABORATION INCREASES SELF-DETERMINATION

Related to the goals of education and the principles of democratic schooling is the concept of self-determination—an individual having the freedom, authority, responsibility, and support to be in charge of his or her life (Wehmeyer, Abery, Mithaug, & Stancliffe, 2003). As defined by Marks (2008), "Self-determination is simply the idea of being a 'causal agent' in one's life, being able to make things happen" (p. 56). As with democratic schooling, it involves participation in the community in order to influence community decisions. As with the goals of education represented by the Circle of Courage (see Figures 1.1 and 1.2), essential skills associated with self-determination include problem solving, decision making, goal setting, self-knowledge, and self-regulation (Mithaug, 2003).

Proponents of self-determination, including Marks (2008), argue that although some children may develop self-determination without formal instruction, it involves a critical set of skills all students should acquire as part of their schooling experiences. Thus, teachers are compelled to structure opportunities for students to collaborate in instruction, decision making, and self-advocacy. How else do students learn about who they are (i.e., self-knowledge), what they like and don't like, and what the consequences are of the choices they make (i.e., self-regulation)? How else do children take the first steps on the lifelong journey of developing self-determination skills tied to each of our differing and ever-changing life priorities, such as securing a desired education, raising a family, pursuing career goals, or achieving financial security for retirement?

RATIONALE #4: STUDENT COLLABORATION INCREASES ACADEMIC AND SOCIAL COMPETENCE

The fourth rationale for educators to collaborate with students spotlights achievement. What if each child were expected to become an expert in something? This book is about students becoming experts in strategies that help them to achieve academically and socially. As students become experts in the strategies offered in each chapter (i.e., cooperative group learning, peer tutoring and partner learning, the mediation of conflict and controversies, co-teaching, self-discipline and self-determination, and the planning of their own futures), their achievement expands beyond mere mastery of academics to mastery of self-conduct. Further, students who collaborate with their teachers to transcend self-concern by caring and taking responsibility for what happens to their classmates in school and in their neighborhoods (e.g., being a dependable peer tutor or a responsible peer advocate) acquire dispositions of social responsibility as well and richer and broader reasons for staying in rather than dropping out of school (Solomon et al., 2000). Finally, more than two decades ago, Benjamin (1989), a well-known educational futurist of the time, predicted collaboration would be the essential skill for 21st century citizenship. We agree with Benjamin's prediction of the importance of collaboration. We argue that, by collaborating with students, educators can model and support students to achieve competence and confidence in essential collaborative skills for living responsibly in 21st-century society. Stated otherwise, achievement through student collaboration embraces the whole of the Circle of Courage and yields academic and social achievement across the breadth of the goals of education—mastery, independence, belonging, and generosity.

RATIONALE #5: STUDENT COLLABORATION FACILITATES OTHER SCHOOL REFORM EFFORTS

A constant concern of administrators and school boards is the quality of teachers who are teaching. Professional development and teacher preparation programs are implemented with the purpose of improving the quality of instruction. When teachers collaborate with their students, they are also showing their competencies in meeting state standards for teacher certification. All general and special educators can celebrate the fact that, when they collaborate with their students, they are demonstrating at least three sets of standards[1]—Interstate New Teacher Assessment and Support Consortium (INTASC) for beginning general and special educators, Council for Exceptional Children (CEC) for beginning special educators, and National Board for Professional Teaching Standards (NBPTS) for veteran teachers at all levels), as shown in Table 1.1.

When students and teachers collaborate with each other, teachers often experience a new appreciation for what their students actually can do. This shifts the teachers' attention from the typical focus on deficits and deficiencies toward a strengths-based perspective, which opens up new roles and responsibilities. For example, when students are trained to work as peer tutors, they can often be tapped to provide extra tutorials to their classmates, who may benefit from that support. In fact, classwide peer tutoring has been found to be an effective method to increase reading and math achievement. Thus, teachers and administrators

Table 1.1 Analysis of Professional Standards Demonstrated When Teachers Collaborate With Their Students

Classroom Teachers INTASC (2006)	Special Educators CEC (2003)	Both (Veteran) Teachers NBPTS (2006)
Standard 3 requires teachers to understand *how learners differ.*	Knowledge and skills in understanding characteristics of learners with *different cognitive, physical, cultural, social, and emotional needs.*	Teachers adjust their practice according to *individual differences in their students.*
Standard 4 requires teachers to *use a variety of instructional strategies.*	Competencies related to *knowledge and skills for instructional content and practice.*	Teachers show multiple methods to engage student learning and to enable students to reach goals.
Standard 10 asks teachers to *collaborate and communicate* with parents, families, and colleagues to support student learning.	Competencies related to *communication and collaborative* partnerships.	Teachers *collaboratively work with others* and coordinate services.

---

[1] Council for Exceptional Children (CEC). (2003). *What every special educator must know: Ethics, standards, and guidelines for special educators* (5th ed.), Arlington, VA: Author.

Interstate New Teacher Assessment and Support Consortium (INTASC). (2006). *Interstate New Teacher Assessment and Support Consortium standards.* Washington, DC: Council of Chief State Schools Officers. Retrieved November 16, 2009, from http://www.ccsso.org/projects/Interstate_New_Teacher_Assessment_and_Support_Consortium/Projects/Standards_Development

National Board Professional Teaching Standards (NBPTS). (2006). *Performance-based teaching assessments.* Princeton, NJ: Educational Testing Services.

often turn to peers when they implement Response to Intervention (RTI) approaches in their schools, sometimes at every tier of the RTI pyramid (general education classroom, extra personnel support, and specialized personnel support). Working with students as collaborators is a capacity-building process that strengthens the general education classroom instruction for all students.

Several other school reform efforts can be facilitated when students and teachers collaborate. High-stakes testing and the movement to establish communities of practice are two examples. There are even some long-term benefits to those who learn to be generous and generative—they tend to live a longer and happier life. In fact, recent research shows that generosity and gratitude are both big contributors to happiness, according to Dr. Todd B. Kashdan (Froh, Kashdan, Ozimkowski, & Miller, 2009; Froh, Kashdan, & Yurkewicz, 2009), director of the Laboratory for the Study of Social Anxiety, Character Strengths, and Related Phenomena at George Mason University in Fairfax, Virginia.

RATIONALE #6: STUDENT COLLABORATION IS AN UNTAPPED RESOURCE IN TIMES OF LIMITED FISCAL AND HUMAN RESOURCES

Even in better economic times or at schools with vast economic and human resources, it is unlikely that school personnel will tell you that they have all the resources that they need to educate our students effectively and facilitate the attainment of the desired outcomes of education (i.e., belonging, mastery, independence, and generosity).

Unfortunately, in the current economic situation, many schools are losing precious resources, and school personnel, families, and students are frustrated at the quality of education being provided. But there is one resource that they will never take away from educators: that is the *students* themselves. Regrettably, this precious resource is wasted every single day in many of our nation's schools and classrooms.

What is it that students say at the end of the day when parents ask, "What did you do in school today?" You likely answered, "Nothing!" You might think this answer represents students not wanting to share their day with parents and others. However, our interviews with students suggest that "nothing" is an accurate summation of many students' daily experience of being passive learners in teacher-directed classrooms.

In contrast, in schools where educators collaborate with students in instruction, advocacy, and decision making, students' answers to the "What did you do in school today?" question are quite different. Rather than "nothing," they respond with descriptions of exciting, engaging, and self-determined experiences. At any time, but particularly during difficult economic times when human and fiscal resources are limited, we are compelled to collaborate meaningfully with our students and tap into the untapped and most valuable educational resource of all: the students themselves.

CONCLUSION: SO WHY *NOT* COLLABORATE WITH STUDENTS?

We hope that after reading the rationales for student collaboration provided in this chapter, you agree with us that rather than asking, "Why collaborate with students?" the question that educators, parents, and students should be asking is "Why *not* collaborate with students?" What is there to lose? What are the potential gains? What rationales can you envision? If there is a big enough reason to do something, you will be more motivated to create the procedures necessary for doing it. We invite you to read on and learn how to teach and support students to join educators and other adults as teachers, decision makers, and advocates.

Part II

Teaching With Students

In Part II, we provide an overview of the concepts and principles that undergird the strategies you will explore in Chapters 2, 3, and 4. Have you observed classrooms where students are teaching each other? Do you wonder how teachers develop the instructional roles of their students as members of cooperative learning groups, peer tutors, and co-teachers? The purpose of the chapters in this part of the book is to help you answer these questions.

DEFINITION OF TEACHING

First, what is your definition of teaching? We believe that the broadest possible definitions of teaching should guide our discussion of how to develop the instructional roles of our students. The English language attributes multiple meanings to the word *teaching*. For example, to teach is to impart knowledge or skills. To teach is to cause to learn by experience or example. To teach is to advocate or preach. To teach also means to instruct or to tutor, which implies methodological or procedural knowledge (how to teach) in addition to content knowledge (what to teach).

In Chapters 2, 3, and 4, you will discover how to develop your students' skills to instruct and to tutor. You will see how students can effectively embody all the verbs that are associated with the word *teaching*. They can tutor, instruct, impart knowledge, assess progress, demonstrate examples, act out the procedures as a model, and so on. There are many ways that students can teach. They can teach each other when they learn together in small cooperative groups. They can tutor each other in one-to-one partner learning or reciprocal teaching situations. They can influence the learning of all their classmates when they co-teach with their classroom teachers.

WHAT IS THE INSTRUCTIONAL CYCLE?

Given the above definition for teaching, what should students know about the instructional cycle? To help students understand their roles in the instructional cycle, we begin by describing how teachers think about the instructional cycle. Teachers engage in an ongoing recursive instructional cycle, shown in Figure II.1. When teachers decide to involve their students as partners in the teaching process, students will learn to go through this iterative cycle to develop, deliver, and reflect on the impact of the lessons.

First, as shown in Figure II.1, students need to know that their teachers *plan.* Planning includes getting to know the students in the class, the content that is to be delivered and the state standards that the content addresses, what students are expected to know or do and how this will be assessed, as well as what experiences or activities will be arranged to help students learn or make sense of the content.

Figure II.1   The Instructional Cycle

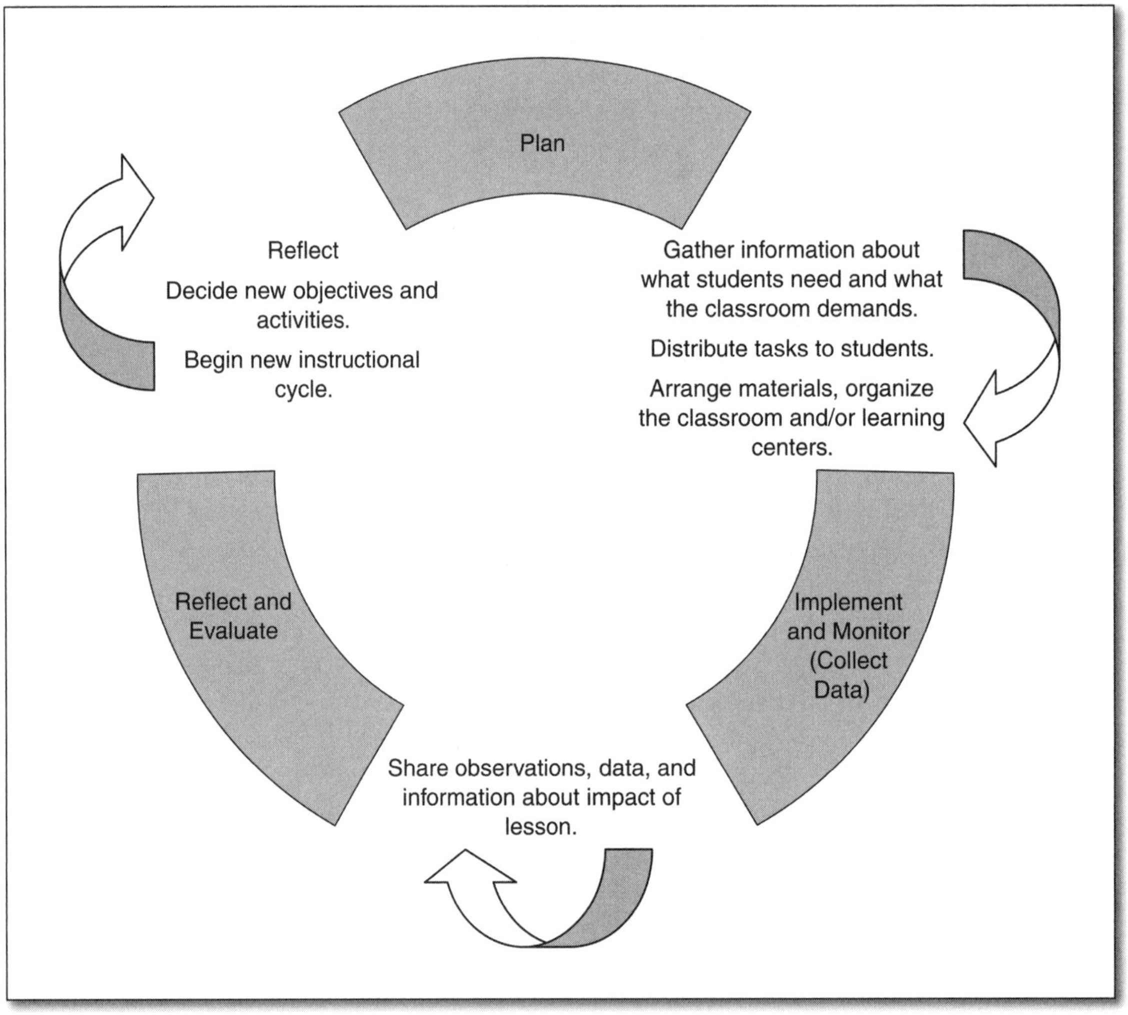

Then, students need to know the importance of the specific part(s) of the planned lessons they will *deliver* or *implement.* While they are doing this, they monitor and adjust their instruction during the lesson as they observe and collect data on the impact of the lesson. Finally, after the lesson, students meet with their teachers to reflect on the lesson and evaluate how successfully they achieved the intended learning outcomes.

When teachers teach *with* their students, they may ask their student co-teachers to assist in instruction at any point of the instructional cycle. Students may be asked to plan, teach, monitor progress, collect data, and reflect upon and evaluate instruction; and this may be done at the individual student level or for all of the students in a particular group.

When students assist in the planning point of the cycle, they often are asked to assist teachers to adapt what typically has occurred in a classroom in order to allow a classmate who learns differently to access the general education curriculum. To determine what to adapt, educators must have information about both the learning characteristics of a student of concern and the characteristics of classroom instruction. This requires gathering data about the classmate and data about the content, product, and process demands of the classrooms.

Addressing Mismatches Between Student Characteristics and Classroom Demands

Often when students are struggling, students as well as the educators they assist may be tempted to focus upon and gather information primarily about classmates' perceived deficits. It can be too easy to ignore or downplay information about what classmates do well and under what conditions classmates perform best. Instead, we suggest a strengths-based perspective. This begins with gathering information about classmates' strengths, learning preferences or styles, multiple intelligences, and interests, as well as the classroom demands. This is the first step in determining how to develop adaptations that use and build upon student characteristics and strengths.

Figure II.2 offers a template that students and teachers can use to gather information as a starting point for discovering and addressing mismatches between a classmate's characteristics and typical classroom demands (also see Resource F). The left-hand side of the template first prompts the discovery of *positive* information, as well as specific goals and needs. The right-hand side of the template prompts planners to examine the content, product/assessment, and process/instructional dimensions of the typical demands of the classroom.

The next step in the process of crafting adaptations is to compare the classmate and classroom information in order to identify mismatches between the two. It may be discovered that there is mismatch between how the classmate accesses content and the typical materials used (i.e., content demands). For example, a seventh-grade student reading at a fourth-grade level may have only seventh-grade-level textbooks available in the classroom. This represents a materials mismatch. There may be a mismatch between how classmates best show what they know and how achievement is typically assessed. This is a product mismatch. There may be a mismatch between how the classmate best

Figure II.2   Template for Gathering Information About Student Characteristics and Classroom Demands

Student Characteristics	Classroom Demands
Strengths Background Knowledge & Experiences Interests Learning Style(s) Multiple Intelligences Important Relationships Other: _____ Other: _____	**Content Demands** How is the content made available to the learners? What multilevel materials are used?
(continued above)	**Process Demands** What processes or instructional methods do the co-teachers use to facilitate student learning?
Goals Does this learner have any unique goals related to academic learning, communication, English language acquisition, and/or social-emotional functioning? Are there particular concerns about this learner?	**Product Demands** How do the students demonstrate what they have learned? How are students assessed or graded?

acquires knowledge or skills and how instruction typically has occurred. This would be a process mismatch (explained in detail in Chapter 6).

Armed with information about these identified mismatches, a team then can collaboratively consider possible ways to provide support or change the task demands—the content and material (content demands), how the student is asked to show what he or she knows (product demands), and/or what is done during instruction (process demands). Students are assisting other educational personnel—classroom teachers, special educators, teachers of English language learners. In other words, they have many people with various knowledge bases and experiences with whom they can brainstorm solutions to mismatches.

When generating potential solutions, it is important to avoid solutions that might lead to stigmatization of a student. Thus, we suggest whatever you consider as a possible solution for a mismatch for a struggling student also should be considered and made available to any student who might benefit. We further suggest that when prioritizing solutions to mismatches, a team first considers solutions that meet at least three criteria: (a) the solution is the least intrusive—that is, least likely to disrupt what goes on in the classroom with all of the other students; (b) the solution is only as special as necessary—that is, you do not oversupport a student; and (c) the solution is the most natural (e.g., natural peer supports, use of already existing technology) to the context of the classroom. Armed with this information about the instructional cycle, strategies, and tools for adapting instruction through comparing information about students and typical classroom demands, in the chapters in this part, you will see how students learn to engage in the instructional cycle.

What Is the Theoretical Framework
for Teaching With Students?

What is the theoretical base for peer tutors, partner learners, cooperative group learners, and student co-teachers? First, cognitive psychologists have verified that when students become reciprocal teachers to each other, the reading comprehension scores of poor readers increase (Palincsar & Brown, 1984). In a reciprocal teaching exchange, both students alternate being the teacher who coaches the comprehension skills they are learning.

Second, the zone of proximal development, or ZPD (Vygotsky, 1934 & 1960/1987), provides theoretical insights about the success of peer-mediated learning. The ZPD refers to an individual's potential level of learning if helped by a teacher or peer and is defined as a particular range of ability with and without assistance from a teacher or a more capable peer. Vygotsky emphasized that what children can do with the assistance of others is even more indicative of their mental development than what they can do alone. When scaffolding students effectively within their ZPDs, teachers are aware of the range of reciprocal roles that can be assumed throughout the teaching-learning exchange. They use a variety of procedures to make sure that (a) the tutor models the behavior for the tutee (and vice versa), (b) the tutee imitates the peer's behavior, (c) the peer gradually removes instruction, (d) and the tutee practices reciprocal teaching (scaffolding others) until the skill is mastered.

Third, social learning theorists have also explained the success of students as teachers in cooperative learning groups. When students work together in cooperative groups, they form interdependent relationships that allow them to learn from each other as they complete assignments. They also acquire friendships and decrease their negative stereotypes about each other, especially if they are learning and working with classmates who are different from themselves (Johnson & Johnson, 1989, 2002). In summary, learning theorists agree that learners construct knowledge and invent meaning through interactions with others.

WHAT IS THE RESEARCH BASE
FOR TEACHING WITH STUDENTS?

When students co-teach in peer tutoring or partner learning situations, they are more likely to experience the academic and social benefits that have been documented by many researchers. Perhaps the strongest rationale for implementing these strategies is the research base for achieving the goals of education related to the Circle of Courage outcomes of belonging, mastery, independence, and generosity. As shown in Table II.1, students have helped their peers acquire skills and knowledge in all areas of the school curriculum (e.g., mathematics, language arts, physical education, science, health, art, and social studies).

Teachers, administrators, and parents alike can be assured that when their children and youth serve in tutor or teaching roles, they are increasing their own mastery of the content, as well as learning valuable communication skills

Table II.1   Peers Help Peers Acquire Skills Across the Curriculum

Mathematics—ratios, proportions, perspective taking	Fuchs, Fuchs, Yazdin, & Powell (2002)
Language arts—comprehension strategies Phonemic skills, vocabulary acquisition Story grammar Reading fluency practice General decoding skills Sight word identification	Barbetta, Miller, & Peters (1991) Fuchs et al. (2001) Giesecke, Cartledge, & Gardner (1993) Palincsar & Brown (1984) Wheldall & Colmar (1990) Wheldall & Mettem (1985)
Science Health Art Social studies	Anliker, Drake, & Pacholski (1993) Maheady, Sacca, & Harper (1988) Rosenthal (1994) Thurston (1994)
Physical education	Block, Oberweiser, & Bain (1995)

(for a review of the impact of peer-mediated instruction, see Hall & Stegila, 2009). For example, students in urban multicultural and disadvantaged neighborhoods, those most at risk for school failure, increased their reading skills when the whole class engaged in peer tutoring (Kourea, Cartledge, & Musti-Rao, 2007). Peer-tutoring arrangements allow students more opportunities to respond and practice academic content compared to more conventional teacher-directed lessons, and positive changes in students' social behaviors and school adjustment often occur (Fuchs, Fuchs, Mathes, & Martinez, 2002; Kourea et al.).

When students learn with each other during cooperative group activities, they show more frequent and open communication, deeper understanding of other perspectives, more clearly differentiated views of each other's contributions, improved self-esteem, greater achievement and productivity, and increased willingness to interact with others who are different from them (Johnson & Johnson, 1989, 2000, 2002). The bottom line is that teachers can be assured that there is a research base for students' taking on instructional roles. In fact, educational researchers have identified cooperative group learning as one of the top nine best educational practices correlated with increasing student achievement on standardized tests (Marzano, Pickering, & Pollack, 2001).

Many positive effects (social and academic achievement) have been reported in the research on the different types of peer-mediated instruction—peer tutoring, partner learning, reciprocal teaching, and cooperative group learning. For example, peer-mediated instruction provides important scaffolding for students who are acquiring English as their second language (e.g., Faltis, 1993; Gersten & Baker, 2000; Walter, 1998).

Would it surprise you to discover that students are as effective as their teachers in teaching social skills to their peers? Prater, Serna, and Nakamura (1999) studied how teenagers with learning disabilities acquired social skills. Many students with learning disabilities may lack the social skills necessary for effective peer interactions. A special education teacher taught 12 students with learning disabilities the following social skills: (a) how to give positive feedback, (b) how to contribute to discussion, and (c) how to accept negative feedback. A random sample of five students previously taught by the teacher then instructed five other students with learning disabilities. Results indicated that both groups, the students taught by their teachers and those taught by their peers, improved in all three social skills! However, both groups did not show as much improvement in accepting negative feedback as in the other two skills. The authors concluded that social skill instruction taught by peers may be as effective and efficient as that taught solely by teachers.

Students with disabilities form another source of tutor support. When students with disabilities served as reciprocal tutors/tutees, they showed more achievement compared to when they were tutees only, and they experienced increased student self-esteem when in the teacher role (Elbaum, Vaughn, Hughes, & Moody, 2000). These studies help all of us better understand what we mean by students as the untapped resource in our classrooms. The most important point to remember is not to stereotype your students into only one role—tutor or tutee. Be sure that all students learn to serve as tutors and have the opportunity to learn as tutees from their peers. This is especially important for students who are considered gifted or talented, lest they become typecast as tutors only. They too can benefit from being tutored. Students with talents and gifts, like all learners, should receive a challenging education filled with diverse activities and opportunities. Tutoring other students can be one, among many, exciting components of their day.

Do you agree that peer-mediated instruction provides alternatives to traditional teaching methods such as lectures, demonstrations, or independent study? What do teachers need to do to implement a system that results in effective peer tutors, partner learners, cooperative group learners, and student co-teachers? There are at least six components: identification, recruitment, training, supervision, evaluation, and reinforcement. Each is described in detail in the following chapters in this part.

Why should we make the effort to implement peer-mediated learning strategies? Van Bockern, Brendtro, and Brokenleg (2000) point out that children in every culture need to belong. Peer-mediated learning techniques help students *know* that they belong, *know* that their presence makes a difference to their classmates, and *know* that they can contribute. Students who learn and practice peer-mediated strategies are more likely to grow into adults who are effective in advocating for themselves, participating as members of work teams, and being family members.

Students as Co-Teachers in Cooperative Learning Groups 2

In this chapter, as you discover the answers to the following questions, you will learn how to unleash student academic and social potential to realize the research promise described in the introduction to this part of the book.

1. What are common attributes to all approaches to cooperative learning?

2. What does the acronym PIGS Face mean? What are the five essential ingredients of the Learning Together approach to cooperative group learning?

3. What are quick cooperative structures? What are base teams? How can you use them in your teaching?

4. How does a teacher translate the five essential ingredients of a cooperative learning experience—positive interdependence, individual accountability, group processing, social skills, and face-to-face interaction—into a viable and cohesive lesson?

5. What are the 14 decisions teachers must make when planning and implementing cooperative group lessons?

6. What is an example of a cooperative group lesson that accommodates the learning challenges of a diverse group of students?

7. What do students say about cooperative group learning? What does cooperative learning do for them?

WHAT IS COOPERATIVE LEARNING?

Cooperative learning is the umbrella term used to refer to a family of instructional methods in which the teacher instructs and guides groups of students to work together. This instructional practice can be challenging to master and even counterintuitive to some teachers. Yet the extensive and overwhelmingly positive international research results yielded over the past several decades clearly indicate that

> teachers can increase their pupil's performance on academic tasks if they have their pupils work on the tasks in groups of two to six under rules by which the pupils teach each other, coach each other, and succeed as a group. These gains occur only if teachers show their pupils how to do and think about these things. (Murray, 2002, p. 179)

Cooperative learning has been recognized as the sixth most powerful instructional strategy to increase student performance (Marzano et al., 2001). In other words, it is more than worth a teacher's while to learn *how* to design lessons effectively to engage their students as teachers in cooperative learning groups. Further, cooperative learning allows students to access the Circle of Courage and 21st-century educational goals of belonging and generosity through their support and coaching of one another for the purpose of achieving mastery and independence with regard to the content they study.

There are several major approaches to engaging students in cooperative group learning that are recognized as effective. Each approach has unique features or strengths. All share the common attributes of (a) students engaging in a shared learning activity in small groups and (b) students being interdependent and accountable for one another (Davidson, 2002). We value all of the cooperative learning approaches that have emerged over the past several decades because they result in increased student engagement and learning. However, we are most attracted to David and Roger Johnson's Learning Together approach (Johnson & Johnson, 1999; 2009; Johnson, Johnson, & Johnson Holubec, 1994a, 1994b), because it is the one approach that focuses upon the direct teaching of interpersonal and small-group social skills—the civic behaviors needed for survival in school and the larger society (Johnson & Johnson, 2002). Thus, this is the approach we share with you in this chapter. We encourage teachers to use the Learning Together cooperative learning approach because it most naturally aligns with the rationale for student collaboration outlined in Chapter 1; that is, the approach directly teaches and holds students accountable for the skills that promote belonging, mastery, independence, and generosity shown in Figures 1.1 and 1.2 (Brendtro, Brokenleg, & Van Bockern, 2002). We also encourage teachers to use this approach because it has been recognized as one of the "great success stories based on theory, research, and practice over the past 11 decades" (Johnson & Johnson, 2009, p. 365). Teachers who use this approach empower their students to learn and use the democratic virtues and social competence required of well-rounded citizens (Johnson & Johnson, 1996b).

WHAT COOPERATIVE LEARNING GROUPS ARE *NOT*

There is a huge difference between simply having students work in groups and structuring effective cooperative group learning among students. Four students sitting at the same table doing their own work and talking while they work is not cooperative learning; it is individualistic learning with sidebar conversations. When students work together with teacher instructions such as "Help others if you finish first," this is not cooperative learning; it is individualistic learning with an expectation that some students will tutor others without any training or teacher direction. When students are assigned a project on which one student does all of the work while the others put their names on it to receive a group grade, this is not cooperative learning; it is one student working and others getting away with what is known as academic hitchhiking or what David and Roger Johnson called "free riding" and "social loafing" ((Johnson & Johnson, 1999, p. 74).

For students to be empowered to instruct one another in cooperative groups, the teacher must have a solid understanding of the critical ingredients for success, as well as how to translate those ingredients into a recipe for success—a clear and structured lesson plan. In this chapter, we first examine the five critical ingredients of a cooperative group. Then we learn how to use a one-page cooperative group lesson plan that ensures all of the ingredients are included. Lastly, we examine a couple of examples of cooperative group lessons in action.

FIVE ESSENTIAL INGREDIENTS OF COOPERATIVE GROUP LEARNING: PIGS FACE

David and Roger Johnson have used an acronym, PIGS Face, as a mnemonic to help teachers and students remember the five essential ingredients of the Learning Together cooperative learning approach. *P* represents "positive interdependence"; *I*, "individual accountability"; the *G*, "group processing"; the *S*, "social skills"; and *Face* represents "face-to-face interaction." All five ingredients must be included in a lesson if students are to be more productive than if they were to work alone or in competition with one another. Let's first briefly define each of these ingredients in terms of teacher actions and then look more closely at what each ingredient looks and sounds like when students are teaching one another cooperatively.

1. *Positive interdependence* involves clearly structuring and communicating to students that they are linked with one another in ways such that they cannot succeed unless all members succeed.

2. *Individual accountability* involves structuring ways to assure that each group member is taking personal responsibility for contributing to accomplish the group's goals and assisting other group members to do likewise.

3. *Group processing* involves guiding students to reflect (group process) on how well the group members (a) accomplish the tasks and (b) maintain and develop their interpersonal skills to work effectively and enjoyably in small groups.

4. *Social skills* involve providing instruction, guided practice, and expectations to use the interpersonal skills that are needed to make collaborative work effective and enjoyable.

5. *Face-to-face interaction* involves structuring the cooperative groupings (e.g., group size and membership) and the environment (e.g., the room arrangement) so students have frequent opportunities to engage in positive and promotive interaction with one another face-to-face.

Quick Cooperative Structures. Although these five ingredients are essential to formal cooperative learning groups, a host of quick cooperative structures take just a few minutes to set up and employ in any lecture, lesson, or review activity. Quick cooperative structures ensure that students have frequent opportunities to be positively interdependent and individually accountable through brief yet meaningful face-to-face interactions. Table 2.1 offers a dozen flexible, diverse, and easy-to-implement quick cooperative structures described by Kagan and Kagan (2008) that are favorites of the authors. In what ways might you or a teacher you know use these 12 structures? How could they be adapted to work with younger or older students or students not yet very experienced with cooperative learning?

Long-term Cooperative Structures. In contrast to quick cooperative structures, teachers can establish long-term cooperative face-to-face interactive structures referred to as base groups or base teams (Davidson, 2002; Johnson, Johnson, & Smith, 1998). Base teams have stable, long-term (e.g., semester- or year-long) membership of a small number of students who provide one another with personal and academic support. Students who work together in long-term relationships learn to motivate one another's efforts by providing clarification on assignments, updating absent members on missed material, providing feedback on papers, and preparing each other for assessments. Because base teams meet frequently (e.g., daily, weekly, biweekly), as with quick cooperative structures, the structured positive interdependence allows students to develop social skills, such as empathetic listening, and academic and nonacademic problem solving while being individually accountable to one another for ongoing support.

Cooperative Group Lesson Ingredient #1: Positive Interdependence

The heart of any effectively designed cooperative group lesson is that students in the group perceive they will "sink or swim together." As with the three musketeers, it is "All for one, and one for all." Positive interdependence exists when students believe they must coordinate their efforts; that is, they are linked with one another in such a way that they cannot succeed unless every team member succeeds. There are many specific methods for overtly structuring ways to help teammates feel connected and committed to learning cooperatively. Some of the methods shown in Table 2.2 (page 39) are examined more closely later in the chapter when we explain the teacher's role in structuring positive interdependence.

Table 2.1 A Dozen Quick Cooperative Learning Structures

Name	Description
1. Think (optional: Write)-Pair-Share	Students think to themselves about a teacher-provided question or topic and (optionally) summarize by writing or illustrating thoughts/answers. They partner to share thoughts and then are called upon to share their own or their partners' responses.
2. Formulate-Share-Listen-Create	Begin as above. Then after partners have shared thoughts/answers, they formulate a new answer/idea that incorporates both members' contributions.
3. Numbered Heads Together	Students in small teams count off in each team (e.g., 1, 2, 3). The teacher asks a question; teammates consult to make sure each member knows the answer. Then a student in each group (e.g., "all number 3s") is called upon to answer.
4. Mix-Freeze-Pair or Cocktail Party	Students stand and "Mix" (move around the room) until the teacher signals (e.g., says "freeze") or stops the music. At the signal, students turn to the closest person to form a pair. The teacher asks a question, which pairs discuss until the music resumes or the teacher says, "Mix."
5. Say and Switch	A student is asked to relate information or answer a question. At the end of a sentence or midsentence, the student is stopped, and another student is asked to pick up where the other student left off. This process is continued for several students. This structure can effectively advantage students with limited English or communication by starting with a word, picture, or idea upon which classmates then can build.
6. Say Something	Given a piece of text, partners decide together how far to read silently before stopping to "say something" that is a summary, a question, or an interesting connection. At the chosen point, both partners say something. Partners repeat this process to the end of the selection. The whole class then discusses the text. Thinking out loud, supported by attentive listening, helps connect prior and new information and promotes interpersonal relations.
7. Roundtable or Round-Robin	Each student in turn writes an idea or answer, as paper and pencil are passed around the group. Each idea is to expand upon previous entries. With "Simultaneous Roundtable," more than one pencil and paper are passed at once.
8. Graffiti or Carousel	With "Graffiti," each group is given chart paper and a different topic to write about. At a designated time (e.g., three minutes), sheets are rotated (e.g., clockwise). Rotations continue until all groups see each sheet and each sheet returns to the home group. "Carousel" is a variation of Graffiti where students move among topical sheets posted on the wall or placed at tables around the room.
9. Three-Step Interview	Groups of four divide into partnerships of two. Then (1) students interview their partner about a question posed by the teacher, (2) the students reverse roles so that interviewers become interviewees, and (3) they debrief in a round-robin fashion in the original group of four by taking turns sharing what they learned from interviewing.
10. Talk Walk	Engage in both physical and mental exercise by discussing a question or problem-solving an issue while walking outdoors. Walking increases freethinking, creativity, and expression by decreasing inhibitions and inducing a relaxed and physiologically healthy state. Talking while walking also provides a change of environment and kinesthetic stimulation. "Talk walk" can occur indoors, with partners taking a walk around a room or up and down a hallway.

(Continued)

(Continued)

Name	Description
11. Inside-Outside Circle	Students stand in two concentric circles, with the inside circle facing out and the outside circle facing in. Inside/outside partners discuss a question/topic posed by the teacher. When signaled, the outside circle of students rotates clockwise to face a new partner, and they discuss the same or a new question/topic. This is repeated for several rounds.
12. Toss-a-Question	Each group generates a question on a piece of paper, wads up the question into a ball, and tosses it to another team, which then answers the question and tosses it back to the originator to evaluate.

Cooperative Group Lesson Ingredient #2: Individual Accountability

In a cooperative group lesson, teachers structure group and individual accountability.

- *Group accountability* occurs when the teacher (a) assesses the overall performance of students in the group as a whole against a standard of performance and (b) lets the students know how they did with regard to the standard.
- *Individual accountability* involves increasing individual members' level of concern to be personally responsible for contributing and learning by (a) assessing the performance of individual students in the group, (b) providing feedback to individuals and the groups so they can celebrate success and remediate problems, and (c) structuring ways for students in the groups to hold each other responsible for their contributions.

A major goal of cooperative group learning is to prepare group members to be better able to complete tasks independently by first completing them with the cooperative support of others. Individual accountability is what ensures that all group members, in fact, are strengthened by the cooperative experience.

How is individual accountability built into a cooperative learning? As with positive interdependence, teachers have many choices of methods to monitor and hold individual students accountable for their learning. Table 2.3 (page 43) offers 10 such methods. In addition to structuring ways to monitor members' contributions, teachers also need to plan in advance ways in which to intervene should group members have difficulty with the task or their communication or if a member does not pull his or her own weight and engages in social loafing.

Cooperative Group Lesson Ingredient #3: Group Processing

A major goal of using cooperative group learning is to help students become consciously aware of their own behaviors in a group. Group processing explicitly helps develop students' awareness of the interpersonal and task-related behaviors they need to use when they work together in groups through self-examination and feedback. Group processing first requires a teacher to monitor students while they are working in groups by (a) systematically observing each group, (b) analyzing strengths and challenges members experience in using small-group interpersonal skills, and (c) providing support to each group when needed. Group processing also requires a teacher to structure time for students to reflect on their own behaviors in their small groups and/or as a whole class. Their reflection focuses on how well group members interacted with one another. During this group processing or reflection time, the teacher (a) shares formal and informal observations of students' behaviors, (b) guides students to identify their strengths, and (c) helps students and groups to set goals for improvement. Group-processing reflections may focus upon a particular social skill targeted for the lesson (e. g., active listening, soliciting ideas from others), particular aspects of the task itself (e. g., how well members performed their designated roles), or particular problems groups encountered and how they solved those problems.

Group processing is a reflective technique that promotes students' sense of self-determination and empowerment, because they learn to recognize how they have worked through conflicts in ideas and opinions, overcome their struggles in learning new content, and gained new understandings of complex or difficult material. A critical aspect of the teacher's role in structuring the group processing reflections, whether in small groups or as a whole class, is to make sure that students celebrate their contributions as well as their groups' accomplishments. By structuring frequent opportunities for students to experience appreciation and to receive public acknowledgment for collaborative work, a teacher builds students' enthusiasm for and commitment to learning cooperatively.

Cooperative Group Lesson
Ingredient #4: Social Skills

Social skills are learned. We are not born with them, nor do they magically develop. Simply placing students in groups and telling them to cooperate in no way guarantees that students will know or use the social skills they need to collaborate to accomplish their learning goals. Consequently, directly teaching and expecting and motivating students to use the small-group interpersonal social skills needed for quality teamwork is the fourth essential ingredient for successful cooperative group learning. Student achievement in cooperative groups increases when a teacher teaches, monitors, and acknowledges (e.g., offers praise, gives points, assigns grades) students' use of social skills (Johnson & Johnson, 1994).

There are literally hundreds of social skills that students can be taught and then expected to apply when collaborating in cooperative groups. In the authors' view, students' development of these interaction skills is equal in importance to students' achievement of the academic goals of a lesson. Social skills personally and professionally benefit a person for a lifetime; they enable students to develop more sophisticated, supportive, and satisfying relationships with others.

Cooperative Group Lesson
Ingredient #5: Face-to-Face Interaction

The fifth critical cooperative group ingredient is the structuring of regular opportunities for students to be positively interdependent in face-to-face interactions. Promotive social behaviors, such as motivating one another to strive to achieve the group goal, exchanging ideas and materials, and providing help and feedback to improve performance, can only occur if students spend time engaged in face-to-face interactions.

This fifth ingredient requires the teacher to make decisions about how to engineer the classroom environment to optimize positive student interactions during cooperative group work. It includes determining how the room and work materials will be arranged, which students will be grouped together, and how large the groups should be. Face-to-face interactions can take the form of quick cooperative structures, which require only a few minutes (see Table 2.1, page 31), long-term base teams, or formal cooperative groups that last an entire lesson or series of lessons. The bottom line is to structure frequent opportunities for students to interact face-to-face in positively interdependent and promotive ways.

THE FOUR PHASES OF PLANNING AND IMPLEMENTING FORMAL COOPERATIVE GROUP LESSONS

How does a teacher translate the five essential ingredients of the cooperative learning experience—positive interdependence, individual accountability, group processing, social skills, and face-to-face interaction—into a viable and cohesive formal cooperative group lesson? Planning and guiding students to collaborate in formal lessons has four distinct phases that translate the five essential ingredients into action.

In Phase I, the teacher makes a set of decisions about academic and social skills objectives and the face-to-face organizational logistics of the lesson. Phase II involves decisions about how to open the lesson, communicate academic and social skill expectations, and ensure that positive interdependence and individual accountability are structured. In Phase III, the teacher sets the face-to-face interactions among students into motion and makes a set of decisions about how best to monitor group work and intervene, as needed. In Phase IV, the teacher provides closure to the lesson by deciding how to share observations and provide feedback to groups and individuals on their academic and social performance and guide students to reflect on their own academic and social performance.

TEACHER DECISIONS AT EACH PHASE OF PLANNING AND IMPLEMENTATION

Figure 2.1 offers a one-page template for planning a formal cooperative group lesson and illustrates the relationship between the five essential ingredients and

Figure 2.1   Cooperative Group Learning Lesson Plan Template

Author(s):   **Subject(s):**   **Grade Level(s):**

Phase I. ACADEMIC AND SOCIAL OBJECTIVES and ORGANIZATIONAL DECISIONS

Academic Objective(s):   **Social Skills Objective(s):**

Group Size:

Group Membership:
☐ Heterogeneous
☐ Homogeneous
☐ Other Considerations for Membership:

Room Arrangement:
☐ Desk Clusters ☐ Chair Clusters
☐ Floor Clusters ☐ Tables
☐ Other:

Materials Needed:

Distribution:
☐ Shared
☐ Individual
☐ Jigsaw

Phase II. OPENING AND SETTING UP THE LESSON

Structuring of Positive Interdependence	Explanation of Steps of Academic Task	Explanation of Success Criteria	Explanation of Individual Accountability	Explanation of Social Skill Expectations
☐ GOAL ☐ INCENTIVE ☐ RESOURCE ☐ ROLE ☐ SIMULATION ☐ SEQUENCE ☐ OUTSIDE FORCE ☐ ENVIRONMENT ☐ IDENTITY ☐ INTERGROUP COOPERATION				

Phase III. MONITORING AND INTERVENING DURING FACE-TO-FACE INTERACTION

Who Monitors:
☐ Teacher(s)
☐ Teacher(s) & Students

How Students Are Monitored:
☐ Informal Notes
☐ Formal Observation Sheet

Intervening:
☐ What are likely tasks or social problems?
☐ How do you plan to intervene?

Phase IV. EVALUATING ACADEMIC PERFORMANCE AND GROUP PROCESSING OF SOCIAL SKILL PERFORMANCE

Academic Feedback

(How and when is academic performance evaluated?):

Social Skills Processing (How do students reflect on social interactions?):

Student Self-Evaluation, by: _____

Small-Group Processing, by: _____

Whole-Class Processing, by: _____

SOURCE: Adapted from Bennett, B., Rollheiser-Bennett, C., & Stevahn, L. (1991). *Cooperative learning: Where heart meets mind.* Toronto, Canada: Educational Connections. [Out of press; publisher no longer exists].

the four phases of lesson planning and implementation. The template clearly shows the decisions a teacher makes at each of the four phases of cooperative group lesson development and delivery. This section of the chapter describes and provides examples of each of these decisions.

Phase I Decisions: Academic and Social Objective and Organizational Decisions

In the first phase of planning, teachers make five decisions. They determine (1) the academic objective(s), (2) the social skills objective(s), (3) how many and which students are in each group, (4) the room arrangement, and (5) the materials needed and how these materials are distributed among groups.

Decision #1: What are the academic objectives for the lesson?

In cooperative group learning, the teacher specifies two types of objectives: academic and social. The academic objectives reflect state content standards and relate to one or more curriculum areas (e.g., language arts, mathematics, social studies, science). Academic goals can be group and/or individual in nature. For instance, as part of a government unit, students might be expected to develop a survey about an upcoming election and then poll students throughout the school. Group objectives might be for each group to (a) submit a list of 10 questions and (b) graph the polling results by grade and gender with correct labeling and numeration. An individual objective that would ensure individual accountability might be for each student to compose a paragraph interpreting the polling results.

As part of determining academic objectives, the teacher also asks, "What, if any, are differential academic objectives for students with unique learning needs, such as English learners or students with disabilities?" A reminder at this point is that all students do not need to have the same objectives or performance criteria (Thousand, Villa, & Nevin, 2007). Differentiation based upon students' gifts and challenges is desired and needed in order to communicate that, in a cooperative classroom, "fair is not equal; fair is everyone getting what they need in order to succeed." Of course, differentiated objectives and criteria must be clearly communicated in advance to students.

Consider the following example of how academic and social objectives were adapted to include Marissa, a seven-year-old girl with multiple disabilities, in a cooperative group lesson. When this lesson took place, Marissa was a full-time member of her local school's multiaged first- and second-grade classroom. Although she occasionally vocalized, she was not yet using vocalizations to communicate. Therefore, increasing Marissa's use of various switches on communication devices, such as CD players and tape recorders, was an Individual Education Program (IEP) goal aimed at developing an augmentative communication system. Two IEP social skills goals for Marissa were to (1) remain with the group throughout an activity and (2) refrain from taking neighbors' materials when in groups.

In this lesson, students were assigned to learn together in groups of four. The social skill objectives expected of all students, including Marissa, were to sit in a circle, remain with the group through the lesson, and keep voices at a conversational level. The academic task was to listen to an audio recording while following the text and illustrations in the corresponding storybook. Students in each group were assigned roles, one of which was to turn the storybook pages when the recording signaled. Another role was to turn the tape player on or off. Marissa was assigned this role for her group. The role was adapted so that she continuously pressed the recorder's play button, with physical assistance from teammates if needed. Marissa's role was not only needed, but it allowed her to work on her IEP goals. Having Marissa operate the tape recorder button created an opportunity to assess the potential for using similar devices in the future. The act of holding down the button also inhibited Marissa from reaching for others' possessions and kept her with her group, helping her to accomplish her social IEP goals.

Decision #2: What are the social skill objectives for the lesson?

In the Learning Together cooperative learning approach, the social objectives are *as important as* the academic objectives. The teacher is responsible for diagnosing and selecting which social skills to focus upon for instruction and practice. Each class of students has its own unique social competencies and needs. Often the nature of the academic task determines which social skills are needed (e.g., use of "friendly disagreeing" skills during a structured academic controversy).

One-shot instruction and practice does not result in skilled collaborators. Cooperative groups provide a rich arena in which students can practice using the social skills they are being taught. It takes repeated application in cooperative lessons, along with feedback and goal setting, for students to internalize and spontaneously use even the simplest of social skills.

Social skill objectives can range from the basic to the complex and sophisticated.

- Basic social skills that help students build trust among one another include using people's names, looking at the speaker, encouraging others to participate, and staying with the group.
- Skills that help group members to communicate effectively and get the task completed include contributing ideas, asking for help, asking for clarification, offering ideas on timelines and ways to complete a task, checking for understanding, active listening by paraphrasing others' contributions, expressing verbal and nonverbal encouragement, energizing the group with humor and enthusiasm, and expressing feelings.
- A third set of skills helps students to formulate creative solutions to problems and include brainstorming, elaborating, probing for more detail about the reasoning behind a perspective or position, and summarizing.
- A final interpersonal skill set prepares students to engage in constructive academic controversy or conflict resolution. Skills in this category include criticizing ideas rather than people, differentiating differing perspectives, building on others' ideas or conclusions, integrating divergent perspectives into a single position, and checking that team members can live with an agreement or solution.

Decision #3: How are students grouped?

In designing a cooperative lesson, a teacher decides how many students are in each group and which students are assigned to which groups. Cooperative groups range in size from two to six, with two to four being the preferred group size. Group size is influenced by several factors. Time is one factor. The shorter the time period, the smaller the group; small groups take less time to organize and operate faster because there are fewer people to share air time.

The nature of the task or the materials used is a second factor influencing group size. For example, in a science experiment in which several liquids are applied to a substance to determine its reactions to the liquids, two is an ideal group size. Each partner can alternate applying the liquid and recording data. If there were more members, they would be left without a role (except observing) until it was their turn to record or manipulate materials.

Expertise is a third factor in determining group size; the more group members, the more likely there will be members with knowledge or skills to help accomplish the task. A team's level of social competence also influences group size. Larger groups require more sophisticated social skills to coordinate actions, ensure everyone meaningfully participates, and reach consensus.

Deciding which students to assign to which groups is another important teacher grouping decision. An overarching goal in cooperative learning is to capitalize upon the diversity within the classroom. Therefore, for the most part, students should be assigned so that the group membership is heterogeneous along all dimensions of difference—gender, ethnicity, language, and perceived academic or social strengths and challenges. More frequent explanations, more elaborative thinking, and greater perspective taking occur in heterogeneous versus homogeneous groups ((Johnson & Johnson, 1999). This, in turn, increases depth and accuracy of understanding. At times, students may be grouped homogeneously; for example, when they are to practice and master specific skills that may differ among classmates (e.g., basic math skills, targeted literacy subskills such as decoding, encoding, or fluency). However, homogeneous grouping should be limited in frequency and to the learning of specific critical skills.

In deciding which students to assign to which groups, teachers new to cooperative group learning often are challenged by students who want to select the members of their groups. Does the teacher determine group membership? Why? Student-selected groups tend to be homogeneous (e.g., girls selecting girls, high achievers selecting high achievers), which compromises group performance. A teacher may deliberately assign particular students as teammates for various reasons. For example, a teacher may assign a student with learning challenges to work with students who are particularly supportive, or a teacher may assign a non-task-oriented student to work with students who are task oriented to promote on-task behavior. The teacher also may deliberately assign students randomly so that students eventually get to collaborate with everyone in the class.

Decision #4: How is the room arranged?

How the teacher arranges the room speaks volumes about what behaviors are expected. If students are to communicate without disrupting the learning of other groups, groups must be arranged so members are close enough—"eye to eye" and "knee to knee"—to access all relevant task-related materials and exchange ideas in a comfortable space. Large, rectangular tables and even clusters of desks can cause students to be too far apart to "huddle" and communicate quietly. Given a classroom's configuration, groups may even want to move to the floor so that students can sit in circles.

Decision #5: What materials are needed? How are they distributed or shared?

In planning cooperative groups, it is essential to make sure there are enough materials to distribute across groups. How materials are distributed or shared enhances a sense of positive interdependence among teammates. When a group is given one set of materials, the students need to work together to share these materials. This is especially effective with teams new to cooperative learning. Once students become accustomed to collaborative work, they can be given their own copies of materials. A second way to create positive interdependence via materials is to jigsaw information. Each group member gets different resource materials that collectively are needed to jigsaw together to complete the group assignment. The process of jigsawing materials also increases a sense of individual accountability, because each team member must be prepared to share his or her piece of the puzzle when the group comes together.

Phase II Decisions: Opening and Setting Up the Lesson

In Phase II, the teacher introduces the lesson requirements to the students and makes the five additional decisions (i.e., decisions #6 through #10) shown in the Phase II section of Figure 2.2 (page 50). Three decisions involve how three of the five essential ingredients of cooperative learning—positive interdependence, individual accountability, and social skills—are communicated to students. The other two decisions concern how to explain (a) the academic task and (b) the criteria or performance standard to which students are held.

Decision #6: How is positive interdependence structured?

As a reminder, *positive interdependence* is the perception of students in a cooperative group that they are linked with one another such that they each succeed only if all members succeed. A teacher can create a sense of positive interdependence among students in a variety of ways. Table 2.2 identifies 10 ways to structure positive interdependence into a lesson. It should be noted that it is not necessary to use all 10 strategies in a lesson for students to feel bound together.

The more strategies a teacher employs, the more likely students will feel that they need one another to succeed, and the more likely they will put forth effort to coordinate with teammates to get the task done and use their small-group social skills to encourage one another to participate and learn. The paragraphs that follow further define and expand examples of the 10 ways to increase commitment to learning cooperatively (i.e., positive interdependence). Please refer to Table 2.2 as you read the following paragraphs.

Table 2.2 Ten Ways to Structure Positive Interdependence

1. **Goal:** What is the group goal? What is the common purpose, single product, or shared outcome?

2. **Incentive:** Are you structuring group recognition or a reward? If so, what form will it take? (Examples include celebration, work display, free time, choice activity, fun experience, or other preset privilege for meeting a criterion; a group grade; dual points for individual and group products or dual recognition for academic and social skill performance; bonus points if preset criteria are exceeded.)

3. **Resource:** Are materials arranged to promote positive interdependence? If so, will groups share one set of shared materials, or will materials be jigsawed, with different group members studying or preparing different content in advance of face-to-face group work?

4. **Role:** Are complementary and interconnected student roles structured to promote positive interdependence? If so, name and define each role using the words you will use with the students. How will you determine which role each student in each group will perform?

5. **Sequence:** Is the overall task divided into a sequence of steps, each of which the group must complete before moving on to the next? If so, what are the steps?

6. **Simulation:** Are you structuring a positive fantasy mission or hypothetical situation? If so, what is the simulated mission?

7. **Outside force:** Are you using a time limit or competition with an actual or hypothetical group to create within-group cohesion? If so, how?

8. **Environmental:** Are you using the physical space (e.g., table groupings, carpet squares or chairs in a circle, round table, a special meeting place) to bind group members together? If so, what does it look like?

9. **Identity:** Are you having groups establish a mutual identity through a group name, motto, logo, flag, secret signal, song or rap, etc.? If so, which are used?

10. **Intergroup cooperation:** Are you structuring cooperation among groups by having students share resources or ideas across groups? If so, how and when will you build this into the lesson?

Goal interdependence exists when members of a group perceive they have a mutual outcome to achieve. Success depends on all teammates reaching the common goal. Common goals include (a) creating a single group product, (b) completing a group task, (c) conducting a group analysis of a set of information, (d) all group members performing at a minimum performance criteria (e.g., 85 percent or more correct answers on the next day's quiz), (e) improving a previous group score, or (f) meeting a minimum criterion for an assigned social skill.

Incentive interdependence exists when teammates get the same recognition only when every teammate succeeds. Table 2.2 suggests various group incentives. Whether to assign group grades is controversial. We recommend that grades not be used as an incentive until students are familiar with the concept of cooperative learning and, through training and experience, have developed the skills to work successfully in cooperative learning arrangements. Remember when considering the use of incentives that they need to be genuinely appealing to students or they will not motivate students to unify their actions. Extrinsic rewards (e.g., stars, free time, all members of the group earning bonus points on a quiz, or a night without homework if each member scores at least 80 percent on individual quizzes after group work) can be powerful motivators when first introducing cooperative learning. However, instilling intrinsic motivation (e.g., pride in showing a group report to parents and the principal) to cooperate is the ultimate goal, so fade the use of external motivators whenever possible.

Resource interdependence exists when materials—one text, one pencil, one answer sheet—are shared in a way that brings members together. Resource interdependence also exists when materials are jigsawed. For example, when studying a culture, one student studies the folklore; another, communication; another, economic issues; and another, agricultural issues.

Role interdependence exists when each group member is assigned a complementary and interconnected role that helps the group accomplish the task and interact more effectively. Roles emphasize the value of each person to the group and may be task related or social. For instance, reader, recorder, summarizer, timekeeper, and materials manager are task-related roles. Encourager, feelings watcher, energizer, and process observer (i.e., watcher of teammates' use of social skills) are examples of social roles. When thinking about using roles, let the academic task and the group members' proficiency with social skills guide what roles actually are needed.

Sequence interdependence exists when a task is accomplished by completing a series of subtasks in a step-by-step order. For example, in analyzing a poem, the team might

1. read or hear the poem;

2. generate options to answer a series of questions;

3. come to consensus on the agreed-upon group answer;

4. check for everyone's ability to articulate the answer;

5. sign the answer sheet to indicate that each person contributed and is prepared to be quizzed by the teacher; and

6. finally call the teacher over to quiz students individually.

Simulation interdependence exists when a group has a fantasy situation with which to grapple. For example, students are part of an architectural firm with a $20,000 contract to design a school playground. Their task is to identify the materials and quantities required to design the playground that meet certain criteria. In another example, students become a hypothetical scientific team charged with identifying the first four steps needed to find a cure for a deadly disease threatening to wipe out the world's population.

Outside force interdependence exists when a team is placed in competition with some outside force. As the examples in Table 2.2 suggest, an outside force could be a time limit; a team's previous score; or a hypothetical outside enemy, such as a total number of creative ideas generated by a hypothetical previous class. We strongly suggest that groups not compete with other groups within the same class to prevent the potential negative effects of within-class rivalry.

Environmental interdependence exists when the physical environment—desk cluster, carpet squares, chairs in a circle, a round table, a hula hoop, a special meeting place—unites group members. Environmental interdependence promotes active face-to-face interactions as students work elbow to elbow and knee to knee.

Identity interdependence exists when group members create a shared identity to instill pride. Just as with sports teams, a student cooperative learning team can strengthen its sense of oneness by creating symbols that represent the team. Some ideas for establishing identity interdependence are listed in Table 2.2. The teacher also can facilitate team identity by assigning names of famous inventors, explorers, governmental leaders, or international heroes/heroines to each team for a science or social studies lesson. We all need to belong; identity interdependence addresses this need.

Intergroup interdependence exists when different groups cooperate with one another by sharing resources, ideas, or a collective goal. A teacher can construct intergroup interdependence by (a) pausing a lesson to have a "runner" from each group go to other groups to get ideas on how to solve a problem or (b) pausing a lesson in which teams have been brainstorming ideas to have teams "cross-pollinate" by sharing their favorite, wackiest, or last-generated ideas. A teacher might unify group efforts classwide by compiling and graphing the collective scores of all the groups and recognizing the class for improving their scores as a whole class from one week to the next. By structuring intergroup interdependence, a teacher can use cooperative learning to promote a sense of community within a class.

Decision #7: What are the steps of the academic task and how is it explained?

As in any effective lesson, clear and specific instructions ward off student confusion and resultant frustration or conflict. Effective explanations include definitions of relevant concepts, explanations of steps of procedures, providing relevant examples, explaining the learning objectives, and connecting to students' prior learning and experiences. Checking for understanding—asking specific questions to check that students in fact understand what they are to do—is the final step of effective explanation. One distinct advantage of cooperative learning is that students who are confused can first ask teammates rather than the teacher for clarification.

Decision #8: What are the criteria for success, and how are they explained?

In cooperative group lessons, assessments are based upon predetermined criteria. For students to understand what they need to do in order to be considered successful by the teacher, the teacher must be explicit, clear, and detailed in explaining performance expectations. The performance expectations or success criteria may be as simple as completing the task within a designated time limit, answering a minimum number or percentage of questions correctly, or demonstrating the use of a procedure to solve a problem. Alternatively, criteria may be more complex. For example, multiple criteria may be identified in a rubric that specifies a set of quality standards or benchmarks.

Success criteria may be the same for all group members or differentiated for some. Teachers can and should differentiate and individualize performance expectations within a group and across groups. If certain groups of group members need additional encouragement or help, the teacher teaches, models, and coaches how to provide that encouragement and assistance. For some learning situations, all members may be working to achieve the same criteria; for other tasks, different members may be assessed on different criteria. For example, on a spelling list of graduated difficulty, Jamie, a student with an IEP, may be expected to learn the 10 core words while other teammates are expected to learn all 20. Criteria must be tailored to be challenging and realistic for each individual group member, and whatever the criteria, they must be structured so students can reach them without penalizing other students in the group. This is a challenging but essential role of the teacher in crafting successful cooperative lessons.

Decision #9: How is individual accountability structured, and how is it explained?

A group is not genuinely a cooperative learning group if individual members fail to learn what they are expected to learn, socially loaf and fail to contribute their part, or let others do all of the work. Stated otherwise, a teacher has not designed a genuine cooperative lesson if individual accountability, one of the five essential ingredients of cooperative learning, has not been structured into the lesson and effectively communicated to the students. Table 2.3 lists a sampling of 10 common ways in which a teacher can structure individual accountability into a lesson. These are but a few strategies for holding students individually accountable. Students can be very helpful in generating additional strategies for checking learning. We know students are more likely to buy into and take seriously the accountability strategies if they themselves have devised them.

As with our discussion of success criteria, we emphasize that not every cooperative group member needs to be held to the same performance level. For example, Carlotta, a student with Down syndrome, is expected to learn and recall 5 rather than 15 facts about the Amazon rain forest. She is held accountable for this differentiated expectation just as other team members are held accountable for their targeted outcomes.

Decision #10: How are the social skill objectives expectations explained?

Of equal importance to communicating the academic objectives and success criteria is communicating what social behaviors the teacher expects of students as they strive to achieve their academic objectives. The words *cooperation* and *collaboration* have very different meanings to different people, including students. In fact, they encompass hundreds of different skills. Therefore, teachers need to define operationally exactly which social skills are expected by explicitly explaining and modeling and/or reviewing what the expected social skills "look like" and "sound like." Social skills expectations that are clearly and specifically communicated prevent confusion and conflict among teammates. Additionally, if the teacher solicits rationales for the use of the social skill from students or the teacher's explanation clarifies how the social skills will help the

---

Table 2.3 Ten Ways to Structure Individual Accountability

1. **Keep the group size small.** It is difficult to socially loaf in a group of two!

2. **Observe group member participation.** Roam among groups, pause near each group, observe group members, record the frequency of each member's contributions, and/or make note of examples of positive words or actions of individual members.

3. **Spot-check**. While groups are working, stop and check for understanding with individual team members. Ask teammates to check for understanding with one another.

4. **Use colored pens or markers.** When brainstorming, each group member uses a different colored pen to write ideas on a team idea page.

5. **Assign a team member the role of "checker."** The checker's job is to check for understanding by asking each member to explain the group's answers or rationale underlying the answer.

6. **Have team members sign to verify participation and mastery**. Members and teams are only assessed after they agree and verify (by having a checker check) that they each know or are able to do what they are collectively and individually expected to know or do.

7. **Have team members teach what they learn to someone else outside of the group.** It is said we remember and understand 20 percent of what we hear, 50 percent of what we see demonstrated, 70 percent of what we actually try, and 90 percent of what we teach to another person. If materials are jigsawed, when team members explain their part, they are teaching someone else!

8. **Individually assess each member of the group.** There are several variations on this accountability strategy. Individual assessments can include "practice tests" to see who is ready and who needs more help or practice. One assessment can be selected to represent the entire team. The team can earn "bonus" points or privileges if every team member scores above a set criterion. The team can also earn extra points for an individual member's personal improvement on his or her performance (e.g., getting 10 rather than 7 answers correct after studying with the team).

9. **Randomly call on a group member to answer for the group.** The representative can report out within the group or to the entire class. Each team can be numbered and teammates assigned a letter, A, B, C, etc. The numbers and letters then are used to select group reporters randomly. For example, "Let's hear from Team 6, Person B."

10. **Public presentation of work.** Have teammates present their learning or product to other groups or the class. Be sure each member has a role in the presentation.

students be successful in this and future work, students are more likely to use the skills, as they will see their relevance to their work on the task and/or in their lives in general. Social skills generally are assigned to all members of a group. Sometimes, however, select skills are assigned to certain groups or individual students who may have individual social skills goals or needs (e.g., Rich is told the teacher is specifically looking for him to raise his hand to signal his desire to contribute as an alternative to interrupting teammates).

Phase III Decisions: Monitoring and Intervening During Face-to-Face Interactions

In Phase III, students are engaged in face-to-face interaction in their groups. The teacher's primary job at this point is to monitor group work and intervene, as needed. The teacher needs to plan in advance how to monitor (i.e., Decision #11) and how best to provide task assistance and prompt the use of social skills (i.e., Decision #12).

Decision #11: How are students' behaviors monitored? Who monitors?

Once students are engaged in collaborative work, the teacher's role intensifies. Students may be engaged in a task; however, there is no guarantee that they are performing the task correctly or using small-group social skills. Therefore, the teacher must circulate among groups and monitor performance to determine if interventions are needed.

To monitor, a teacher may use a formal observation sheet to tally the frequency with which students use assigned social skills or other interpersonal skills. It is wise to observe formally only a few social skills (e.g., two or three)—the ones most relevant to the demands of the task. Anecdotal note taking of students' statements and problem-solving strategies also is important for providing meaningful and exact feedback to students. Focus on recording desired behaviors so you can acknowledge students' positive behaviors when sharing observations during group processing at Phase IV.

The teacher is not the only person who can monitor performance; student monitoring promotes student reflection and increases the amount of data collected on each student and group. A student may be assigned to the role of observer within a group or across several groups. When students observe, teachers need to make the task manageable. For example, the teacher can (a) limit the number of skills observed to one or two; (b) limit the observation time to a portion of the lesson (e.g., 5 to 10 minutes); (c) rotate the observer role among students; and, above all, (d) train students to identify accurately the skills they are observing and report their observations in a nonjudgmental way.

Placing a student in the observer role is a powerful way to enhance self-awareness and self-modification of interpersonal small-group behaviors. The observer is in the best position to learn about the impact of small-group social skills. To illustrate, consider placing a student who tends to dominate discussions in the role of the silent observer, watching for equal participation of the students in the group. Through observing other students, the student observer can become aware of the importance of each member having the opportunity to make contributions. This awareness can lead to that student modulating his or her own behavior in the future.

Whether or not a teacher elects to use student observers, the teacher must always engage in some observing, monitoring, and reflection. Among the questions teachers can ask themselves are the following:

- Are students practicing the specified social skills?
- Do students understand the task?
- Are students accepting individual accountability?
- Are the criteria for success appropriate, or are they too difficult or too easy for some or all of the students?

Decision #12: How do you intervene to provide task assistance or prompt use of social skills?

Monitoring and data collection during students' cooperative work enables a teacher to determine when an intervention may be needed—when it is necessary to clarify instructions, review procedures, answer student questions, or teach or review social skills. When problems are detected, the teacher must decide how best to intervene. It is wise to anticipate likely problems in advance in order to be prompt and decisive with interventions.

David and Roger Johnson (1999) are fond of telling two stories about intervening to teach social skills. The first involves a teacher confronted by three members of a group of four with the complaint, "Darin is under the table and won't come out." They demanded, "Make him come out!" Rather than start to solve the problem, the teacher asked the members what they had already tried to get Darin to rejoin the group. When they indicated that they had tried nothing yet, the teacher sent them back to try to figure out a strategy on their own. Moments later, the teacher looked at the group's table and saw no heads above the table. In a few minutes, when she checked again, all four heads had re-emerged, and all four students were working diligently. What had happened under the table? The teacher had no idea, but the group received a perfect score on their paper. Later, when the teacher returned papers, Darin confided with the teacher that this was the first perfect score he had ever received.

The second story involves a teacher who, during monitoring, noted a number of students who dominated group conversations. In the next cooperative group lesson, she gave each member of each group five poker chips with a different color for each group member. She instructed students to place one chip in the basket in the center of the table each time they spoke. The rule was that a student who had spent all of his or her chips could not speak again until everyone in the group had spent their chips. Only after every member's chips were in the basket could they get their five colored chips back and start all over again. Imagine the surprise when certain students discovered their chips were the only ones in the basket. This teacher only had to use this contrived yet highly illustrative device twice to get the message across and change student behavior.

The point of the "under the table" story is to resist the temptation to jump in and problem solve for students. Whenever a teacher answers a question or solves a problem that students can answer or solve themselves (given time, opportunity, practice, and motivation), that teacher takes away the opportunity for students to become independent solution finders. The point of the "poker chip" story is that sometimes a teacher needs to intervene by constructing mechanistic structures to prompt or "teach" the use of a social skill. Cooperative skills can be taught and learned, and often the best time to teach and learn social skills is when they are needed. Teaching skills in context (i.e., in the classroom) and practicing them in context (i.e., in cooperative learning groups) is critical, since the transfer of skills from one situation to another cannot be assumed.

Phase IV Decisions: Evaluating the Product and Group Processing of Social Skill Performance

In Phase IV, the teacher provides closure to the lesson by leading students to summarize what they have learned and how they might apply their knowledge to future learning or life situations. In particular, Phase IV is the time when the teacher gives students feedback on their academic performance (i.e., Decision #13) and guides students' reflection on their academic and social performance (i.e., Decision #14).

Decision #13: How is student academic performance evaluated? How and when do students receive teacher feedback on their academic performance?

When deciding how to explain the criteria for success (Decision #8), the teacher also is determining how the quality of students' academic learning will be evaluated. Additionally, if the teacher decides to structure incentive interdependence (Decision #6), then some type of recognition (e.g., grade, redeemable points, public presentation or display of work) must be attached to the feedback that students receive regarding their academic performance. Teachers need to be crystal clear from the start about the assessments that will be made, the predetermined criteria for success for those assessments, and associated incentives or reinforcement for meeting the criteria. Equally important is to follow through and perform the assessments as defined and provide immediate and specific feedback and contingent reinforcement.

Decision #14: How do you guide group processing of students' social skill performance?

Cooperative learning experiences should be lively, exciting, and fun. If working in a group is not enjoyable, something is gravely wrong. For group experiences to be productive and positive, problems must be discussed and solutions explored and agreed upon. One of the first things many teachers are tempted to do when they run short of time with cooperative groups is to abandon the group processing. However, group processing—one of the five essential ingredients—is necessary. Processing time must be set aside to help students improve the effectiveness of their interpersonal interactions so each member can contribute to the whole to the best of his or her ability. Individuals do not improve without feedback. The same can be said of groups. Group processing provides an opportunity for teams of individuals to reflect, celebrate, and set goals for improvement.

There are two levels of group processing—small-group and whole-group. In preparation for both levels of group processing, a teacher may ask students to self-evaluate their performance in their groups, particularly reflecting upon their social interactions with teammates. Students then have something concrete that they have thought about to bring to the processing discussions.

Small-Group Processing. Small-group processing occurs after each cooperative lesson or at the end of each day in which cooperative learning experiences are used. In small-group processing, members of each group describe what member actions were helpful and not helpful and make decisions (i.e., set goals) about what behaviors to continue or change. The teacher can share formal and anecdotal observations that have been gathered on each group during Phase III of a lesson. If groups had student observers, their observations also are shared with their respective groups and can be used to set goals.

Group processing can be done in many ways. Varying the processing procedures allows for different aspects of the collaborative learning process to be examined from one reflection time to the next, and it keeps group processing interesting and exciting for the students. Table 2.4 offers a wide range of teacher-directed and more student-directed processing methods. The key to successful small-group processing is to provide structure and to make the processing specific and positive.

Whole-group Processing. In addition to small-group processing, the teacher should engage students in whole-group processing. Whole-group processing can follow small-group processing, with the teacher summarizing observations across all of the groups and inviting groups to share success stories about creative ways in which they approached a challenge or solved a problem. A teacher can also convene periodic whole-group processing sessions as a type of class meeting.

Whenever processing occurs, whether small-group or whole-group, a general rule is to describe the *behaviors* observed and avoid naming *who* exhibited the behaviors. Two other general rules are to (a) provide sufficient time so that students see group processing as an important part of their schoolwork and (b) clearly communicate that the purpose of processing is to think positively in order to solve problems and celebrate one another. Group processing is intended to build enthusiasm for cooperative work. This occurs when students reflect upon how they were successful and how they could be even more successful together.

AN EXAMPLE OF A FORMAL COOPERATIVE GROUP LESSON

Let's bring cooperative group learning alive by examining an actual lesson, using the one-page lesson plan template (see Figure 2.2 on page 50) to summarize the

Table 2.4 Group Processing: Procedures, Definitions, and Examples

Procedures	Definitions	Examples
Group share	As a whole group, team members discuss what they did well.	"We all took turns contributing."
My contributions or accomplishments	Each member states what he or she did to help the team.	"I shared my opinions." "I researched my assigned part."
Checklist	Individuals score and discuss a 5- to 10-item checklist of behaviors important to team functioning.	1. I helped clarify ideas. 2. I shared my opinions. 3. I asked others to contribute.
Incomplete statements	Team members are given incomplete statements that they complete to describe their performance.	"We could improve our communication by . . ." "Three social skills we used that helped us work were . . ."
Continua	Team members are given a sheet of paper with a series of statements to which they react on a continuum.	I felt supported. No Somewhat Yes Everyone shared ideas. No Somewhat Yes
Turn to your neighbor	In a round-robin, each team member takes a turn complimenting the person on his or her right regarding a task or relationship behavior used in the group.	"You were a terrific timekeeper; we finished on time!" "I appreciated you asking for my opinion; I was afraid of interrupting."
Oral strength bombardment	One member is selected, and each teammate tells the person how he or she helped the group that day.	"You generated lots of possible solutions to the problems we had to solve."
Yearbook (i.e., written strength bombardment)	Each member passes around a note card with his or her name written on top. This card is a proxy "school yearbook." When everyone has written on each card, cards are returned to the owners to read and enjoy.	"Roses are red, violets are blue. A great idea generator; that would be you." "You came up with wild and crazy ideas that we really could shape into winners." "You are so supportive."
Role evaluation	Individuals and teammates describe how well members performed assigned roles.	"I used my timer to keep us within time limits." "You checked for understanding to be sure we all knew the answers."
Goal setting	Teams or individuals set goals for future behavior.	"We need to ask for one another's perspective." "I will praise others' contributions more."

components of the lesson. This lesson was designed by one of the authors, Jacqueline Thousand, to illustrate for teachers how to include students with identified disabilities and other challenges successfully in cooperative learning groups. As you read about this lesson, embrace this simulation and imagine being one of a group of middle-level students interpreting the poem, "The Little Boy and the Old Man" from Shel Silverstein's (1981) classic book of poems *A Light in the Attic.* Also, refer to the one-page lesson at a glance shown in Figure 2.2 and see how the narrative translates into the four phases of lesson planning and implementation.

Phase I Decisions: Academic and Social Objectives and Organizational Decisions

This language arts and diversity awareness lesson could be taught to students from upper elementary grades through adulthood. The academic objective for students is to interpret a poem that evokes strong feelings and empathy for the alienation that comes when people feel unnoticed or undervalued. For adults simulating this lesson, an additional objective is to experience how a lesson can be deliberately structured to capitalize upon student strengths and work around their perceived challenges or limitations.

Groups work in teams of five. At least one member of the group must be able to read the poem and one must be able to write. Otherwise, groups are heterogeneously mixed by gender, English language proficiency, gifts, and challenges. The teacher strategically groups members and assigns roles with their unique learning characteristics in mind. The room is arranged so students sit close together at a small table or in a circle without a table so they can easily hear each other's contributions. Each group has one poem (see Table 2.5 on page 51), one question-and-answer template (see Table 2.6 on page 51), one sheet of lined paper, and one writing utensil. Now, how is this lesson set up? How does the lesson create a sense of positive interdependence among group members? What interpersonal skills are needed to interpret the poem?

Phase II Decisions: Opening and Setting Up the Lesson

This lesson features 7 of the 10 ways to create positive interdependence (see Figure 2.2). First, each group produces one set of agreed-upon answers (i.e., goal interdependence) to the four questions (see Table 2.6). Each group can earn up to 100 points for the group answer sheet (i.e., incentive interdependence): 20 points for each of the four answers to the questions and 20 points if all members sign their initials on the answer sheet within 30 minutes. Each group shares one poem and one answer sheet (i.e., resource interdependence).

Role interdependence and simulation interdependence are also built into this lesson. Each group member is assigned a different role (i.e., reader, recorder, timekeeper, encourager, and checker), as defined in Table 2.7 (page 52). Each role is specifically designed and assigned to accommodate the needs of a particular group member with a particular challenge. In the case of adults who are undertaking this lesson to learn how they can implement similar lessons in their classrooms, they will simulate assigned challenges.

Figure 2.2 Silverstein's "The Little Boy and the Old Man": One-Page Cooperative Group Learning Lesson Plan

Author(s): Jacqueline Thousand

Subject(s): Language Arts and Diversity Awareness

Grade Level(s): Upper elementary to adult

Phase I. ACADEMIC AND SOCIAL OBJECTIVES and ORGANIZATIONAL DECISIONS

Academic Objective(s): Interpret poem about feelings and diversity by agreeing on answers to four questions.

Social Skills Objective(s): Contributing ideas in response to questions, listening, praising others' ideas, pushing for many answers.

Group Size:	Group Membership:	Room Arrangement:	Materials Needed:	Distribution:
Five	X Heterogeneous ☐ Homogeneous ☐ Other Considerations for Membership: At least two members can read and one member can write.	☐ Desk Clusters X Chair Clusters ☐ Floor Clusters X Tables ☐ Other: _____	1 copy of poem 1 question & answer page 1 sheet of lined paper 1 writing utensil	X Shared ☐ Individual ☐ Jigsaw

Phase II. OPENING AND SETTING UP THE LESSON

Structuring of Positive Interdependence	Explanation of Steps of Academic Task	Explanation of Success Criteria	Explanation of Individual Accountability	Explanation of Social Skill Expectations
X GOAL (Agree to 4 answers) X INCENTIVE (100 points) X RESOURCE (1 poem & questions) X ROLE (5 roles, see Table 2.7) X SIMULATION (Teens with needs) X SEQUENCE (See 7 steps of task) X OUTSIDE FORCE (30 minutes) ☐ ENVIRONMENT ☐ IDENTITY ☐ INTERGROUP COOPERATION	1. Reader reads (Table 2.5). 2. Four questions (Table 2.6); recorder records all answers. 3. Reach consensus. 4. Checker checks. 5. Members sign. 6. Group processing in groups. 7. Teacher quizzes members and gives points and observational feedback.	"Each group can earn 100 points—20 for each question and 20 for signatures within 30 minutes—indicating each person contributed, encouraged, checked for agreement, and is ready to report out each answer."	"When you have signed and your checker is confident you all can answer all four questions, signal me and I will come over and quiz each of you on one of the questions. You get 20 points for each question and another 20 for your signature."	"I expect each of you to contribute at least one idea per question and see and hear you listen to and praise at least one other teammate's ideas. I want to see you push for many answers before deciding on one."

Phase III. MONITORING AND INTERVIEWING DURING FACE-TO-FACE INTERACTION

Who Monitors:

X Teacher: Observe each group 3–5 minutes
 ☐ Teacher & Students

How Students are Monitored:

X Informal Notes: Task and social behaviors
 ☐ Formal Observation Sheet

Intervening:

X What are likely tasks or social problems? Forget roles.
 X How do you intervene? Give reminder of definitions.

Phase IV. EVALUATING ACADEMIC PERFORMANCE AND GROUP PROCESSING OF SOCIAL SKILL PERFORMANCE

Academic Feedback (How and when is academic performance evaluated?):

When the group signals, the teacher randomly quizzes each member on one question, awards points, and shares observations of how the team worked together.

Social Skills Processing (How do students reflect on social interactions?):

Student-Self-Evaluation, by: Verbally answering the four group processing questions (see Table 2.8)

Small-Group Processing, by: Sharing observations with groups after quizzing members

Whole-Class Processing, by: Asking groups to share their answers and social skills they used

Table 2.5   Shel Silverstein's "The Little Boy and the Old Man"

The Little Boy and the Old Man

Said the little boy, "Sometimes I drop my spoon."
Said the old man, "I do that too."

The little boy whispered, "I wet my pants."
"I do that too," laughed the little old man.

Said the little boy, "I often cry."
The old man nodded, "So do I."

"But worst of all," said the boy, "it seems
Grown-ups don't pay attention to me."

And he felt the warmth of a wrinkled old hand.
"I know what you mean," said the little old man.

(Silverstein, 1981, p. 95)

Table 2.6   Question-and-Answer Template for "The Little Boy and the Old Man" Poem

Instructions: Please share your answers to each question. Be sure each team member contributes at least one answer to each of the four questions. Recorder, please record every answer given on the sheet of lined paper. When the group comes to agreement on one answer, please record it on this answer sheet. Be prepared to be quizzed by your teacher on any of the four questions.

Questions:

1. What is the poem saying? (__ minutes)
2. What emotion(s) does the poem evoke in you?
    How does this poem make you feel? (__ minutes)
3. What are two key words in the poem? Why did you select these words?
    Be prepared to defend your choices. (__ minutes)
4. How does this poem relate to diversity? How does the poem relate to the treatment of a person who learns differently or appears different in some way? (__ minutes)

Signature:

_____   _____

_____   _____

_____   _____

Note to group members: When you sign your name, it means you

a) contributed,
b) encouraged others to contribute,
c) checked for agreement on and understanding of the answers, and
d) are prepared to share answers in the large group and with your teacher.

Table 2.7	Roles for Poem Interpretation Lesson
Reader	Reads the poem out loud to the group as many times as needed and requested by group members.
Timekeeper	Notifies the group of approaching time limits on each question. Allots about 5 minutes per question. Moves the group along to the next question. Makes sure signatures are secured within the time limit.
Recorder	Reads the questions. Records all contributions on lined paper. Records agreed upon answer on answer sheet. Secures signatures within the time limit.
Encourager	Encourages teammates to contribute to each question by asking for their ideas and complimenting them on their contributions.
Checker	Checks to make certain each member can state each answer. Checks to make sure members agree on the reasons for the answers. Checks at any time during the discussion. Quizzes each team member on the answers before everyone signs answer sheet indicating they are all prepared to be quizzed by the teacher.

- The reader role is assigned to a member who is told that he has cerebral palsy and uses a wheelchair to get around and a hand stamp to sign his name. He is particularly theatrical and reads with expression, so a good choice for the reader role.
- Another member is told she has a specific learning disability and is unable to read, so she needs a reader to read the poem. This student has no trouble with telling time, so timekeeper is a role she can perform with ease.
- A third member is told he has a lot of energy and needs a role that keeps his mind and hands actively engaged. The *recorder* role is perfect to support this member's engagement.
- The fourth team member is introduced as someone who just transferred from a highly competitive and individualistic gifted and talented program. This member is not accustomed to valuing and complimenting the work of others and benefits socially by being assigned and playing the supportive role of encourager.
- The fifth group member is given a blindfold to wear throughout the task, simulating being a student who is visually impaired. Since this person does not have access to print or to the body language of teammates, the role of checker allows the student to be able to slow down or stop the group when she needs to check for understanding and to ensure that she knows the agreed-upon answers at the end by quizzing everyone in the group on the agreed-upon answers.

The academic task requires sequence interdependence; that is, groups must perform a sequence of steps (outlined in the "Explanation of Steps of Academic Task" section of Phase II of the one-page lesson plan in Figure 2.2) to be successful. First, the reader reads the poem. Next, teammates generate responses to the four questions, while the recorder records all responses on lined paper. Teammates then come to consensus on one answer per question, which the recorder records on the answer sheet (see Table 2.6). The checker checks to be sure all members can articulate the answers before members initial the answer sheet to indicate that each member contributed, encouraged others, checked for agreement, and is ready to report out each answer. Team members then generate answers to the group-processing questions (see Table 2.8) as the recorder records answers on the back of the answer sheet. Finally, the team calls over the teacher to quiz members randomly as to the answers, award points for answering and signing, and offer observations on their collaborative work.

Finally, the time limit of 30 minutes serves as an outside enemy and structures outside force interdependence. This time limit creates a sense of urgency that will focus attention and coordinate actions to contribute answers, encourage divergent thinking, come to agreement, and process team effectiveness.

You can see the exact explanations for the academic task, the expected success criteria, the ways in which individual students are held accountable, and the expectations for students to use the social skills that are identified as objectives for the lesson in the lesson plan presented in Figure 2.2.

Phase III Decisions: Monitoring and Intervening During Face-to-Face Interactions

There are no student observers in this lesson. The instructor is the observer and rotates among the groups systematically, visiting each group to listen in for three to five minutes to (1) ensure group members understand and are following the steps of the task, (2) ensure that students are practicing the social skills of contributing and generating many ideas and encouraging and praising each other, (3) check for group members' performance of assigned roles, and (4) intervene if necessary. No observation form is used; instead, the instructor records anecdotal notes of strategies teams use to come to agreement, particularly interesting responses to questions, and examples of encouraging statements. An anticipated problem is that those assigned the roles of encourager, timekeeper, and checker may get so caught up in the task that they forget to engage in their roles. If this is observed, the instructor will check for understanding and provide a verbal reminder of what the role looks and sound like.

Phase IV Decisions: Evaluating the Product and Group Processing of Social Skill Performance

Teams receive academic feedback when they signal the instructor that they have completed the task. The instructor then randomly quizzes each member on one of the questions and assigns points for each answer and the signatures on the Question-and-Answer Template (for a maximum total of 100 points). Teams also receive feedback on members' interpersonal engagement when the instructor shares specific examples of phrases members used to encourage and extend one another's contributions and how the group approached the task and engaged in roles. Members of each group are prompted to self-evaluate their social skills, roles, and overall performance as a small group by answering the four processing questions listed in Table 2.8. The lesson closes with the instructor asking groups to share with the entire class the secrets to their success; any particular challenges experienced; and answers observed to be particularly insightful, deep, interesting, or unique.

The authors' experience in having taught this lesson to thousands of adults and youth over the years is that those who are asked to simulate blindness and engage in the role of checker often express frustration with how difficult it is to process and retain verbal information and distinguish speakers when blindfolded. In processing, they identify ways teammates could be more supportive by pausing and checking for understanding; identifying themselves before speaking; and noticing that when they communicate nonverbally (e.g., nodding in agreement), this information is lost to the teammate who cannot see. The observations on the part of the checkers are a natural lead-in to a discussion of the fourth question, "How does this poem relate to diversity? How does the poem relate to the treatment of a person who learns differently or appears different in some way?" Group discussion can focus on how this lesson illustrates ways in which roles and cooperative group lessons, in general, can be crafted to ensure that all group members can participate in ways that support their challenges and take advantage of their strengths.

Table 2.8   Questions for Group Processing

1. What small-group interpersonal social skills did we use?

2. What could we have improved upon?

3. How well did we perform our roles of timekeeper, reader, recorder, encourager, and checker?

4. What would help us perform our roles even better next time?

WHAT DO STUDENTS SAY ABOUT COOPERATIVE GROUP LEARNING?

If you ask your students why they like to work in cooperative learning groups, they may share some of the same sentiments that these students shared with us.

Students at John Adams Middle School in Albuquerque, New Mexico, are articulate about why they like cooperative group learning. One student focuses on how much easier it is to learn with a peer: "It is easier for a student to approach a peer than a teacher." Another student adds this perspective: "Since we are being taught right now, we have been taught more recently than they (teachers) have. So, we know what helps and what really doesn't help."

Similarly, high school students are enthusiastic and articulate. A Twin Valley High School (Elverson, Pennsylvania) student says, "It is more interesting to learn with your friends than to sit and listen to your teachers talk." An Etiwanda High School (Etiwanda, California) student explains, "It is more fun."

SUMMARY

You now are thoroughly prepared to empower students as co-teachers through the use of cooperative group learning. You know the common attributes of cooperative group structures. You are familiar with quick cooperative structures, base teams, and the five essential ingredients of cooperative learning experiences—positive interdependence, individual accountability, group processing, social skills, and face-to-face interaction.

In addition, you know how to translate these five ingredients into a cohesive lesson through a series of 14 instructional decisions. You have a one-page lesson plan format at your disposal for designing your own formal cooperative group lessons. You also have examined a model lesson that illustrates how to tailor cooperative group learning to the diversity within a classroom. Now, go give cooperative structures a try! We predict your success in building students' competence and confidence in learning and supporting one another and tapping into students as a resource for themselves and one another as they meet academic and social goals!

Students as Peer Tutors and Partner Learners

3

Another way to deal with more students in the classroom within the context of diminishing resources (especially when the students come from diverse backgrounds and skill levels) is to arrange for students to learn how to be effective peer tutors and partner learners. When students become peer tutors and partner learners, they unleash their potential to delve deeper, learn more, and retain better the content they are tutoring. In this chapter, we pose the following questions frequently asked about peer tutoring and partner learning.

1. What are common attributes of all approaches to peer tutoring and partner learning?

2. How does a teacher arrange for students to learn peer tutoring and partner learning skills?

3. What are the benefits of peer tutoring? Who benefits?

4. What is an example of a peer tutoring/partner learning lesson that accommodates for the learning challenges of a diverse group of students?

5. What do students say about peer tutoring and partner learning? Why do they like learning this way?

MEET SOME PEER TUTORS

There are many ways to collaborate with students and others to create effective peer tutoring and partner learning situations. In this section, we showcase three examples of peer tutoring and partner learning implemented in elementary and secondary classrooms. The examples include a variety of subject matter (math, spelling, and social studies) and illustrate both classwide and dyad approaches.

A Peer Tutoring Program to Support English Language Learners

Julietta and Michelle are fifth graders at a large, urban elementary school. Julietta is a recent immigrant and an English language learner. She is nervous about being in a new country and embarrassed to speak in front of her teachers and classmates. Upon entering her language arts class, Julietta was placed next to Michelle, as an empty desk was available there. Julietta tripped and dropped her books as she neared her desk. She felt her face flush as she bent to pick up her books. Michelle quickly got out of her desk and assisted Julietta with picking up her belongings. Julietta was immediately comforted by the assistance, Michelle's reassuring smile, and the gentle touch of Michelle's hand on her arm.

It soon became quite apparent that Julietta did not understand the teacher. She could not follow Mrs. Robinson's directions and, thus, often did not complete class assignments. Since the two girls were seated at adjoining desks and students in this class frequently worked in pairs or groups, Michelle explained what to do and sometimes modeled what to do for Julietta. Mrs. Robinson noticed how anxious Julietta appeared, except when she was working with Michelle. When the teacher asked Julietta if she liked receiving assistance from Michelle, Julietta beamed and vigorously nodded her head as she said, "*Si. Si.* Oh, she is my *maestra* [teacher] too." Mrs. Robinson arranged for Michelle to receive two 30-minute training sessions to learn how to peer tutor from Mr. La Due, the guidance counselor, who managed a peer-tutoring program. It was important to be sure that Michelle knew how to support and empower Julietta and not simply do the work for her.

The two students really appreciated learning about reciprocal teaching. Reciprocal teaching is a well-researched method of teaching students to be active readers.[1] It was originally developed by Palincsar and Brown (1988) as an explicit metacognitive procedure to increase reading comprehension for students with learning disabilities. Reciprocal teaching has been demonstrated to be effective for normally developing students, as well as students with mental retardation, students with emotional disturbance, and students who are learning a second language. Reciprocal teaching is useful for any task that requires reading comprehension (e.g., reading to solve math problems, reading to gain information from a science or social studies text). Reciprocal teaching can be considered a study skill as well as a strategy because it requires explicit teaching of the procedures.

Each peer models each of the four reciprocal teaching steps. Lovitt (1991) outlined the teaching procedure for each step as follows:

Step 1: Question—Ask a question about the main idea of a selected reading.

Step 2: Summarize—In a brief sentence or two, paraphrase the main idea and details.

Step 3: Clarify—Identify any words or concepts that need to be defined.

Step 4: Predict—Based on the information read so far, ask, "What will happen next?"

---

[1] Teachers in Highland Park, Michigan, decided to implement reciprocal teaching as part of their reading instruction program at the elementary through high school levels (Carter, 1997). At the student level, dramatic improvements were observed on the Michigan assessment instrument in reading comprehension. At the faculty level, teachers themselves used reciprocal teaching on each other to enhance their proficiency in acquiring a second language (a goal for their staff development).

Teachers often ask their students to generate and post on their desks a Reciprocal Teaching Guide (similar to a number line) with the following cues: Question, Summarize, Clarify, and Predict. These cues help students remember to pose the questions to themselves and their partners while they read to learn the content.

Michelle and Julietta were enrolled in the same math class. One day over lunch, Mrs. Robinson was speaking with Ms. Hussein, the math teacher, about how well Julietta and Michelle worked together in her language arts class. Ms. Hussein noted that Julietta had no difficulty at all in math and, as a matter of fact, Michelle was struggling in math. Ms. Hussein decided to speak with the two girls to see if they would like to sit near each other in math so Julietta could assist Michelle with grasping the math facts, principles, and concepts they were learning. They loved the idea! In fact, they decided to use the reciprocal teaching method to help each other solve the word problems that had always vexed them! Michelle's grades on quizzes and tests began to improve.

Michelle and Julietta developed a close friendship. They gained a new respect for each other when the roles of tutor and tutee were reversed and they realized that each had unique strengths. They were both moving to the middle school for sixth grade. Michelle was learning a little Spanish from Julietta. Spanish happened to be one of the electives available to middle school students in the arts rotation. Michelle was planning to take the Spanish class and knew that Julietta would be a great afterschool tutor if she needed support to learn, speak, and practice her Spanish language.

A Classwide Peer Tutoring Program to Acquire Math Facts

Laurie LaPlant was a collaborating teacher who helped Nadine Zane, a third-grade teacher, develop a reciprocal peer tutoring program that allowed all the third graders to learn their math facts. They made sure that the tutors and tutees practiced sequential steps to incorporate auditory, verbal, and writing components in a repeated rehearsal format (LaPlant & Zane, 1994). The teacher scheduled at least one opportunity a day for reciprocal tutoring, which required about 10 minutes to allow for each partner to play the role of tutor and tutee. The students focused on six math facts per session (four known and two unknown or unmastered) and practiced until they achieved mastery using auditory, visual, and kinesthetic activities.

The teacher was concerned about the way in which two of her students were treating each other during their reciprocal tutoring sessions. She noticed they frequently used "put-down" statements and failed to use the reinforcement, feedback, and other appropriate social skills they had demonstrated during training. They fought over the materials as well. However, their progress in acquiring math facts, as well as their written feedback, indicated they perceived the sessions to be going well academically. When the collaborating teacher interviewed them about the teacher's concerns, they each made accusations about the other.

With additional training, modeling, and supervision of the tutoring sessions, these two students developed their skills in making positive statements and sustaining positive interactions with one another. In addition to the math facts, they kept track of two items as part of their data collection procedures:

"saying nice things" and "saying thank you." Both students kept a graphic representation of their performance and set up a contract with their teacher whereby they could collect jointly accrued points based on the number of times they both made positive statements. The points could be traded later for activities they both enjoyed (e.g., learning games, lunch with a favorite teacher, etc.).

With this slight adjustment to the classwide peer tutoring program, the students improved their positive social interactions even as the supervision was gradually reduced. They consistently increased the number of math facts mastered, and they were able to sustain more positive interactions with each other.

An Individual Peer Tutoring Program to Increase Spelling Skills

Teachers often share concerns about specific students in their classrooms. They say, "I'm not sure that peer tutoring could work with all the students in my class!" In this section, we show how a teacher increased spelling accuracy by providing two students with autism a one-to-one learning experience with a peer.

McNeil (1994) designed a cross-age peer tutoring program to increase the achievement of two goals related to both students' IEPs: (1) academic progress and (2) social interactions with another person. John was 13 years old and Ron was 9 years old. Both boys were able to communicate orally and occasionally engaged in noncompliant and self-injurious behavior. Each tutoring session consisted of 10 trials to practice 10 spelling words. A percent correct was calculated for each session. Each session began with John giving Ron a verbal cue (e.g., "Ron, spell the word *car*."). A trial ended after 10 seconds of no response (scored as 0), 1 minute of an actual attempt (scored as 1), or 2 seconds after the word was correctly spelled (scored as 2). This method of recording was intended to make the program seem similar to scoring points for basketball games, a sport that both Ron and John enjoyed. Reliability of the scoring procedures was obtained every session by a student teacher and John, the peer tutor. Their data always agreed 100 percent.

Three different lists of words were used to verify that the peer tutoring program was effective. Initially, to assess level of mastery for list #1, John presented the 10 spelling words one at a time to Ron, who either spelled correctly or incorrectly using magnetic letters placed in front of him. No praise, prompting, or correction was offered during the baseline sessions.

During the peer tutoring interactions, John praised Ron for each word spelled correctly and recorded a score of 2. If a word was spelled incorrectly, John explained, "Ron, the word is spelled. . . ." Ron was then given a second chance to spell the word. If he was successful, John praised him and recorded a score of 1. If he was not successful, John prompted him again until Ron spelled the word correctly. John then praised him and recorded a score of 0.

Ron's spelling accuracy on each list of words improved only when the peer tutoring interactions were used. For the first list, the initial percent correct scores ranged from 0 to 20 percent with an average of 6.67 percent. During the peer tutoring interactions, the spelling scores ranged from 50 to 100 percent with an average of 88.89 percent. For the second list, the percent correct initially ranged from 0 to 40 percent with an average of 14 percent. During peer tutoring interactions, the range was 50 to 60 percent with an average of 55 percent. For the third list, the percent correct initially ranged from 0 to 40 percent with an average of 14 percent. The range for peer tutoring interactions was 60 to 70 percent with an average of 66 percent.

The results showed that John's spelling performance improved as well when he became the peer tutor, and he seemed to be pleased that Ron acted as though he enjoyed the tutoring sessions. John was proud that Ron showed he was able to learn the spelling words much faster with the increased opportunities to respond and the consistent positive feedback. Ron continued this program with a different peer tutor and proceeded to master four-letter spelling words that were related to his own IEP objectives.

Using Peer Tutors to Teach Miranda Rights to Students

Many teachers are interested in making social studies instruction relevant to their students' lives. One way to do that is to use peer tutoring to help students realize the importance of their civil rights. One civil right that is often overlooked is the Miranda rights that all citizens have. All students can benefit if they learn and can teach one another what the Miranda rights are and how to ensure that they are received. Students can learn a teaching procedure known as the cued response in which peer tutors practice a variety of situations followed by discussions of their choices. The cued response is a short, concrete, affirmative statement that the student is taught to say respectfully to each of the Miranda warnings. Because the Miranda warnings themselves often are hard to understand, students first learn how to translate what the statements mean into colloquial language, as shown in the excerpted scripts in Table 3.1 (Sears, Bishop, & Stevens, 1989).

Peer tutoring was found to be an effective way to practice what happens during mock arrests. Peers practiced different lines of questioning with several variations that were conducted by a variety of people, individually and in

Table 3.1 Examples of Traditional and Simplified Miranda Rights

Traditional Miranda Warning: 1. You have the right to remain silent.

Simplified Miranda Warning: 1. It's OK if you don't want to talk; I won't try to make you.

Traditional Miranda Warning: 2. Should you give up the right to remain silent, what you say can and will be used against you in a court of law.

Simplified Miranda Warning: 2. If you do talk to me about what happened, I will use what you tell me to try to send you to jail.

SOURCE: Sears, J., Bishop, A., & Stevens, E. (1989). Teaching Miranda rights to students who have mental retardation. *Teaching Exceptional Children, 21*(3), 38–42.

groups, so as to replicate as closely as possible the real thing. For example, teachers brought in mock uniforms for the peers who played the role of police officer and suits for those peers who played the role of lawyer. As shown in Table 3.2, peers worked together to practice various scenarios (Sears et al., 1989). They made sure that each peer had a chance to be the police officer or the lawyer or the person being arrested.

Once students have learned to use the cued response, then they can use that same procedure to learn other complex material involving procedural knowledge, such as learning how to vote without being unduly influenced by other people.

Table 3.2 Example of Cued Responses for Miranda Rights Role-Play

Scene 1. No Miranda warning is given, but student is asked to state name and address.

Cued response: Give name and address, always followed by "I want a lawyer," and the request to "Please call my (father, mother, friend, guardian) at (phone number)."

Scene 2. A Miranda warning is given.

Cued response: "I want a lawyer."

Scene 3. A Miranda warning is given, and student is encouraged, coaxed, cajoled into talking: "It's really OK; You have nothing to fear if you tell the truth."

Cued response: "I want a lawyer."

Scene 4. A Miranda warning is given, and student is told the police are friends.

Cued response: "I want a lawyer."

Scene 5. A Miranda warning is given, and student is offered candy, food, money as a friendly gesture.

Cued response: "I want a lawyer," followed by polite refusal of anything offered.

Scene 6. A Miranda warning is given, and student is asked to sign for belongings.

Cued response: "I want to wait until my lawyer is here."

SOURCE: Sears, J., Bishop, A., & Stevens, E. (1989). Teaching Miranda rights to students who have mental retardation. *Teaching Exceptional Children, 21*(3), 38–42.

WHAT IS PEER TUTORING/ PARTNER LEARNING?

What do these examples have in common? Peers are teaching and learning from each other, guided by their teachers, and they are learning to be accountable for their own and their partner's achievements. Cross-age and peer tutoring are methods of instruction in which learners help each other and, in turn, learn by teaching. Peer tutoring is the process by which a competent student, with minimal training and with a teacher's guidance, helps one or more students at the same grade level learn a skill or concept. Cross-age tutors are students in higher grade levels who work with younger students. Peer tutoring and partner learning situations can be arranged as a whole-school activity in which all classes are involved during a specific time of day, a whole-class activity, or an activity that involves two specific students. The important components of a peer tutoring/partner learning activity are discussed in the following section.

ESSENTIAL INGREDIENTS OF PEER TUTORING AND PARTNER LEARNING

One reason peer tutoring works may be that tutors and tutees speak a more similar language than do teachers and students. Some researchers have found that students feel freer to ask questions or express their opinions with a peer rather than a teacher (Damon & Phelps, 1989). In other words, peer tutors may simply be good teachers who use instructional strategies known to increase response rates and academic gains, such as increasing on-task behavior, prompting and guiding, praising and encouraging participation, and adjusting to specific needs of the learner.

Six conditions must be met for effectively transmitting knowledge through peer tutoring:

1. The tutor must provide relevant help that is

2. appropriately elaborated,

3. timely, and

4. understandable to the tutee; and

5. the tutor must provide an opportunity for the tutee to use the new information; and

6. the tutee must take advantage of that opportunity (Webb, 1989).

Teachers incorporate these dimensions into clearly structured lesson plans with objectives, instructional procedures, evaluation, and feedback.

GETTING STARTED WITH PEER TUTORING AND PARTNER LEARNING

How do teachers create viable and cohesive lessons that lead their students to become effective peer tutors and partner learners? Planning and guiding students to collaborate in partner learning or peer tutoring lessons requires thoughtful decision making. To illustrate, Laurie LaPlant and Nadine Zane (1994) developed an elegant design framework for recruiting, training, monitoring, and evaluating instruction delivered by students, which is shown in Table 3.3. Laurie and Nadine pose the questions in this framework to anyone planning for peer tutoring. The answers that are jointly developed provide important boundaries for the program and participants.

Table 3.3 A Quick Guide to Establishing Partner Learning Systems

I. Identification	**Who will participate?**
	How will you determine who will participate? Who will be instructed? How will this benefit the person instructed?
	Who will be the peer tutor(s)?
	How will this benefit the peer tutor(s)?
II. Recruitment	**Sources of Tutors and Tutees**
	Same-aged? Within class? Cross-aged? Across classes? Resources outside of the school?
	Method of Informing Potential Participants and Their Families
	Direct contact? Teacher, guidance, parent referral? Class presentation? Other? Will there be a contract between the participants to be partners for a given period of time?
	Who Has or Needs to Acquire Teaching Skills?
	What technical skills do the peer tutors/partner learners need (e.g., direct questioning, checking for understanding, giving feedback, data collection, evaluating each other's performance)? Does the peer tutor have these skills? Does the peer tutor need to acquire the skills?
	What interpersonal skills does the peer tutor need (e.g., giving praise, giving eye contact, assessing another's willingness to participate, problem solving)? Does the peer tutor have these skills? Does the peer tutor need to acquire the skills, and how will the teacher arrange this instruction if needed?
III. Training	**Who will conduct the training?** (Will you or someone else do it?)
	Where will training occur? How many sessions will there be, and what length of time is needed for each session?
	What will be taught in each session? How will the peer tutor teach it; that is, what methods will be used to gain eye contact, state instructions, give recognition (e.g., verbal praise, points, stars, or tokens) and corrective feedback?
	What materials are needed for teaching, and how will the instructor use them?
	What materials are needed to record the tutee's responses, and how will the tutor use them? What materials are needed to summarize and graph the tutee's responses, and how will the tutor and/or tutee use them?
	How will the tutee monitor his or her own progress?
	How will the tutee provide the tutor with feedback regarding the instructor's teaching? How will the tutee be taught how to participate (e.g., greet the tutor, receive instruction, thank and say good-bye to the tutor)?
	How will the peer tutor evaluate the quality and effectiveness of his or her own technical and interpersonal behavior? How will the tutee evaluate his or her own learning and/or interpersonal behavior?

IV. Delivery and Supervision of Peer Tutoring

When, how often, and where will the instructional sessions occur? (The more frequent—daily for 10 to 15 minutes—the better!) When and how will you get a measure of preinstructional performance *before* the peer tutor begins instruction? This is a necessary first step before partners come together for instruction!

Who is responsible for supervision?

Are you and/or someone else responsible? How frequently does supervision—direct observation of the instruction—need to occur (e.g., daily in the beginning? weekly later on?)?

How will you communicate with the classroom teacher, the special educator, and any others who are concerned with the instructors' and learners' performance?

What will you look for in your observations? Which technical and interpersonal skills are you noticing? What forms will you use to record your observations? How will you deliver constructive feedback to the peer tutor and tutee?

Keep a copy of all of the materials that you prepared for training along with the materials the students will use in the tutorial sessions so you can pass it on to others who may want to achieve the same results you did.

V. Evaluation

Is the training content relevant and effective? Are the learner's objectives being met? Are you seeing progress? Is the instruction still necessary? What is the next step in instruction? How might the tutor motivate the tutee?

Is there a need to change in any aspect of a partner relationship? What do the tutor and tutee think about their relationship and progress? How will you arrange for the partners to determine what they did well and what they think they could improve (i.e., engage in reflection)?

Is the frequency of the teacher monitoring and evaluation session adequate or overkill? Include how you plan to get initial performance measures (e.g., pretests) before the instruction on how to tutor begins. Include all data forms and graphing formats that will be used.

VI. Reinforcement and Recognition

How will you provide recognition for partner learner/peer tutoring participation? Will you provide *formal* recognition (e.g., ceremonies, awards, parties, mention in school newsletter)? Will you provide *informal* recognition (e.g., observed and interviewed by a visitor to the school, presentation at a university class, letter from a pleased parent, letter of thank-you to partners, requesting student to tutor a classmate?)?

Tip: Keep an implementation log of what *actually* happened as you carry out your training plan. Also, include any samples of the learner's work, the peer tutor and tutee self-assessments, sample data sheets, comments, or any other anecdotal outcomes that you found interesting. Be sure to craft a graph of the performance to help both tutor and tutee "see" their progress.

(Continued)

(Continued)

VII. Self-Reflection, Analysis, and Redesign	**Here is where you get to interpret what happened.** What did your measures/observations suggest about your planned approach?
	What would you change about your tutoring and/or tutor-training program if you were to go through the process again?
	What recommendations do you have for yourself and other teachers about planning for and carrying out partner learning programs?
VIII. Share Your Results	**Share your strategies and results with other teachers, students, and administrators in your school and school district.** It is always helpful for others to learn what you discovered.

Identifying potential peer instructors can be as simple as noticing when a student may need a partner to tutor her to acquire a skill or more actively participate in lessons, or a student may need to develop skills in a leadership role. A parent, teacher, or other staff member can initiate a request for a peer or partner learning system. Recruitment efforts can be simple or complex, ranging from one teacher noticing who in the classroom might work well with another student to arranging for older students in the school to tutor younger students as part of their educational programs. Methods to recruit can include flyers, announcements, class presentations, and teacher recommendations.

Training and supervision are important starter steps because those who serve in these roles must acquire certain technical instructional skills (e.g., asking questions rather than telling answers, checking for understanding, giving appropriate feedback, etc.). Training can range from having the tutors observe as the instruction is modeled to formal step-by-step procedures whereby tutors learn to set objectives, use instructional materials, state instructions clearly, use respectful age-appropriate language to correct the tutee, praise correct responses, and so on.

Supervision and evaluation go hand in hand with providing appropriate reinforcement and celebration to the tutors and tutees, partners in their respective instructional journeys. Evaluation involves frequent (daily checkups, weekly progress monitoring) assessment to (a) discover whether or not there are any problems to solve (such as missing instructional materials) and develop mutually beneficial solutions, (b) assess the progress of both tutor and tutee and adjust the tasks accordingly, and (c) determine the effectiveness of the instructional methods and the interpersonal interaction between tutor and tutee.

The culminating component is designing and implementing ways to reinforce students for participating in peer tutoring and partner learning relationships. Reinforcement systems can be informal (e.g., on-the-spot "high fives" after a session) to formal (e.g., tutors and tutees having a pizza party during lunch hour at the end of a marking period, recognition in a classroom or school newsletter).

Teachers, as well as peers, need to learn how to avoid the pitfalls of peer tutoring and partner learning situations. They learn what to do and what to avoid, as illustrated in Table 3.4. With frequent opportunities to reflect on their interactions, partners often add their own discoveries about what to do and what not to do.

Peers can become more effective peer tutors when they learn how to think like a teacher. At John Adams Middle School in Albuquerque, New Mexico, prospective peer tutors participate in structured activities to prepare for the tutorial role. They are encouraged to understand what students need from peers. For example, students who are being tutored may need (a) someone to sit next to them during class and explain the work using words that are just right for them, (b) more opportunities to ask questions when they are confused (instead of being embarrassed in front of the whole class), (c) someone who can tell them right away whether their answers are right or wrong, and (d) someone to help and encourage them to finish class work. Prospective peer tutors are also encouraged to think like a teacher. They review the instructional cycle shown in Figure II.1 and discuss how that might show up during a tutorial session. As shown in Table 3.5, they review the list of strategies that show they can think like a teacher, adding some of their own ideas about how they think teachers think.

Table 3.4   Peer Tutoring/Partner Learning: What to Do and What *Not* to Do

What to Do	**What *Not* to Do**
Greet your partner using his or her name.	Do not use labels or nicknames.
Focus on what your partner can do.	Do not focus on what your partner cannot do.
Keep a neutral tone of voice when giving a correction.	Do not use a negative tone of voice to correct your partner's mistakes.
Be on time for your peer tutoring or partner learning sessions.	Avoid being late; every minute counts!
Be flexible if your partner needs extra time or material.	Do not be rigid when implementing the peer tutoring interactions.
Remember that learning is emotional and personal!	Do not take it personally if your partner seems upset when being corrected.
Celebrate every success, no matter how small! Remember to exchange ideas about how to make the session more enjoyable in the future.	Do not skip the celebration and reflection part of the lesson.

SOURCE: Adapted from Villalobos, Tweit-Hull, & Wong (2002), pp. 408–409.

Table 3.5 Peer Tutors Think Like Teachers

Understand the instructional cycle.	Plan, implement and monitor, reflect and evaluate (review Figure II.1).
Lead to the answer instead of giving it away.	Ask leading questions. Guide one step at a time to allow the student to arrive at his or her own answer.
Use examples to "show" rather than "tell."	Give plenty of examples and samples. Ask the student to follow along as you show how to do the task. Then ask the student to do it alone with you observing.
Restate.	Ask, "What comes next?" Clarify the teacher's instructions by using your own words (which may be more understandable to the student).
Redirect.	Refocus the student. Bring attention back to the task at hand.
Chunk.	Assist by showing the general location where an answer may be found (such as a paragraph where a specific comprehension question is addressed).
Check for understanding, often.	Ask Who, What, When, Why, Where, and How questions often. Ask questions that require more than yes or no answers (e.g., Why do you think. . . ?). Encourage the student to share personal opinions about what is being learned.
Be aware of the learning environment.	Consciously observe what other students are doing around you and your student. Anticipate the teacher's next activity. Stay within the time frame.
Use tools!	Use the whiteboard/blackboard, multiplication charts, grammar word lists, spell checker, computer, etc.
Check in to find out how the student is doing.	Ask, "How are you doing?" Ask, "What can I do to make learning easier, more fun, faster?" Ask, "What would you like to do next?"
Understand "kid talk."	If your student says he or she is bored, it may mean he or she is having a hard time—take a break! If a student is discouraged because of mistakes, explain that mistakes are the building blocks of learning.
Celebrate often.	Remember that learning occurs in small steps. Celebrate every achievement.

SOURCE: Excerpted from materials developed by Michelle Allen, seventh-grade life science teacher and co-coordinator of peer tutoring program at John Adams Middle School Academies, Albuquerque, NM; used with permission.

Perhaps the most important demonstration of students' commitment to serve as peer tutors is the opportunity to understand and agree to a code of ethics for how they will behave while peer tutoring. The National Association of Tutorial Services recommends several examples of statements that could be included in a code of ethics. At John Adams Middle School, peers sign the code of ethics shown in Table 3.6.

Peer tutors increase their effectiveness when they are held accountable for their roles as peer tutors. There are many ways to ensure accountability, such as having peers sign learning contracts that specify how often and when they will tutor, working with teachers or guidance counselors to make sure tutors are trained, and asking the tutors' supervising teachers for feedback. Peer tutors at

Table 3.6 Peer Tutor Code of Ethics

I will strive to be responsible, be respectful, be safe, and be a learner. I agree that . . .

1. My major motivation is building the partner learner's self-confidence.
2. My partner learner deserves and will receive my total attention.
3. The language my partner learner and I share must be mutually understood at all times.
4. I must be able to admit my own weaknesses and will seek assistance as I need it.
5. To show respect for my partner learner's personal dignity, I must accept my partner without judgment.
6. My partner learner will constantly be encouraged but never insulted by false hope or empty flattery.
7. I will strive for a mutual relationship of openness and honesty as I tutor.
8. I will not impose my personal value system or lifestyle on my partner learner.
9. I will always understand (and remind my partner learner) that my role is never to do the partner's work.
10. I count on my partner learner also to be my tutor and teach me ways to do a better job.
11. I will do my best to be on time as an example for my partner learner to follow.
12. I will maintain logs, records, and progress data as expected and required.
13. I understand that good tutoring enables my partner learner to transfer learning from one situation to another.
14. An important part of my goal is to make learning real for the partner learner.
15. My ultimate tutoring goal is my partner learner's independence.

_____   _____
Signature of Tutor   Date

SOURCE: Adapted from materials developed by Michelle Allen, seventh-grade life science teacher and co-coordinator of peer tutoring program at John Adams Middle School Academies, Albuquerque, NM; used with permission.

John Adams Middle School in Albuquerque, New Mexico, regularly meet with the supervisor of peer tutors at their school. The supervisor reviews their peer tutor logs and provides specific feedback and advice about how to solve any problems they might be facing. An example of a peer tutor log is shown in Table 3.7.

Table 3.7 Peer Tutor Log

Peer Tutor Log

Directions: The peer tutor will keep the log in a three-ring binder notebook, updated daily and monitored by the supervising teacher.

Date: _____   Tutor: _____

Peers tutored (first name only): _____

Subjects (tasks, assignments): _____

What was completed and/or
accomplished: _____

Peer Tutor Rubric

Directions: Supervising teacher completes the rubric before progress reports and report cards are due. Supervising teacher meets with the tutor to provide feedback and suggestions for improvement.

Up to 10 points can be assigned for each of the 10 areas for a total of 100 points.

_____ Attendance   _____ Willing to learn   _____ Polite and respectful

_____ Is responsible   _____ Establishes rapport   _____ Dedicated to tutees

_____ Shows tutoring skills _____ Completes daily log   _____ Contributes to learning

_____ Peers being tutored rate tutor as helpful (supervisor asks for evaluation from peers).

Comments: _____

_____

SOURCE: Excerpted from materials developed by Michelle Allen, seventh-grade life science teacher and co-coordinator of peer tutoring program at John Adams Middle School Academies, Albuquerque, NM; used with permission.

A Template for Peer Tutoring and Partner Learning Lessons

Figure 3.1 displays a template for preparing a peer tutoring and partner learning lesson. The template is streamlined so that teachers can easily keep track of the lesson objectives, the relevant state or local standard being taught, the materials and room arrangement needed, and the specific tasks that peer tutors are expected to complete. In addition, an evaluation component is included. The template is easy for students to comprehend as well.

Figure 3.1 Peer Tutor and Partner Learning Lesson Plan Template

Lesson Objectives:

Content Standards:

What is the room arrangement? Will other spaces outside of the classroom be used?

What materials do the peer tutors and partner learners need?

How is student learning assessed?

What specific supports, aids, or services do select students need?

What does the tutor and tutor partner do before, during, and after the lesson?

Tasks	Peer Tutor/Tutee	Peer Tutor/Tutee
Before		
During		
After		

Evaluation: Where and when will the lesson be debriefed and evaluated?

AN EXAMPLE OF A PEER TUTORING LESSON

Let's bring peer tutoring and partner learning alive by examining an actual lesson, shown in Figure 3.2, that uses the lesson plan template shown in Figure 3.1.

This lesson was developed by Laurie LaPlant and Nadine Zane (2002). They helped Elise, a third-grade classroom teacher, who wanted to learn how to use a reciprocal teaching process to help her students to acquire math facts to a mastery level. Notice how Elise adapted the peer tutoring lesson to include social objectives for two of the third graders who also needed to practice the social skills of giving and receiving positive feedback.

Figure 3.2 Lesson Plan for Third Graders as Peer Tutors to Learn Math Facts

Lesson Objectives:

Given 10 addition, subtraction, and multiplication math facts (5 known and 5 unknown or as yet unmastered by each partner) and a 10-minute daily practice session with a peer tutor, students will participate in learning activities that match various learning styles (e.g., auditory, visual, and kinesthetic) until all math facts are mastered (i.e., 10 of 10 correct over three consecutive sessions). (Since facts to be mastered are individualized based upon each student's needs, the math facts are different for each partner and change for each partner as facts are mastered.)

(Continued)

(Continued)

Content Standards:

Arizona Standard Mathematics Standard 1: Number Sense: Students develop number sense and use numbers and number relationships to acquire basic facts, to solve a wide variety of real-world problems, and to determine the reasonableness of results. FOUNDATIONS: Understand the meaning for and application of the operations of addition, subtraction, multiplication, and division.

What is the room arrangement? Will other spaces outside of the classroom be used?

Peer tutor partners sit at their desks or on the floor. They sit face-to-face to show the math facts in such way that each student can see the fact without seeing the answer printed on the back. They lay out the flashcards for activities such as Concentration, do Jump Rope Number Facts where they chant the facts as they jump rope, and develop Math Facts Raps based on the particular facts they are acquiring.

What materials do the peer tutors and partner learners need?

Peer tutor partners need their own stacks of math facts, a checklist to record accuracy of responses, a pencil, a graph to display the daily percent or number correct, an oven timer to set the 10-minute time frame, and directions printed on 3 × 5 cards for the learning activities.

How is student learning assessed?

The student peer tutor matches his or her partner's response to the answer on the back of the math fact flashcard. The tutor gives immediate correction for errors and/or immediate praise for correct responses. He or she checks off the selected learning activities that were practiced each day.

What specific supports, aids, or services do select students need?

Dave and Juan will serve as peer tutors to each other. They each have a learning contract that supports each of them in practicing the giving and receiving of positive feedback.

What does the tutor and tutor partner do before, during, and after the lesson?

Tasks	Peer Tutor/Tutee (Dave)	Peer Tutor/Tutee (Juan)
What are the specific tasks that I do BEFORE the lesson?	Collect and bring to the session a set of math cards for partner, the daily checklist to record progress, and the graph of percentage correct responses.	Same as the tutor role, as tutor partners become tutors with partner.
What are the specific tasks that I do DURING the lesson?	Select a learning activity with partner. Show math flashcard to partner. Give correct answer for the partner if partner makes error. Praise, go on to next math fact. Say nice things. (Note: In contract for Dave and Juan.)	Select a learning activity with tutor. Look at math flashcards. Give answer to the tutor partner. If tutor corrects error, repeat the correct answer and thank the tutor for correct answer. (Note: In contract for Dave and Juan.)
What are the specific tasks that I do AFTER the lesson?	Enter number or percent correct on graph. Thank partner for working and celebrate successes. (Note: In contract for Dave and Juan.)	Help tutor enter number or percent correct on graph. Thank tutor for instruction and celebrate success. (Note: In contract for Dave and Juan.)

Evaluation: Where and when will lesson be debriefed and evaluated?

The classroom teacher has brief weekly conferences with specific peer tutor partners on a rotating basis to review portfolios of math facts acquired, check on the tutorial exchanges, problem-solve, and celebrate.

WHAT DOES THE RESEARCH SAY AND WHAT ARE EDUCATORS AND STUDENTS SAYING ABOUT PEER TUTORING AND PARTNER LEARNING?

Peer Tutoring: Benefits and Cautions

As you learned in the introduction to Section II, a strong research base exists for peer tutoring and partner learning systems, perhaps because students experience more opportunities to respond and practice academic content compared to students' learnings only through more conventional teacher-directed lessons (Fuchs, Fuchs, Mathes, et al., 2002). In addition, we can be confident that peer tutoring can prevent early reading failures (Masters, Fuchs, & Fuchs, 2002); inspire high school students to self-identify and self-evaluate the characteristics that are essential to good peer tutoring (Longwill & Kleinert, 1998); and influence students at risk for dropping out of school to attend school, perceive themselves as successful, and increase their sense of belonging in school (Nazzal, 2002).

Students who work together as peer tutors and partner learners do indeed learn to self-monitor their comprehension, integrate new knowledge with what they've learned before, and elaborate and construct their knowledge (Roscoe & Chi, 2007). Perhaps most important, students with disabilities have been successfully taught to work as peer tutors (Elbaum et al., 2000; Giesecke et al., 1993). Elbaum et al. showed clear benefits to students with learning disabilities who worked as reciprocal tutors/tutees, and they found increased self-esteem in students who were practicing the teacher's role. Similarly, Giesecke et al. showed that low-achieving students could be successful cross-age tutors during a six-week tutoring program.

At John Adams Middle School in Albuquerque, New Mexico, teachers regularly evaluate the effectiveness of the schoolwide teen peer tutor program that has been implemented. Michelle Allen, a seventh-grade life science teacher, commented,

Instead of using adults, we like to use peers. Adults create barriers. They create bubbles of isolation. . . . Other students do not want to sit next to an adult.

When speaking of the informal peer tutoring support that Henry provides to a classmate with significant disabilities, Ms. Vanessa Jaramillo, a language arts teacher, said,

In life everyone has to learn work together. We would do our work and Henry would be the first to say, "Miss, I think Leeandra could help me cut this out or how about I write the sentence and she can paste it on the paper. I've learned a lot by just taking his suggestions about how to include her and really make her a part of our classroom, our community. Working with Leeandra has not hurt his grades; it has probably helped him. Not only is he listening to what I am saying, he is breaking it down for Leeandra in a way that helps her understand it better.

The social interaction element of peer tutoring is emphasized by Trindo Martinez, a special education teacher, who said,

> *The kids look up to these older cross-aged peer tutors. It means a lot to them [students] that an older child and a popular kid would sit there and help them. Friendships develop, and it is neat to see the kids get excited when their peer tutors walk into the classroom. There are benefits to the tutor; their teaching skills come out and their creativity. They learn that we are all the same. It is a real learning experience for them.*

However, students can be overzealous in telling rather than helping their peers learn the content. Roscoe and Chi (2007) studied two specific tutoring activities that are commonly believed to support tutor learning—explaining and questioning. Roscoe and Chi discovered that peer tutors tend to show a knowledge-telling bias. In other words, even when trained, they want to focus more on delivering knowledge than on helping their peers develop or discover knowledge. Teachers need to be aware of this tendency and help their peer tutors and partner learners to guard against it! They can do this by adding the specific skills of explaining and questioning to the peer tutoring lessons.

Students' Views of Peer Tutoring and Partner Learning

What do students themselves say about their experiences as peer tutors or partner learners? The experiences or perspectives of peer tutors or partner learners have not been reported in the literature; researchers typically focus on academic achievement gains, and social interaction outcomes have not generally been reported. One study by Mastropieri and colleagues (2002) at George Mason University involved interviewing middle school students who assumed the roles of peer tutor and tutee during daily reading periods. The students said they enjoyed tutoring more than their traditional instruction, and they wanted to include tutoring as part of their science and social studies classes.

Practitioners are more likely to poll their peer tutors and partner learners as part of the feedback process after a lesson. In a series of videotaped interviews, Rich Villa (1991) captured the feedback from students who shared their experiences of giving or receiving tutoring when their teachers asked, "What did you like about today's lesson?" For example, Elise's third graders were asked, "What can the fifth graders do to improve their tutoring?" Chad raised his hand and said,

> *They can make stuff harder.*

Elise paraphrased him and asked for other comments. Paul said,

> *Make something more easier.*

This comment gave the teacher a chance to comment on how important it is to make sure that the lesson fits the individual needs of each person. Later, Elise asked both groups to share what they liked about the lesson. Amber said her tutee

just kept on working . . . no fidgeting!

And Dan said about his tutor,

He listened a lot!

In another feedback session, the fifth graders who served as cross-age tutors were asked about their experiences with the third graders. Jon reported,

Some kids will doze off into the blue, and you have to get their attention.

This gave the teacher a chance to brainstorm ways to keep students focused. Ryan explained,

I learned you gotta pay attention. It's hard to teach if you don't pay attention.

This remark made the teacher smile broadly because Ryan, himself, had a difficult time paying attention. The bottom line was expressed over and over when students emphasized,

"So many kids just like it! They like to listen and learn."

These statements were echoed at John Adams Middle School in Albuquerque, New Mexico, where a schoolwide teen peer tutoring program has been implemented. For example, Selina, an eighth-grade peer tutor, said,

I see more progress with her [Cassey] because she works harder and doesn't get mad.

Another student mentioned,

I enjoy helping him because I think it is fun to help others.

SUMMARY

Take a moment to reflect on all that you have discovered from this chapter. Do the common attributes to all approaches to peer tutoring and partner learning make sense to you? Can you now arrange for your students to learn peer tutoring and partner learning skills? Do your students experience the benefits of peer tutoring? What examples of peer tutoring and partner learning might you add? And what do *your* students say about peer tutoring and partner learning? Do they like learning this way?

Students as 4 Co-Teachers

In this chapter, you will learn the answers to the following questions about the emerging practice and concept of students as co-teachers:

1. What is co-teaching?

2. How did the idea of students as co-teachers emerge?

3. What might student co-teaching in a classroom look like and sound like? What variations might you see and hear?

4. What are examples of programs in which students become co-teachers?

5. What training, supervision, and supports are needed for students to become effective co-teachers?

6. What do student and adult co-teaching team members say about their co-teaching experiences? What do the students that they co-teach say?

7. How might students participate as co-planners with teachers? Where and how do they fit into the lesson planning cycle?

8. If you are interested in students co-teaching with adults at your school, how might you begin?

WHAT IS CO-TEACHING? WHAT ARE SOME EXAMPLES OF ADULTS CO-TEACHING WITH STUDENTS?

Co-teaching is two or more people sharing instructional responsibility for the students assigned to a classroom. Two common co-teaching arrangements are (1) a general education teacher (a master of curriculum) co-teaching with a special educator (a master of access) and (2) a general educator co-teaching with a paraeducator (Nevin, Thousand, & Villa, 2009; Villa, Thousand, & Nevin, 2008). Although these are prevalent co-teaching configurations, anyone can co-teach. Co-teachers might include reading specialists, speech and language pathologists, occupational or physical therapists, teachers of students who are English language learners, teachers of students identified as gifted and talented, psychologists, counselors, administrators, university personnel, parents, local businesspeople, or other community volunteers.

An emerging practice is for students to serve as co-teachers with their own credentialed classroom teachers. Consider the following teacher-student co-teaching scenarios.

Jessica, a senior at Etiwanda High School, co-teaches with Ms. Boykins, a math teacher. While Ms. Boykins provides an overview of what the students will do during the day's algebra lesson, Jessica engages in supportive co-teaching by passing out materials to students. When Ms. Boykins transitions into direct instruction of the content, Jessica walks among the students, checking for comprehension of the new concept and skills being taught. Next, students are given problems to solve. At this point, the co-teachers switch to team teaching; students in the classroom hold up whiteboards showing their answers and receive a "yes" or "no" response from either co-teacher. To assist students in finding the correct answer, Jessica is masterful at providing prompts such as "Look at your signs—be sure they are correct," or "Talk to your neighbor and see if you agree." Later in the lesson, Ms. Boykins and Jessica instruct the whole class together as they alternate the complementary co-teaching roles of problem explainer and the person who creates a visual representation of the algebraic equations on the board.

In another classroom in the school, while Ms. Landy, the art teacher, refers to the grade book and informs students of any unfinished work, Kimberly-Anne, the student co-teacher, returns graded assessments of those who have completed assignments. Then Ms. Landy and Kimberly-Anne both walk among the students in the art class, monitoring individuals working at tables and answering individual questions.

In yet another class, Mr. Kyle, a drama teacher, co-teaches with Reanna and Ryan, two advanced drama students who have previously taken the class in which they co-teach. The students and drama teacher have met and co-planned the lesson. During the lesson, all three co-teachers rotate, explaining and modeling drama exercises to the class of 45 students. While the class members move around the room and engage in the exercises in pairs and triads, all three co-teachers walk among the groups to provide feedback and encouragement. Periodically, the three huddle together to adjust their lesson on the spot based upon what they are observing through their joint monitoring.

How Did Student Co-Teaching Emerge?
An Evolutionary Tale

We acknowledge that the three scenarios above may stretch the imagination. Certainly, a student functioning as a co-teacher represents a cutting-edge practice. At this point in time, student co-teaching is an example of practice informing the research rather than research informing practice. However, rest assured that at this school and other schools in this country, cadres of students are successfully engaging in similar co-teaching partnerships.

How has the practice of student co-teaching emerged? It emerged as a natural outgrowth of general and special education teachers co-teaching and students serving as peer tutors (see Chapter 3) in one of the nation's first inclusive school districts—a school district in which Richard Villa, a co-author of this text, was an administrator. As you read the following evolutionary tale of student co-teaching emerging in this district, imagine how this evolution might happen in your school community.

In the early 1980s, to support the education of diverse learners in mixed-ability classrooms, the school district in which Dr. Villa worked initially relied upon adult collaboration in planning and teaching. Over time, those assigned to co-teach expanded beyond just general and special educators to include all related service personnel (e.g., speech and language pathologists) and para-educators. Subsequently, students collaborated in their own education, initially by working in cooperative learning groups, then as peer tutors, and eventually as co-teachers.

Formal peer tutoring began in the fourth grade when one fourth-grade teacher and her supporting special educator were trying to think of ways to gain additional support for the classroom on a regular basis. The special educator suggested that she could train some students to serve as within-class peer tutors. Starting with a few students tutoring classmates in math, the interest of class members grew so that by the end of the year, most students were tutoring one another. The classroom teacher saw the tutoring successes and noted that, while some of the students in the class might need tutoring in an area of need (e.g., math), they were perfectly competent to tutor a classmate in another subject area at a different time during the day (e.g., language arts). Most of the students in the class expressed a desire to be peer tutors, so the number of students in this class trained to tutor rapidly expanded.

A first-grade classroom teacher in the same school was the parent of one of the peer tutors in this fourth-grade class. Her son's enthusiastic dinner table comments about his role as peer tutor led her to ask if the fourth-grade peer tutors could come to her first-grade class once a week during literacy instruction to tutor her students in letter sound-symbol relationships. The fourth-grade team jumped at the request, and the special educator trained all of the fourth-grade class members to tutor the younger students. With parental permission, each fourth grader in this class served as a cross-age peer tutor in the first-grade classroom one afternoon a week for the remainder of the school year.

Given this initial success, over the next three years, the peer tutoring program expanded so that over 90 percent of all elementary students had been trained and were serving as within-class and cross-age peer tutors (Villa & Thousand, 1992). Even after the elementary-aged students transitioned to middle school, they volunteered to be assigned as peer tutors in elementary classrooms at the end of the day. With students more frequently collaborating in instruction (i.e., working in cooperative learning groups, serving as same- and cross-aged peer tutors), the idea of students serving as co-teachers seemed to evolve naturally in the school district. Bill and Christine were two pioneer high school-aged co-teachers in the district. Let's discover how they became co-teachers.

Bill was a high school student who, having completed all areas of his high school mathematics curriculum, attended a nearby university where he completed the university's most advanced math classes with As in all four classes. Knowing this, a school administrator recruited Bill to be a co-teacher in a high school mathematics class. At first, he moved among students checking comprehension and offering assistance. His role quickly expanded. At times, he and the math teacher, Sharon, worked with separate groups of students in the classroom. At other times, he recorded the steps of solving a problem on an overhead or blackboard while the teacher explained the steps to the class. Eventually, Bill and Sharon met outside of class to plan lessons and divide instructional responsibilities throughout the lesson.

Feedback from students in the class indicated that they valued Bill's presence as a co-teacher. In fact, some students said that he was the better teacher because he used age-appropriate vocabulary and examples. Sharon, the adult member of this co-teaching team, smiled at the student feedback and noted that her ego was not fragile and that she was pleased to use all the resources at her disposal, including co-teaching with a student, to meet the needs of the learners in her math classes. Bill reported that students frequently called him at home at night if they were having difficulty with the lesson. After graduating from high school, Bill went to Harvard, on a complete four-year academic scholarship, where he majored in math and science. At the end of his freshman year, he addressed over 200 educators attending a weeklong summer institute on inclusive education. In response to concerns about "gifted" students and inclusion, Bill noted that he learned more about mathematics when he was co-teaching than he had at any other time, including in the courses that he had just completed at Harvard.

Christine, another high school student in this school, also co-taught. As a 16-year-old student with Down syndrome, Christine was academically included in all core academic classes. She also was socially included, as evidenced by her membership on the school's cheerleading squad. In her inclusive school, Christine was accustomed to witnessing collaborative teaching and learning among adults and students. When she overheard a third-grade teacher asking her health teacher for ideas and materials to teach basic nutrition to her third-grade class, Christine said, "I know that stuff. I can co-teach with you." Christine co-taught health in the third-grade class, and the third-grade teacher reported that she did an excellent job.

CO-TEACHING APPROACHES

There are four approaches to co-teaching—supportive, parallel, complementary, and team teaching. Each approach is described and illustrated in the examples that follow.

Supportive Co-Teaching

Recall the opening scenario with Jessica, a student co-teaching in algebra with Ms. Boykins. Jessica is engaged in supportive co-teaching when she distributes materials to students as the classroom teacher provides an overview of what the students will do during the lesson and when Jessica moves among the students to check for understanding of the new concepts and skills being introduced by Ms. Boykins. Supportive co-teaching is when one co-teacher takes the lead instructional role and the other(s) rotates among the students providing support as needed. The co-teacher(s) taking the supportive role watches and listens as students work together, stepping in to provide one-to-one tutorial assistance when necessary, while the other co-teacher continues to direct the lesson. Teachers new to co-teaching with students often choose to begin with this approach. It is important to note that who is in the lead versus support role may change over the course of the lesson.

Students often appreciate the extra help that is available when an extra support person is available in the classroom. Whoever is in the supportive role should avoid becoming "Velcro-ed" to individual students, because this can be stigmatizing for both the targeted student and the supportive co-teacher. If one member of the team is always locked into the supportive role, maximum use may not be made of that individual's expertise and creativity in planning, instructing, and evaluating student progress.

Parallel Co-Teaching

Do you remember Mr. Kiley, the drama teacher, and his two student co-teachers? The three co-teachers were engaged in parallel co-teaching when they all moved among students performing drama exercises, monitoring and providing feedback and encouragement. Parallel co-teaching is when two or more people work with different groups of students in different sections of the classroom. Co-teachers may rotate among the groups, and sometimes one group of students may work without a co-teacher for at least part of the time. Parallel co-teaching has many variations, including those described in Table 4.1.

It is important when using parallel co-teaching approaches that, whenever possible, students are grouped heterogeneously and regrouped frequently. This ensures that all students have the opportunity to benefit from the experiences of different classmates and the expertise of different instructors. Ms. Boykins and Jessica followed this advice; they assigned their algebra students to work in mixed-ability pairs.

Complementary Co-Teaching

Ms. Boykins and Jessica were engaging in complementary co-teaching when Jessica created a visual representation of the algebraic equation on the board to assist students in understanding the concept and procedure Ms. Boykins was explaining. Complementary co-teaching occurs when a co-teacher does something to enhance, supplement, or add value to the instruction provided by the other co-teacher. For example, one co-teacher might paraphrase the other co-teacher's statements, provide additional examples, or model note-taking strategies. When employing a complementary co-teaching approach, it is important to remember to monitor the progress of the students in the class. In other words, co-teachers must be mindful of avoiding the "sage on the stage" syndrome of both co-teachers being at the front of the classroom and forgetting to roam among and monitor the students.

Table 4.1 Seven Variations of Parallel Co-Teaching

Split Class

Each co-teacher is responsible for a particular group of students, monitoring understanding of a lesson, providing guided instruction, or reteaching the group if necessary.

Station Teaching or Learning Centers

Each co-teacher is responsible for assembling, guiding, and monitoring one or more learning centers or stations.

Co-Teachers Rotate

The co-teachers rotate among the two or more groups of students, with each co-teacher teaching a different component of the lesson. This is similar to station teaching or learning centers, except in this case, the teachers rotate from group to group rather than groups of students rotating from station to station.

Cooperative Group Monitoring

Each co-teacher takes responsibility for monitoring and providing feedback and assistance to a given number of cooperative groups of students.

Experiment or Lab Monitoring

Each co-teacher monitors and assists a given number of laboratory groups, providing guided instruction to those groups requiring additional support.

Learning Style Focus

One co-teacher works with a group of students using primarily visual strategies, another co-teacher works with a group using primarily auditory strategies, and yet another may work with a group using kinesthetic strategies.

Supplementary Instruction

One co-teacher works with the rest of the class on a concept or assignment, skill, or learning strategy. The other co-teacher (a) provides extra guidance on the concept or assignment to students who are self-identified or teacher identified as needing extra assistance, (b) instructs students to apply or generalize the skill to a relevant community environment, (c) provides a targeted group of students with guided practice in how to apply the learning strategy to the content being addressed, or (d) provides enrichment activities.

Team Teaching

In the co-taught drama class scenario, Mr. Kiley, Ryan, and Reanna offer an excellent example of team teaching, a co-teaching approach in which two or more people do what the traditional teacher has always done—plan, teach, assess, and assume responsibility for all of the students in the classroom. Team teachers divide lessons in ways that allow students to benefit from each co-teacher's expertise. The key to successful team teaching is that co-teachers simultaneously deliver the lessons. The co-teachers are comfortable alternately taking the lead and being the supporter. The bottom line and test of a successful team-teaching partnership is that the students in the class view each team teacher as knowledgeable and credible and the co-teachers move in and out of all four approaches (i.e., supportive, parallel, complementary, team teaching) based upon student needs and curriculum demands. As with complementary co-teaching, when team teaching, co-teachers must guard against getting so caught up in co-delivering instruction at the front of the classroom that they fail to monitor students closely.

The authors emphasize that no one co-teaching approach is better than another. All four approaches share the goal of marshalling additional human resources to support diverse learners. Although many adult-student co-teaching teams begin with the student in a supportive role, student co-teachers should not be limited to this role. As with adult co-teaching partners, when provided with appropriate training, coaching, and shared planning time, student-teacher co-teaching partners can develop the competence and confidence to engage in parallel, complementary, and team-teaching roles.

Two Examples of Co-Teaching Programs: Etiwanda and Twin Valley High Schools

A school system interested in establishing student co-teaching programs must attend to the same dimensions described for peer tutoring and partner learning programs; namely recruitment, training, monitoring, and evaluation of student co-teachers and evaluation of the co-teaching program. Although students may function as co-teachers, they do so under the supervision of a licensed and qualified teacher.

The next section of this chapter describes two co-teaching programs, one on the West Coast and one on the East Coast of the United States. As you read about the two programs, notice the similarities and differences in how they address the recruiting, training, supervision, and evaluation dimensions of their programs.

Etiwanda High School's Co-Teaching Program

Etiwanda High School, located in Etiwanda, California, educates 3,300 9th through 12th graders. The student body is diverse, with the student population divided roughly evenly among Hispanic, African-American, and Anglo origin or heritage. At the time of the writing of this book, the student co-teaching program at Etiwanda High School is in its second year of operation. In Etiwanda's student co-teacher program, juniors and seniors are eligible to be co-teachers and participate in a two-semester, five-credit elective co-teaching course.

Recruitment. The program's coordinator is the high school's assistant principal, who at the start of the program's second year offered answers to frequently asked questions about student co-teaching at the school. The memo, reproduced in Table 4.2, is an excellent example of how to share information about a student co-teaching program and how to recruit faculty and student participation. Distributing these frequently asked questions and responses to those questions is one way to inform staff and students about the program and recruit potential co-teachers. Other recruitment strategies include promotional flyers, such as the one presented in Table 4.3; discussions about the benefits of

Table 4.2 Frequently Asked Questions About Student Co-Teachers at Etiwanda High School

1. What is co-teaching?

Co-teaching is utilizing our largest resource (students) to assist teachers in the classroom in an instructional capacity. It is "two or more people sharing responsibility for teaching some or all of the students assigned to a classroom" (Villa, Thousand, & Nevin, 2008).

2. Isn't *co-teacher* just another term for *teacher's assistant* (TA)?

No. TAs typically do clerical work for the teacher. They do not always, if ever, help teachers with instruction. A co-teacher does not run to make copies, sit and watch, or only function as a tutor or homework helper when needed. A co-teacher is involved in instruction in some way every day. This requires a collaborative relationship between the teacher and the student co-teacher in all areas of the classroom and a commitment from both participants to each other and their classroom. The student co-teacher may progress at a pace that works best for him or her. This necessitates the direction and support of the classroom teacher.

3. What do student co-teachers do?

A co-teacher is involved in the instruction in some way, ideally every day. In most cases, the student co-teacher will tutor, support, or complement instruction. At Etiwanda, student co-teachers routinely do the following: tutor, provide individual attention/clarification, answer questions, and monitor student progress in math and science during independent practice and labs. Some provide a component of a lesson (warm-up, review) under the direction of the regular classroom teacher and serve as a resource to the students. Students will earn 5 credits of elective credit per semester.

4. Is this a class for credit?

Yes, this is a class for credit. It is a two-semester course, and the students can earn 5 credits for successfully completing the course.

5. Where did the idea to bring this to Etiwanda come from?

Several teachers from Etiwanda attended the collaboration training with Dr. Villa provided by the district in the spring of 2007. The concept of using students as collaborators was discussed during the inservice, and teachers agreed that students could be a positive and powerful instructional resource in the classroom.

6. How many students have signed up to be co-teachers?

Currently there are 24 students working with 16 teachers. Teachers came forward at the end of last year with students who they thought would like to be co-teachers. The program is not imposed on anyone.

7. What do you do to support student co-teachers?

Since our school is an AVID school, we ask the students to attend AVID tutor training. Most have done that. We also have seminars and guest speakers with co-teachers to cover the curriculum in the co-teaching course outline. Additionally, I provide pull out training that covers basic teaching concepts (e.g., checking for understanding). Currently, I meet with the student co-teachers five or six times a year, and we plan to expand that training into monthly meetings. The bulk of the training comes from the collaboration between the student co-teachers and the classroom teachers.

8. What training can the regular classroom teacher get?

They are encouraged to attend collaborative planning and teaching training provided by the district when it becomes available. We sent six classroom teachers last year along with six of our student co-teachers. Classroom teachers will also be provided with a copy of *A Guide to Co-Teaching* by Richard Villa, Jacqueline Thousand, and Ann Nevin. This is a useful resource for teachers who are interested. Teachers are also welcome to attend the tutor training that is provided to the students.

9. **How do we get a co-teacher?**

The co-teaching relationship must be initiated by the student co-teacher and the classroom teacher. I will not recruit and assign student co-teachers to teachers. I believe it works best when the two have a mutual and serious desire to work together.

10. **Are there issues that need to be addressed with co-teaching?**

Of course. While this approach has a lot of potential, there are issues with time, training, etc. Teachers who want to be involved need to be patient and creative and find ways to address the challenges that confront them. It is not for everyone.

SOURCE: Adapted from materials developed by James Cronin, high school administrator at Etiwanda High School, CA; used with permission.

Table 4.3 Sample Recruitment Form

Would you like to be a teacher?

Next year, select students will have the opportunity to co-teach with one of Etiwanda High School's classroom teachers.

As a student co-teacher, you will work directly with a teacher on a daily basis. In the role of co-teacher, you will tutor, instruct, model, demonstrate, and perform other tasks to assist in the instruction of students in a classroom.

Co-teachers will do the following:

Assist the teacher in classroom instruction.

Provide tutoring to individuals and small groups.

Assist the teacher in planning and setting up activities.

Receive instruction, training, and experience in the teaching profession.

Develop and apply interpersonal skills.

Help a teacher in a subject area you have excelled in.

And more.

This course is ideal for someone who is considering a career in teaching or who has simply wanted to help others. In addition, student co-teachers will earn 5 elective credits each semester (Course: Peer Tutoring I/II). If interested, talk to a teacher you would like to work with next year. Then, complete the form below to get started. (Co-teachers must meet certain qualifications, including B or better in subject area, recommendation from teacher, and availability to attend AVID tutor training).

Yes, I am interested in working as a co-teacher next year!

Name: _____

Signature: _____

Teacher I would like to work with: _____

Subject area: _____

Teacher signature: _____

Parent signature: _____

"I support my son/daughter in this endeavor."

SOURCE: Adapted from materials developed by James Cronin, high school administrator at Etiwanda High School, CA; used with permission.

student co-teachers; and the identification of potential student co-teachers at departmental meetings. At Etiwanda, classroom teachers, rather than the program coordinator, take the lead in recruiting the particular student co-teachers with whom they would like to co-teach.

Training. At Etiwanda High School, initial training of student co-teachers involves attendance at peer tutor trainings provided by the Advancement Via Individual Determination (AVID) program, which began in San Diego, California, three decades ago. AVID programs currently operate in over 1,000 schools in 16 states and 13 countries (McNeil & Hood, 2002; San Diego County Office of Education, 2009). The AVID program is a high school elective course with three components: academic instruction, in-class peer tutoring from peers or college students, and motivational activities. AVID students learn instructional strategies such as (a) cooperative group learning, (b) how to question and facilitate inquiry, and (c) how to use writing and written expression as a learning tool.[1]

Following AVID training, student co-teachers receive ongoing support and coaching from their adult co-teacher partners. They also attend periodic meetings facilitated by the assistant principal, who coordinates the program, and other staff members, who deliver the course curriculum (see the syllabus presented in Resource D). At these meetings, they learn other instructional and motivational strategies (e.g., anticipatory set, closure, presentation of new material, use of technology). Students are expected to demonstrate an understanding of the approaches to co-teaching (Villa et al., 2008), Bloom's taxonomy (Bloom, Englehart, Furst, Hill, & Krathwohl, 1956), levels of questioning (Costa, 2000), AVID methodologies (San Diego County Office of Education, 2009), and strategies for increasing student achievement (Marzano et al., 2001).

The school district also brings in outside consultants, such as the authors, to provide schoolwide professional development inservice events on collaborative planning, co-teaching, and differentiation of instruction. Student co-teachers attend these professional development events with their co-teachers.

Monitoring. At Etiwanda High School, primary responsibility for monitoring the student co-teacher resides with the classroom teacher, although the assistant principal in charge of the program periodically observes and holds conferences with student co-teachers. Classroom teachers meet with their student co-teachers before or after school or during lunchtime to share feedback, as well as plan future lessons. The observation form used when observing student co-teachers appears in Table 4.4.

Evaluation. Evaluation of student co-teachers for the co-teaching elective course is based upon attendance and participation in training seminars, self-assessments, assessment by the teacher, classroom surveys of the students being taught, and a portfolio. The teacher and student negotiate the contents of the portfolio and the rubric to assess it. As far as program evaluation, it is ongoing and takes the

---

[1] Participation in AVID training is one of many ways that students can be taught basic instructional skills, as evidenced by the subsequent example from the Twin Valley School District. Other school districts decide to use different programs.

Table 4.4   Sample Student Co-Teaching Observation Form

Etiwanda High School Co-Teaching Observation

Name: _____ Date: _____ Observer: _____

Co-Teacher Behavior Observed	Notes and Comments
Provides individual tutoring during class, before school, and/or after school.	
Provides clarification, examples to whole class or individual.	
Conducts group tutorials.	
Answers students' questions.	
Monitors and checks for student understanding.	
Presents warm-up activity.	
Provides feedback on work.	
Brings closure to the class or reviews.	
Shows, models, demonstrates.	
Teaches alongside the teacher, assisting with delivery of the lesson.	
Teaches part of the lesson.	
Plans lessons with the teacher.	
Sets up and monitors labs and other learning activities.	
Other:	

Overall Comments:

***** **Place This Observation in Your Co-Teaching Portfolio** ****

SOURCE: Adapted from materials developed by James Cronin, high school administrator at Etiwanda High School, CA; used with permission.

form of feedback on surveys from the classroom teachers and student co-teachers participating in the program.

Twin Valley High School's Co-Teaching Program

Twin Valley High School, located in Elverson, Pennsylvania, is part of a school district where one of the authors has provided ongoing professional development to implement inclusive education strategies. The content of the professional development includes co-teaching, differentiated instruction, student partner learning, and student-adult co-teaching arrangements. At Twin Valley, all special education students are enrolled in general education classrooms. Classes are not tracked. Any student can choose to participate in honors or Advanced Placement (AP) classes.

Twin Valley educators established a peer tutoring program as an elective credit course open to all seniors. Although called peer tutors, these students function as co-teachers. They are not assigned to work with specific students but to support their adult co-teachers. As the school leadership team notes, this program is a way to maximize human instructional resources, assist classroom teachers in planning and implementing differentiated instruction, and promote the school district's philosophy of inclusive education. In addition, the peer tutoring program allows students an opportunity to serve others—to exhibit generosity, one of the "Circle of Courage" goals of education.

One indicator of the effectiveness of the Twin Valley Student co-teaching program is the growth in its enrollment. In its first year, 21 students participated; in its third year, 48 participated with 40 teachers in 48 classrooms. Entering the fifth year of implementation, over 50 students were enrolled.

Recruitment. Twin Valley student co-teachers enroll in a peer tutoring/co-teaching course that is an open enrollment course limited to seniors. Posters and informational meetings are used to recruit students into the course. Additionally, guidance counselors recommend the course as an elective for students planning on entering human service-related careers. Perhaps the most successful recruitment vehicle has been students' positive experiences of having a student co-teacher as a co-instructor in a freshman, sophomore, or junior class. It should be noted that even in the first year of the program, over a quarter of the school faculty requested a student co-teacher. This number has grown to the majority of teachers in the school.

Training. Student co-teachers at Twin Valley receive training in the 12 competency areas shown in Table 4.5. Training begins in the week prior to the start of school and continues throughout the year via periodic seminars with the program coordinator and guest speakers and ongoing coaching of student co-teachers by their partner adult co-teachers. Seminars are augmented with technology-based forums, such as podcasts, blogs, and chat rooms, as well as Web site reviews.

Student co-teachers are matched to classroom teachers by the program coordinator based upon considerations such as which classes or students

Table 4.5   Student Co-Teacher Competencies

1. Role of peer tutors and student co-teachers (Thousand, Villa, & Nevin, 2002, 2008)

2. Understanding inclusive education (Villa & Thousand, 2005)

3. Effective instruction (Cummings, Nelson, & Shaw, 2002)

4. Checking for understanding (Fisher & Frey, 2007)

5. Teaching to diverse learning styles (Thousand, Villa, & Nevin, 2007)

6. Personality types (Pauley, Bradley, & Pauley, 2002)

7. Multiple intelligence theory (Armstrong, 2009)

8. Bloom's taxonomy of educational objectives (Bloom et al., 1956)

9. 21st-century learning (http://www.21stcenturyskills.org)

10. Classroom management; that is, dealing with challenges in the classroom and handling difficult students

11. Leadership roles in a school community (Conduct interview of district and school administrative staff.)

12. Technology as an instructional tool (Use online learning.)

SOURCE: Adapted from materials developed by Amanda Pierce, high teacher at Twin Valley High School, PA; used with permission.

within classes need extra support, the student co-teachers' academic strengths, and their academic and nonacademic interests outside of school.

Monitoring, supervision, and evaluation. Supervision and evaluation of Twin Valley student co-teachers is performed once a week through meetings with each student's cooperating co-teacher. Additionally, student co-teachers are required to keep and share with the program coordinator a professional journal that contains entries related to each week's co-teaching experience. Further, the program coordinator observes the student co-teachers at least once a quarter, and the cooperating co-teacher completes a student co-teacher evaluation midterm and at the end of the semester.

CHALLENGES FACED BY STUDENT CO-TEACHERS

When student co-teachers are asked about the challenges they typically face, they are remarkably candid. The top four issues student co-teachers identify are (a) role clarification, (b) time to meet and plan with their adult co-teaching partner, (c) being perceived by students in the class as a teacher and not another student, and (d) motivating students in the co-taught classes. Not unexpectedly, these are the same top issues identified by adult co-teachers (Villa et al., 2008). Table 4.6 identifies common issues most co-teachers are likely to encounter.

Table 4.6 Issues for Discussion and Planning

Instruction

What content standards will we teach?

What content is the student comfortable teaching?

Which co-teaching approaches will we use?

What are our strengths in the area of instruction and assessment?

Do we rotate responsibilities?

How will we assess the effectiveness of our instruction?

What instructional and motivational strategies will we use to engage and motivate our learners?

Time for Planning

How much time do we need?

Where will we find the time that we need?

How long will we meet?

How will we use our time together?

Communication

How will we explain this collaborative teaching arrangement to the students?

How will we maintain frequent and open communication with one another?

How will we communicate with the person in charge of training and supervising student co-teachers?

Evaluation

How will we monitor students' progress?

How will we assess our own effectiveness?

Logistics

How will we refer to each other in front of the students?

Other

As with adult co-teachers, student co-teachers and their adult partners are encouraged to meet and attempt to address these and other issues of concern at the very start of the co-teaching partnership. They also are encouraged to seek advice and assistance from veteran co-teachers and the program supervisor. When students and their co-teachers collaborate in the identification of challenges and in the development of ways to address the challenges, they are more likely to assume ownership of the solutions.

A tool developed at Etiwanda High School to help with role clarification is shown in Table 4.7. Using this Co-Teaching Interest Survey, a student identifies his or her current level of comfort in performing various instructional roles. The student then meets with the assigned adult co-teacher to clarify current role expectations and set goals for their future role expansion. Job descriptions also assist in role clarification for everyone. See Table 4.8 for Twin Valley's outline of job expectations for student co-teachers, their partner classroom teachers, and the co-teaching program faculty advisor.

Table 4.7 Student Co-Teacher Assessment of Level of Comfort With Co-Teaching Roles

Etiwanda High School

NAME _____

Co-Teaching Interest Inventory   teacher

Below is a list of activities commonly performed by student co-teachers. Circle the number that indicates your level of interest for each of the following using this scale:

1—not at all interested 2—uncertain 3—may want to try 4—interested 5—very interested

Provide individual tutoring during class, before school and/or after school.

    1   2   3   4   5

Provide clarification, examples, etc.

    1   2   3   4   5

Conduct group tutorials.

    1   2   3   4   5

Answer students' questions.

    1   2   3   4   5

Monitor and check for student understanding.

    1   2   3   4   5

(Continued)

(Continued)

Present warm-up activity.

| 1 | 2 | 3 | 4 | 5 |

Provide feedback on work.

| 1 | 2 | 3 | 4 | 5 |

Bring closure to the class/review.

| 1 | 2 | 3 | 4 | 5 |

Show/model for students how to do something.

| 1 | 2 | 3 | 4 | 5 |

Teach alongside the teacher.

| 1 | 2 | 3 | 4 | 5 |

Assist the teacher with a lesson.

| 1 | 2 | 3 | 4 | 5 |

Teach part of a lesson.

| 1 | 2 | 3 | 4 | 5 |

Plan lessons with the teacher.

| 1 | 2 | 3 | 4 | 5 |

Set up and monitor labs and other learning activities.

| 1 | 2 | 3 | 4 | 5 |

Are there other things you see yourself doing as a co-teacher? Explain.

SOURCE: Adapted from materials developed by James Cronin, high school administrator at Etiwanda High School, CA; used with permission.

Table 4.8 Co-Teaching Roles, Responsibilities, and Expectations

Student Co-Teacher

Attendance and punctuality

Respectful student interactions

Support of student learning

Support of teacher instruction

Support for differentiation

Maintainance of data (i.e., journal and portfolio)

Dressing professionally

Regular communication with cooperating classroom teacher and faculty advisor

Cooperating Classroom Teacher

Regular communication with student co-teacher and faculty advisor

Quarterly evaluations of student co-teachers

Meet to plan and reflect on co-taught lessons

Faculty Advisor

Training of student co-teachers

Placement of student co-teachers, considering student interests and needs and teacher invitations for student co-teachers in their classrooms

Observation of student co-teachers

Review of student journals, data collected, portfolios

Review of quarterly evaluations

Assignment of grades

SOURCE: Adapted from materials developed by Amanda Pierce, high teacher at Twin Valley High School, PA; used with permission.

A Co-Teaching Lesson Plan to Clarify Roles and Guide Instruction

When student/adult co-teaching teams engage in purposeful, regularly scheduled lesson planning, everyone is more likely to communicate effectively, avoid role confusion, maximize the potential to differentiate instruction to reach students, and make progress in using all four co-teaching approaches. Resource C (page 197) offers a simple co-teaching lesson plan format that has been adapted to identify what each co-teacher does during a lesson. The format works for all four co-teaching approaches (i.e., supportive, parallel, complementary, team). Table 4.9 displays an actual co-taught drama lesson plan developed by a student-teacher co-teaching team using this lesson plan format. Any lesson plan format can be adapted in a similar way to differentiate what each co-teacher does during the lesson.

WHAT ARE STUDENT CO-TEACHERS, ADULT CO-TEACHERS, ADMINISTRATORS, AND LEARNERS IN CO-TAUGHT CLASSES SAYING ABOUT CO-TEACHING?

The authors interviewed several groups who have been involved with establishing students as co-teachers with their teachers. The adult co-teachers, the student co-teachers, school administrators, and learners themselves offer a variety of perspectives. Listen to what they have to say (personal communication, January 9, 2008, for Etiwanda and March 24, 2009, for Twin Valley participants).

Table 4.9 Sample Drama Lesson Using the Co-Teaching Lesson Plan Format

Lesson Name: Content: Drama	When one co-teacher does this . . .	Who	The other co-teacher does this . . .	Who
Anticipatory Set Motivate and focus students.	Set lesson objectives. Maintain general focus of instruction.	Mr. Kiley	Directly engage with specific students, helping them connect to their emotions.	Ryan & Reeana
Input Teach to objectives; model; actively engage all students.	Initiate lesson by giving task instructions. Make observations.	Mr. Kiley	Encourage students to challenge themselves. Make observations.	Ryan & Reeana
Guided Practice Students practice under co-teacher's guidance. Check for understanding.	Side-coach class members to express emotion. Side-coach student co-teachers.	Mr. Kiley	Push students to engage in emotional memory and expression.	Ryan & Reeana
Closure Summary of learning by students.	Ask students to define terminology. Ask students to journal about the lesson in response to "What emotions did I feel?"	Mr. Kiley	Offer personal examples of terminology and emotions felt. Relate to everyday student life. Monitor students' journaling in response to "What emotions did I feel?"	Ryan & Reeana
Independent Practice/Transfer Structured opportunities for independent practice and transfer of learning.	Gently and politely state observations and provide prompts as students write in journals.	Mr. Kiley	Gently and politely state observations and provide prompts as students write in journals.	Ryan & Reeana
Reflection After the Lesson What went well? What changes will we make to improve the next lesson?	The co-teachers will review journals and debrief together after class.			

SOURCE: Adapted from a drama lesson created by Mr. Kiley, drama teacher high teacher at School, CA; used with permission.

Student Co-Teacher Comments

Reena, a student co-teacher in a drama class at Etiwanda High School, explains,

> *It has just been a wonderful experience. I am learning so much from the kids in the class and from being able to teach material that I have already learned.*

Jamie (a pseudonym), a student co-teacher for an art class at Etiwanda High School, notes,

> *I think it is a really great way to help students because some students are really scared about talking to teachers.*

Briana, a student co-teacher for an English class at Etiwanda High School, states,

> *It is everything that I thought it was going to be. It is fun.*

Dave, a student co-teacher for a chemistry class at Twin Valley High School, touches on the benefits of giving back when he says,

> *I really enjoy the one-on-one that I am able to do in co-teaching. Not only does it [student co-teaching] help to build relationships with your peers . . . it is a rewarding experience giving back to your peers. I really like co-teaching. . . . It allows me to gain experience for the future. . . . I want to be a teacher.*

Classroom Co-Teacher Comments

Christian Kiley teaches drama classes at Etiwanda High School. He says,

> *I am extremely proud of both of them (his student co-teachers). So, it becomes very emotional and edifying. And, let's be honest. It does alleviate some of the burden in that, if I miss something, they can pick it up. It is like a subject matter spell check.*

A co-teacher in an art class at Etiwanda High School explained,

> *I now have the benefit of having a second person in the classroom who has the experience and the knowledge and who can answer questions the same way that I would. I would love to have a [student] co-teacher every class period.*

This idea is echoed by an English teacher from Etiwanda High School who says,

> *I like having someone to prepare lessons with beforehand. As a student, Briana [my student co-teacher] has skills in anticipating where a student might have a problem whereas as an adult I might think something is going to be really easy for a student.*

Michelle Maio is an English teacher at Twin Valley High School. She explains the value of having a different perspective from her student co-teacher.

I like co-teaching with students because it allows us to get a different perspective and to gain insight into what the students really want. And I think students respond differently when students work with them versus when teachers work with them.

A chemistry teacher at Twin Valley High School explains how valuable it is to have a student co-teacher who can quickly get around to students. This

alleviates frustration that can then turn into inappropriate behavior. It [co-teaching with students] just keeps the class moving and flowing more easily.

Another chemistry teacher at Twin Valley High School explains,

I do not know what I would do without my co-teacher. She has really helped as far as answering questions and dealing with discipline for students who are struggling.

Administrator Feedback

Jim Cronin is the assistant principal of Etiwanda High School and coordinator of the co-teaching program. He nicely sums up feedback obtained from the student co-teachers:

The feedback I get at the end of the year is that they [the student co-teachers] are more confident. They are not shy like they used to be. They feel like they know the subject matter better because they have been compelled to prepare every day to be an asset in the classes where they are co-teaching. . . .

We have received very positive feedback on the program. The teachers really enjoy it. They see it as a resource and an additional challenge. Some have said that it has inspired them, transformed them, and made them better teachers.

Learner Feedback

The students in the classes where other students worked as student co-teachers were willing to share their perspectives.

Drama Class at Etiwanda High School

One student says,

It is a lot easier to relate to your student teacher than your regular teacher because they are more like your age and you also can see them around school and talk to them personally. You have more of a connection.

Another explains,

I just really like that when they are giving you advice, they are not giving you advice from a teacher's standpoint trying to get you to be like this model student. They are trying to get you to be the best that you can because they are not going to be responsible for your future. They are trying to get you to be the best that you can for the short term.

Still another student emphasizes,

The ones [student co-teachers] that I have had give their perspectives. That makes it easier for me to learn. Some teachers can't always get to you. That's when a student co-teacher comes in handy.

Chemistry Class at Etiwanda High School

One student notes,

I like having a student co-teacher in the class. When the teacher is up there giving a lecture, you can call her over if you do not understand it. She'll break it down and, like, explain it to you in a different way—in an easier way.

English Class at Etiwanda High School

A student describes the benefits this way:

You have someone your age telling you what to do and at first you can be a bit more resistant to them. But when you get to know them, you build a relationship with them. You don't have a problem with them telling you what to do and you have more respect for that person.

Another student smiles when he says,

It is fun and she [the student co-teacher] doesn't get as angry [as the teacher] sometimes.

A third student chimes in,

It's cool that she is our age and she knows what she is talking about!

SUMMARY

Now that you have read this chapter, you know what co-teaching is, what it might look like when students and adults co-teach together, and how student co-teaching tends to evolve from successful implementation of other peer empowerment strategies, such as cooperative group learning and peer tutoring. We hope that you have found the experiences and advice of the students, teachers, and administrators whom you met in this chapter insightful and informative.

You have learned that the challenges that student co-teachers identify (i.e., finding time to meet and plan, clarifying their roles, and motivating reluctant learners) are the same that all co-teaching teams face. You learned how students can participate in the lesson planning cycle. Now we hope that you are wondering how you might expand the role of students in your classes and school, so we share the following thoughts about how you might begin to co-teach with students.

Where Might You Begin?

We suggest starting somewhere; rather than waiting for a full-blown program to be developed, consider starting a partnership with one or two students as your co-teachers. It is very likely that your school is new to the notion of student co-teaching and is not quite ready to establish a formal co-teaching program. Yet you have students who have mastery of content, a period available, and an interest in co-teaching. Why not approach these students and begin a partnership that will benefit the students in your class(es) as well as you and your student co-teacher? What are you waiting for?

Part III

Decision Making With Students

We begin this introduction by asking you to read the poem shown in Table III.1, entitled "Whose School Is This, Anyway?" Keep two questions in mind as you read:

1. What thoughts, feelings, or emotions do you think the author is trying to elicit from you, the reader?

2. What is the relationship between the theme of the poem and the topic for this part, decision making and advocacy?

What emotions did you experience? When we ask the first question of audiences, the responses most often heard include emotions such as *frustration, confusion,* and *guilt.* For us, the overarching emotion elicited by the poem is *hope.* We are hopeful that if we are not satisfied with the answer to the questions in the poem, that the school does not belong to all of our children, we will be motivated to do things differently—to create schools that welcome, value, support, and empower all learners.

With respect to the second question, we are sure that many of you correctly identified the theme of the poem as *belonging.* Belonging is an essential component of any theory of motivation. And implementing a student Bill of Rights designed to create a sense of belonging and foster a positive relationship between adults and students and students and students will make it more likely that we have created schools where all stakeholders, especially the students, will answer that it is *their* school. In other words, the school belongs to them. At a minimum, we believe that your students deserve and are likely to agree to the following rights:

- The right to be actively involved in learning activities
- The right to effective instruction
- The right to personalized support for learning

Table III.1   Whose School Is This, Anyway?

Whose school is this?

Is it the principal's?

Is it the teachers'?

Is it the paraeducators'?

Is it the secretaries' and custodians'?

Is it the smart kids'?

Is it the pushy kids'?

Is it the popular kids'?

Is it the native English-speaking kids'?

Is it each kid's equally?

Is it the parents'?

Is it the greater community's, or the state's?

Is it the kids', the teachers', the principal's, and the community's equally?

For whom does school go on?

Does it go on for the kids who go to college?

Does it go on for the kids who go to work?

Does it go on for the kids who have nowhere to go?

Does it go on for all kids equally?

Does it go on for the teachers?

Does it go on for the principal?

Does it go on for the kids, the teachers, the principal, and the community equally?

Who decides what goes on here?

Who determines what is learned?

Who determines how it is learned?

Who determines how students show what they learn?

Who teaches whom?

Do only the adults teach the students?

Do students work together in cooperative groups?

Do students receive training and provide peer tutoring?

Do students co-teach the classes?

Who tells whom what to do?

Who makes the rules?

Who must follow the rules?

Who must see that the rules are followed?

Whose school is this anyway?

SOURCE: Adapted from Curwin, R., & Mendler, A. (1988). *Discipline with dignity.* Alexandria, VA: Association for Supervision and Curriculum Development.

- The right to experience a motivating school climate
- The right to participate in life-related decisions (self-determination)

The goal of Part III is to show how teachers, by collaborating with their students, can actualize this student Bill of Rights. In addition, we explore a variety of answers to the question, *Whose school is this, anyway?* We consider how students can become decision makers on issues that affect their own and one another's education and learning environment. As shown in Figure III.1, the idea is to focus on students as the stars in the teaching relationship. The five chapters in the part provide practical how-to tools and strategies to facilitate their roles as peer supporters.

This is a densely packed part that will help you help your students achieve the Circle of Courage goals of education—belonging, mastery, independence, and generosity (Brendtro, Brokenleg, & Van Bockern, 2002). This part balances the focus on student mastery and independence, on students who are interdependent and generous as well as reassured of their value as members of a community of learners. You will examine the processes and outcomes associated with engaging students in all of the various roles that help them become effective peer supporters. Namely, you will learn how to engage students to

Figure III.1   Advance Organizer for Part III: Decision Making With Students

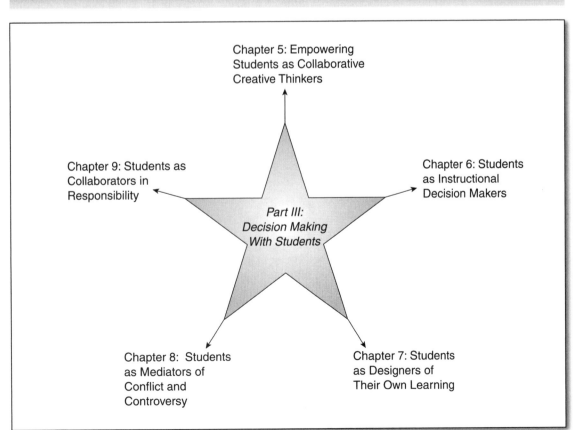

(a) think in novel ways to generate ideas and solutions to challenges collaboratively and creatively (Chapter 5); (b) design differentiated access to the content, products, and processes of learning (Chapter 6); (c) design their own personal learning plans (Chapter 7); (d) become peer mediators and conflict resolvers (Chapter 8); and (e) develop personal responsibility and self-discipline through collaborative problem solving (Chapter 9). Throughout the chapters, we sprinkle various lesson plans, checklists to monitor student progress, and stories or vignettes that explain the essence of the experiences students enjoy.

Empowering Students as Collaborative Creative Thinkers 5

The principal goal of education in the schools should be creating men and women who are capable of doing new things. . . . who are creative, inventive, and discoverers.

—Jean Piaget (as cited by Sennett, 2004, p. 9)

Unleashing the potential of students involves tapping the creativity and imagination in ways that stimulate problem solving. In this chapter, you will discover the answers to the following questions:

1. What blocks to creative thinking and action exist, and how can you teach yourself and your students to overcome them?

2. What are awareness plans? What are awareness plans that can facilitate your students' and your own creative thinking and problem solving?

3. What is the Osborn-Parnes Creative Problem Solving (CPS) awareness-planning process? In what ways does using CPS with students and others help them learn to solve problems and make improvements?

4. What will you do to use the creativity tools you have learned about in this chapter?

In Chapter 1, we explained several reasons for collaborating with students, the first being that it leads students to attain the Circle of Courage goals of education of belonging, mastery, independence, and generosity. What do you believe mastery and independence include? Can you agree that mastery and independence include dispositions and skills to (a) effectively communicate, (b) identify and confront challenges, (c) individually and collaboratively problem-solve in creative ways, and (d) be flexible and adaptable in conceptualizing possible alternatives to challenges? Although there is disagreement about the extent to which creativity as a disposition and skill is innate versus acquired (Abdel Hamid Soliman, 2005), what is known is that creativity can be taught to and learned by children and adults alike. Further, instruction in creativity processes can increase the measured creative thinking abilities of students, including students with disabilities (e.g., Jaben et al., 1982).

As with conflict resolution and other social skills (see Chapter 8), small-group interpersonal and collaborative skills (see Chapter 2), tutoring (see Chapter 3), and co-teaching skills (see Chapter 4), teachers can use tried-and-true processes that help students to overcome the many potential barriers to creative thinking and problem solving (Adams, 2001; de Bono, 1985, 1992; Leff, 1984; Osborn, 1953/1993; Parnes, 1992a, 1992b; Thorpe, 2000; Treffinger, 2000; von Oech, 1986, 1998). We believe that we have an obligation as teachers to model how to use these processes and to guide students to apply them, because they are tools for negotiating life's challenges during and after their school years. Further, students who know how to use these tools are empowered to collaborate with their teachers to develop accommodations and modifications in curriculum, instruction, and assessment for themselves and their classmates (see Chapters 6 and 7), when what we as teachers have typically structured is not working.

This chapter focuses on how to promote creativity in student imagination and actions, with *creativity* defined simply as the process of being inventive, productive, and "imaginative" (*Merriam Webster's Collegiate Dictionary*, 2003, s.v. "creative"). We first identify common barriers to creative thinking and action. Next we introduce a dozen strategies, known as *awareness plans*, for busting these barriers so that imaginative improvements and solutions can be found. We then describe and provide examples of a particular problem-solving awareness plan—the Osborn-Parnes Creative Problem Solving process—which can be adapted to deal with a broad range of educational, interpersonal, and life challenges that students and adults confront.

In contrast with the other chapters in this book, this chapter is conceptual in nature. In subsequent chapters, readers learn about how the creative problem-solving processes explained in this chapter are applied when students are instructional decision makers (Chapters 6 and 7), mediators of conflict (Chapter 8), and collaborators in taking responsibility for their own behavior (Chapter 9). The creative thinking processes presented in this chapter are those that teachers also need to develop to become more flexible and responsive in their own instructional decision making. Hence, we use both adult and student examples to illustrate these thinking tools.

As students of creative processes, we wish to acknowledge the mentors and eminent thinkers in the field of creativity—James Adams, Edward de Bono, Herbert Leff, Alex Osborn, Sid Parnes, and Roger van Oech—upon whose works we draw heavily in crafting this chapter for you. We also have drawn upon our own past work on creativity and collaborative learning (Thousand et al., 2007) and the work of our close colleagues (Giangreco, Cloninger, Dennis, & Edelman, 2002), who have conceptualized variations of the Osborn-Parnes Creative Problem Solving process for sparking student engagement in creative solution finding.

BARRIERS TO CREATIVE THINKING AND ACTION

Barriers to creative thinking and action abound. Barriers can be internal, driven by negative assumptions about ourselves and others. Barriers also can be external, imposed by societal values. This is particularly true in contexts such as public schools, where there are strong spoken and unspoken social norms and rules, cultural and historical traditions, and habits of mind and behavior.

What are potential barriers to creative thinking and action for children, our students? James Adams, in his well-known book *Conceptual Blockbusting: A Guide to Better Ideas* (2001), identified several sets of creativity blocks that students as well as adults can experience. The first set of blocks has to do with perception—how we perceive a situation. Among perceptual blocks are adding extra rules that aren't really there and not being able to picture something differently or from another viewpoint. There are many examples of these blocks from famous and brilliant individuals. For example, consider the following (Goleman, Kaufman, & Ray, 1993, p. 128). The president of the Michigan Savings Bank, advising Henry Ford's lawyer not to invest in the Ford Motor Company, stated, "The horse is here to stay; but the automobile is only a novelty—fad." In 1927, Harry Warner, the president of Warner Brothers at the dawn of the "talkies," asked, "Who the he[ck] wants to hear actors talk?" Two decades later, in 1946, Daryl Zanuck, head of 20th Century Fox, commenting on television, stated, "Video won't be able to hold on to any market it captures after the first six months. People will soon get tired of staring at a plywood box every night."

Another set of blocks are cultural and environmental in nature. Children can experience a variety of cultural barriers in school—unspoken norms that fantasy, playfulness, humor, fun, imagination, and wild and crazy ideas are a waste of time or taboo to the serious business of learning via reason, logic, and seriousness. An environmental block could be a classroom in which students have little opportunity for collaborative learning (e.g., cooperative learning, partner learning, co-teaching) or peer dialogue and problem solving (e.g., via class meetings), all experiences that allow for the "two heads are better than one" phenomenon of synergy.

Language can be a creativity block. A barrier to creative thinking as well as learning and engagement in school is not having been taught the language needed to understand a problem or conceive a solution. For example, the language of mathematics is required to conceptualize and solve mathematics problems; the language of instruction is needed for a peer tutor to think about and talk with others about how to design a lesson.

Finally, emotional blocks are possibly the most common and invisible of the creativity barriers for students. Fear—fear of failure, fear of thinking and being different, fear of looking or sounding foolish—is a strong emotional block. The preference to come to quick conclusions rather than relax, be tentative, incubate, or "sleep on it" and the preference to judge and negate rather than generate ideas are two additional emotional blocks, blocks that can be fostered inadvertently in classrooms where quick and correct responding is reinforced over reflective, imaginative, and fanciful thinking.

Assisting students to learn new ways of thinking takes commitment and energy. In fact, a subtle, but pervasive, barrier to creativity is the amount of mental effort and intellectual commitment it takes to learn and practice anything new or unfamiliar. So expect some student reluctance or resistance as you introduce and practice with students the following awareness plans and problem-solving processes.

AWARENESS PLANS FOR BUSTING BARRIERS AND IMAGINING IMPROVEMENTS

For most readers the term *awareness plan* likely is a new one. The term originated with Dr. Herbert Leff of the University of Vermont, who defined an *awareness plan* as simply a person's mental procedure for selecting and processing information (Leff, 1984). Any thinking activity uses some type of awareness plan. However, people usually do not consciously think about or deliberately select the way in which to process information, examine ideas, or explore possible actions in response to a problem.

In this section, we describe a dozen awareness plans that can be used at any time to imagine an improvement that can lead to actions to respond to a problem. All are drawn from Herbert Leff's (1984) book *Playful Perception: Choosing How to Experience Your World* and his ideas and subsequent applications to inclusive educational challenges (Leff, Thousand, Nevin, & Quiocho, 2002). When Dr. Leff's 1984 book was published, the three coauthors of this book were Dr. Leff's students and professional colleagues. This section of Chapter 5 honors his playful genius by describing awareness plans and how they can be used with students.

Figure 5.1 shows Leff's dozen awareness plans. The power of the 12 awareness plans, identified by number below, is that they address common barriers to creative thinking. They

- break traditional or usual perceptions and assumptions about what is and is not possible (i.e., 2: Ask, "What if . . . ?" questions; 4: Think of unusual, nutty things; 6: Use magic wand wishes as guides to feasible ideas.).
- take on new and different perspectives (i.e., 7: Take on different roles of people, animals, things; 8: Use all senses and emotions.).
- conceptualize new and unusual combinations (i.e., 3: Reverse goals; 11: Form new mental connections; 12: Invent games that inspire thinking.).
- generate many ideas (i.e., 5: Force yourself to think of many alternative ideas; 10: Break the problem into smaller problems.).
- expand ways of defining a problem (i.e., 9: Define the goal in different ways.).

The more quickly and thoroughly thinking aides, such as these awareness plans, are incorporated into your and your students' automatic thinking and problem-solving repertoire, the more often they can be activated deliberately and spontaneously inside and outside of the classroom. Experimentation will inform you and your students what works best for you and for them.

Figure 5.1 A Dozen Awareness Plans

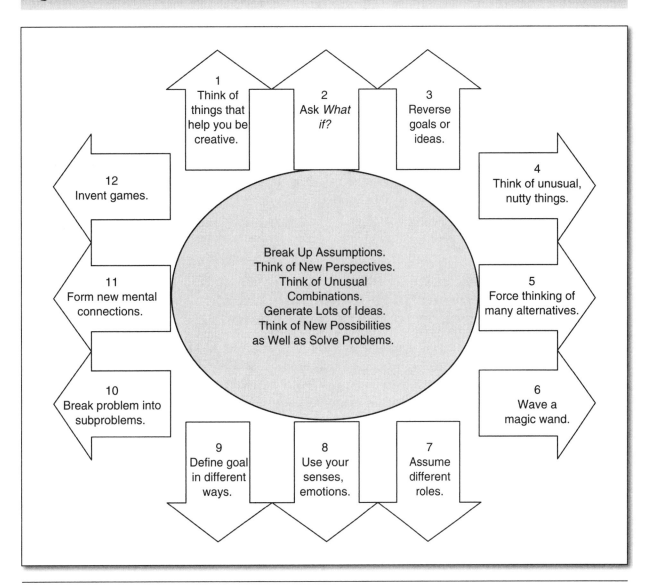

SOURCE: Adapted from Leff, H. L., *Playful Perceptions: Choosing How to Experience Your World*, p. 89. Burlington, VT: Waterfront Books, 85 Crescent Road, Burlington, VT 05401-4126. [Out of print.] © by Herbert L. Leff: reprinted by permission.

Awareness Plan 1: Think of Everything That Helps You to be Creative

When is your creativity at its peak? During what activities are you most inventive in your thinking? Which people and what feelings or states of mind help you to be creative? Make a list! Now vividly imagine experiencing something on your list or actually do something on the list. Things that appear on our list include these:

- Falling asleep
- Waking up
- Sitting by the ocean, listening to the waves
- Thinking out loud
- Running
- Becoming totally immersed in a problem
- Driving long distances with no destination
- Meditating
- Listening to music from other cultures and countries
- Walking and talking with a friend

Many people report that simply imagining being engaged in a preferred activity has led to creative ideas. In fact, this type of visualization has been deliberately used to increase athletic performance (e.g., Janssen & Sheikh, 1994), ensemble music performance (e.g., Hiraga, Mizaki, & Fujishiro, 2002), and reading comprehension (e.g., Johnson-Glenberg, 2000).

Awareness Plan 2: Use "What if. . . ?" Questions to Challenge Usual Assumptions and Expectations

The purpose of the "What if. . . ?" awareness plan is to remove limitations or added rules we consciously or unconsciously assume operate in the situation we are trying to improve. This awareness plan is particularly useful with groups. Suppose, for example, you are on a committee of teachers, students, and community members charged with imagining remodeling options for your school building and playground. "What if. . . ?" questions to help committee members abandon traditional assumptions about what a school could "look like" might include the following:

- What if nothing could touch the floor?
- What if rooms had multiple layers or stories?
- What if rooms allowed for dancing, running, and leaping at a moment's notice?
- What if only students with no sight were to use the building or playground?
- What if infants and toddlers attended school daily?
- What if senior citizens, some of whom use wheelchairs, were part of the school staff and student body?
- What if everyone spoke a different language?

Each question triggers different ideas for new and nontraditional changes—having furniture that folds out from the walls and hangs from the ceiling, having all furniture on wheels, having walls that recede into the ceiling at a flip of a switch, having wide doors that automatically recede into the walls when people approach, having the playground indoors as an integral part of the classroom.

"What if. . . ?" questions are particularly helpful in coming up with alternative actions for change. For example, what possible actions regarding school redesign are suggested by these questions?

- What if everything we did to get this done had to be fun?
- What if we had half (or twice) as long for the change to get done?
- What if we could not spend money to accomplish the change?
- What if this change was the most important thing in all of our lives?

As with all awareness plans, there is no guarantee that "What if. . . ?" questioning will jog ideas. But surely flights of imagination sparked by the "What if. . . ? questioning will be fun!

Awareness Plan 3: Reverse Goals or Ideas

This awareness plan stretches mental flexibility as well as stimulates constructive alternatives by interpreting things as being the opposite of what you normally think they are. Let's use the school redesign challenge again to illustrate how reversing works. Suppose the design team thinks of replacing old window shades with new, more colorful ones. Reversing the idea takes away all window coverings and decorating windows in ways that never block light. Reversing the view of what is inside and outside brings buses, flowers, and trees in as interior furnishings, while whiteboards, computers, DVDs, and iPods become potential playground equipment.

Thinking of possible actions for improving education, imagine working against this goal. Imagine the school as the most uninviting environment (e.g., a prison, a place where emotional and physical garbage is dumped on students). How could this imaging offer insight into actual schooling issues and possible constructive solutions? Suppose the goal is to have a more harmonious relationship with a new principal with whom several teachers have had conflict. Reverse the goal and ask, "What are ways we could decrease harmonious relationships?" Teachers could storm into the principal's office pronouncing a long list of his or her failings or call out his or her failings in front of the superintendent and the school board. Now, imagine reversing these actions to achieve harmonious relations by sending flowers to the office, dropping in one by one for no particular reason but say, "Have a good day," delivering public praise for positive actions, or writing a letter to the superintendent and school board praising the principal for (carefully selected) actions that represent more effective communication with school staff.

The only limit to the creative possibilities of reversals is a willingness to contemplate the usually "unthinkable" or "unthought of." So go for it and enjoy the endless possibilities thought reversal awareness plans can provide!

Awareness Plan 4: Deliberately Think of Unusual, Nutty Things

How absurd can thinking be? The awareness plan of deliberately thinking of unusual and nutty things is a starting place for generating useful ideas that depart from assumptions of what is acceptable or possible. In imagining classroom improvements, in how many ridiculous ways could walls, floors, and ceilings be designed? What are the strangest furnishings possible? Could furnishings be from history, the future, or other cultures? What unexpected activities—a space walk, wrestling, ballet, opera, shopping, art show—can be envisioned for classrooms?

Wild ideas can suggest feasible actions. Focus on making a school's playground more interesting: What are some wacky ideas? Teachers and students could quit school and work full-time on the playground. The school building could be sold to pay for the playground. Students could be hypnotized into thinking the playground already has been made more interesting. Teachers could apply for a federal grant. How could these ideas be massaged to become feasible? Could teachers, students, parents, and members of the community work after school, on weekends, or on a special community service day to renovate the playground? This has been done in many communities. Could parts of the school building be rented out for classes or meetings at night or over the summer, thus raising money for improvements? Why not engage students to play more imaginative games and make more imaginative use of existing equipment? Might a special student fitness project worthy of city, state, or federal funding be written with help from a parent or community member with grantwriting experience?

Awareness Plan 5: Force Yourself to Think of Many Alternative Ideas

Brainstorming is the now commonplace term for the awareness plan of generating a large number of alternative ideas. Alex Osborn first described the procedure in 1953 in *Applied Imagination: Principles and Procedures of Creative Problem-Solving* (1953/1993). Brainstorming adheres to five rules.

Rule 1. Quantity is desired; the more the better. Avoid talking about details, as it slows down the process. Details come later.

Rule 2. Freewheeling is welcomed. Wild ideas are desired. Ideas are critically examined later.

Rule 3. No negative reactions to ideas are allowed. Any premature judgment interrupts the flow of ideas or stops new ideas from being expressed.

Rule 4. The time limit must be short. A few minutes are about as long as the mind can stay intensely creative in a group.

Rule 5. Assign a recorder. The job of the recorder is quickly to jot down a key work or phrase to represent each idea and then to move on. Do not let the recording slow down the idea generating. It may be helpful to have two recorders alternately jotting down the ideas.

Quantity is critical to brainstorming. First- and second-round ideas usually represent the "same old ideas." It is important to get past these usual solutions—to clear out the cobwebs, so to speak—in order to make way for more novel imagined improvements. An aid to brainstorming is to force each new idea to be as different as possible from the previous. For example, if a school team has imagined four ways of making money to improve the playground, try a fifth and sixth way that has nothing to do with money (e.g., use already available recycled materials, such as tires and railroad ties; motivate community members to volunteer time and materials to construction).

Awareness Plan 6: Imagine Having a Magic Wand

What if a magic wand allowed all things to be possible and removed all barriers? How fantastic and fanciful could your imagination become? The magic wand awareness plan is intended to help us forget the genuine barriers to change and defer judgment so the imagination can run wild. In our work with students and adults, we actually issue "magic wands," which are passed over group members while barriers are verbally banished. We suggest banishment invocations such as

"All of the people who would oppose your ideas or think they're crazy have been beamed away to a remote island, and none can be voted off the island."

"You have all the money, time, and resources you could ever want or need."

"Your principals, superintendent, and school board think your ideas are the most ingenious they've ever heard and could never vote against them."

The purpose of the banishment invocation is to remove conscious limitations or barriers that people bring to problem-solving activities.

After thinking of magical wishes "under the spell" of the magic wand, the next step is to identify features of the wishes that are appealing and figure out feasible ways to embody them. Suppose the goal is to get the principal to be more open to student and teacher suggestions. A magic wand-inspired idea might be to spike the principal's coffee with a magic pill that opens minds to new ideas for up to eight hours. Appealing features of this idea is that it is simple, fast, effortless, and nonthreatening. What are real actions that share these features? One action could be to send the principal a gift of a CD, DVD or book on the advantages and skills of open mindedness. Bookstores are full of such self-help literature! Another action might be to anonymously distribute in everyone's mailbox a current article that deals with open-mindedness. How about gift wrapping suggestions and slipping them in with the principal's morning coffee as presents? What other actions resemble a "magic pill" effect? Given a magic wand, what more could be imagined?

Awareness Plan 7: Take on Different Roles While Imagining Improvements

Taking on roles of other people, creatures, or things expands our capacity to view a situation or imagine actions from another's point of view. The idea is to switch among different roles and note how thinking changes. This self-observation while taking on new mental roles helps develop empathy for others' perspectives. To illustrate, the authors suggest that teachers who are planning for differentiation of instruction take on roles other than teacher. Become the student challenged by his or her gifts and talents, the student with a disability, an English language learner. Now stretch your imagination and become the student's parents, a playground supervisor, a lunchroom cook or supervisor, the principal, a community businessperson. Switching among roles several times allows for a broad exploration of potential materials, classroom arrangements, and instructional delivery and assessment options. We have noticed that teachers who take on different roles tend to get to know their students more closely, design instruction that is more reliant on students supporting one another, invite parents and others into the classroom to share their experience, and structure learning experiences that are more engaging and fun.

To activate this awareness plan, de Bono in his book *Six Thinking Hats* (1985) suggests looking at ideas and solutions by literally trying on different colored hats that represent different ways of thinking and perceiving (i.e., white hat—information, facts; red hat—feelings, emotions, and intuition; yellow hat—positive logic, why it works, benefits; black hat—negative logic, judgment, and cautions; green hat—creative, provocative; blue hat—thinking about the thinking process itself). The visual representation of the different ways of thinking in the form of color-coded hats forces ideas to be explored from a variety of angles. The hat wearing also can be quite a wacky activity that can activate playfulness.

Leff and Nevin (1994) suggested that teachers instruct and guide their students to take on thinking patterns associated with various academic and work roles. How would a student think in the role of a mathematician, champion race car driver, historian, environmental activist, sky diver, or crime scene investigator? For a mathematician, logical thinking and tenacity are important, as solving a problem may take years. In contrast, for a race car driver, speed, excitement, and competitiveness are keys to success. To increase students' flexibility in taking on perspectives, combine the different roles and reversal (Awareness Plan 3) awareness plans to switch between a role and its opposite. For example, first think like a competitive race car driver; then reverse the role to experience cooperation as the most important behavior in a team. Think first like a historian, preserving the past; then reverse and think as a visionary futurist. How would a historian's school look and be different from that of a futurist?

How about taking on the roles of animals or other creatures? What would be different in schools if the students and teachers were dogs, birds, or pigs? What would a dog, bird, or pig want or need to learn? How best would you teach a dog, bird, or pig? Now, imagine being an object. If you were the school building and everything in it, what thoughts, feelings, and other sensations might you experience? How might these thoughts, feelings, and sensations inform you on how to create a school culture or environment that allowed you to be a healthy and happy school?

Awareness Plan 8: Use Different Senses and Emotions to Suggest New Possibilities

In the United States, we tend to use only two of our senses (i.e., vision and hearing) when we process information. Why not use the senses of touch, taste, and smell to enhance creative thinking? If in redesigning a school building, we focused on touch, we might focus on using fabrics and textures to soften the atmosphere. Focusing on taste sensations (e.g., hot, cool, spicy, sweet, salty) might suggest ethnic lunch menu options and lunchroom décor, or it might evoke different color schemes, from hot and spicy reds and oranges in one wing to cool blues in another. Similarly, imagining smells, such as the aroma of baking cookies and the scent of flowers, might prompt ideas for having periodic "breakfast club" gatherings for students and staff, or it might suggest starting a school flower and plant garden that could provide floral arrangements and plants for classrooms and educate students about native plants or organic gardening.

Activating any and all emotions can also suggest new possibilities for finding solutions to problems. Does the emotion of excitement suggest vibrant colors and wild décor? Does the emotion of joy suggest flowing and open halls, rooms, and spaces? What if everyone assigned a task had to think of humorous and funny ways to accomplish the task? Even sadness can be used to benefit a goal. In one high school, students grieving the loss of a classmate with disabilities who had suddenly and unexpectedly died took up an advocacy campaign for a student with similar disabilities who was denied access to her local school 1,000 miles away (Villa, 2005). Students wrote letters to the school board and submitted letters to the local paper advocating for her admission to general education classes. Three students even traveled to her town to address a crowd of hundreds about the benefits of including all students in general education. These loss-inspired actions helped classmates to deal with their grief and simultaneously did a public service of heightening a community's awareness of the contributions a student with disabilities can make in the lives of others.

Awareness Plan 9: Define Your Problem or Goal in Many Ways

To activate this awareness plan, begin by restating the problem or goal in a positive way with the starter phrase "In what ways might we. . . ?" Suppose coteaching partners come to you with their problem framed as "We don't have enough time to plan together, much less even go to the bathroom." Restatements of the problem might include "In what ways might we . . .

- use part of a professional development day for time to plan?"
- hire a permanent substitute teacher to cover for us twice a month?"
- rearrange our schedule so we have a common preparation period?"
- schedule specials (e.g., art, music, physical education), clubs, and tutorials during the same time blocks (e.g. first and second period) so that co-teachers have at least that extra time block to plan.
- engage parents and community members in conducting half-day or full-day exploratory, craft, hobby (e.g., iMovie making, photography), theater, or other experiential programs to free up time for co-teachers to plan.

Each positively termed redefinition of a problem is a kernel for a novel potential solution. Each new definition points thinking toward different options, increasing the overall number of possible options for achieving a goal or solving the problem.

Awareness Plan 10: Break the Problem Into Subproblems

Have you ever had the experience of being charged with an overwhelming and seemingly insurmountable project? Have you encountered such a huge and complex problem that it was hard to think even of where to begin? The awareness plan of breaking a problem into smaller subproblems is designed especially for these situations. By breaking a task or problem into its component parts, it is possible to focus on one part at a time and generate more bite-sized actions you personally can take to deal with that aspect of the problem. Once you have thought of these actions, you then can imagine the consequences of each action, select the most promising, and try them out.

This awareness plan may appear to be an obvious one, as we engage it unconsciously for smaller challenges, such as preparing for a dinner party, where there are subproblems of shopping for the food, preparing the linens, cooking and timing the food preparation to meet the schedule for serving courses, and matching beverages to the liking of the guests and the flavor of the food. For some family-related challenges, we likely are conscious of using the subproblem awareness plan. Such a challenge might be planning and executing a wedding. Most of us know at least the categories of the subproblems (e.g., ceremony, reception, clothing, transportation) for which actions need to be imagined. But still, even with this knowledge, many of us seek assistance to tackle the subproblems. We might get a little help from a wedding planning Web site or hire a wedding planner who has extensive experience in defining wedding subproblems, thinking of actions to plan and execute the wedding subproblems, imagining the consequences of each option, and advising the wedding party as to the most promising actions for the big day to come off to the satisfaction of all. How might you teach your students to become problem-solving planners who know how to break a big problem into subproblems?

Awareness Plan 11: Form New Mental Connections

One way to jog new ideas is to think of things similar to what you want to change or do. When thinking about the redesign of a school, what might be applied from features of a majestic old hotel lobby, a modern architectural marvel (e.g., the five-star Burj al Arab hotel in Dubai designed to resemble a sail; see www.burj-al-arab.com), a historical wonder (e.g. the Angkor Wat temple complex in Cambodia; see the UNESCO World Heritage Web site at http://whc.unesco.org/en/list/668), or the designs of your favorite architect (e.g., Frank Lloyd Wright, see www.loc.gov/rr/print/list/103_flw.html). Going further afield, why not derive ideas from parks and homes of animals and birds? Or use the reversal awareness plan (Awareness Plan 3) and think of undesirable habitats, such as prisons or refugee camps, and reverse their features for inspiration.

Another method for jogging novel ideas is to connect two things that seemingly have nothing to do with one another. For example, suppose you have a goal of making the community center safer at night, and you see on your nightstand a deck of playing cards. What does the card deck suggest regarding safety? Perhaps a casino night could be hosted to raise money to install additional parking lot and street lights. Safety tips could be printed on cards and distributed to stores and households in the neighborhood, as well as the children who frequent the center.

Analogies and metaphors also promote the forming of new mental connections. If you are trying to envision new ways of having fun, why not look for analogies in the animal kingdom? How do puppies, lions, or seals seem to have fun and play? What might their play look like for human children and adults?

Awareness Plan 12: Invent Imaginative Games to Inspire Thinking

Games can help people solve problems and learn something new or make reaching a goal more fun. Games can increase students' motivation and appreciation of subject matter. So why not invent games to liven up thinking? For example, let's consider a grammar lesson on adjectives. Rather than having students identify adjectives on worksheets provided by a textbook publisher, why not engage students in an "Adjective Game" with the goal of seeing how many real-life adjectives student teams encounter in a day? First, invite students to detect and list all of the adjectives they hear or see in a day. In teams (e.g., triads or quads), they then verify that their examples are in fact adjectives, create flash cards of each adjective, and receive points equal to the number of adjectives the team collectively identifies. Flash cards can be hung from the ceiling and posted around the room, where all can see them and use them to practice adjectives in sentences over the course of the next week. The game can start over again the next week, this time perhaps as the "Adverb Game."

Games can be created by combining awareness plans. Consider a game designed to imagine improvements to a community library that engages people gathered together in the library in a series of awareness plans. First, group members ask one another "What if. . . ?" questions (Awareness Plan 2). What if there were no books and everything was electronic? What if we had a wealthy benefactor? What if everyone who came to the library used a wheelchair? Next, the group takes on roles of various creatures (Awareness Plan 7). How would each animal want the library to change? Finally, the group turns "What if. . . ?" and animal role suggestions into feasible ideas for improving the library.

Consider a game developed by co-teachers of a combined first- and second-grade class in an inner-city school. The game combined several awareness plans to help students solve real-life problems the class had identified. About 70 percent of the students in the class had identified "eating vegetables" as a problem in their lives (e.g., "I don't like peas (or corn, or broccoli, or carrots) but hafta eat them at dinner.") The teachers guided students to brainstorm (Awareness Plan 5: Force thinking of many alternatives.) ideas for solving the problem. Then students then put on the thinking caps of known characters, such as Popeye and Peter Rabbit (Awareness Plan 7: Assume different roles.). Partners brainstormed in their new role. For example, Popeye might ask for spinach instead of peas, and Peter Rabbit might ask for carrots instead of broccoli. After students shared their "role" solutions, the teachers waved magic wands (Awareness Plan 6) to signal that all dinner rules were removed and asked the students to "redesign supper" to deal with the despised vegetables. When students returned to class the next day, several students shared that they had actually used the Redesign Supper plan to negotiate vegetable alternatives to their personally dreaded entrées!

An Invitation to Use and Model Awareness Plans

A barrier to using awareness plans is assuming that students (and adults) know how to engage awareness plan thinking. Teachers, therefore, must learn, model, teach, and coach students in the application of awareness plans, showing students how a plan actually accomplishes the goal of inspiring thinking in novel ways.

OSBORN-PARNES CREATIVE PROBLEM SOLVING (CPS) PROCESS

One awareness plan for addressing a variety of challenges that has had extensive application in education and business over the past several decades is known as the Osborn-Parnes Creative Problem Solving process, or simply CPS. The six stages of the CPS process presented here are based upon the process described by Alex Osborn (1953/1993) and his protégé, Sid Parnes (1992a, 1992b), as well as our own applications (Thousand et al., 2007) and the applications employed by Giangreco et al. (2002). We would like to emphasize that it is the process of using CPS and other awareness plans as part of students' daily routines that helps to develop the creative disposition and spirit that are lifelong assets (Parnes, 1992a).

In this section, we first describe the six stages of the CPS process— Challenge Finding, Fact Finding, Problem Finding, Idea Finding, Solution Finding, and Acceptance Finding. We then briefly describe three variations of the CPS process: (1) CPS as a retrofit approach to differentiated instruction (detailed in Chapter 6), (2) the SODAS IF problem-solving approach, and (3) the "Quick Brainstorm With the Kids" CPS process. All three variations are intended to empower students to think in more creative ways to solve their own problems.

Stages of the Osborn-Parnes CPS Process

A key feature of the Osborn-Parnes CPS is that at each stage of the process, problem solvers alternate between divergent and convergent ways of thinking. Each stage begins with divergent thinking activities—the broad exploration of possible issues, problems, options, criteria, and actions. Each stage closes with convergent thinking activities—a narrowing of focus through the sorting, organizing, evaluation, and selecting of preferred ideas or actions. The ability to move easily back and forth between divergent and convergent thinking is an identified attribute of highly creative people (Parnes, 1992a, 1992b). Highly creative people also have the ability to defer judgment. Hence, not until stage five of the six stages of CPS are problem solvers invited to evaluate options critically and select among them.

Stage 1: Challenge Finding

At the first stage of the CPS process, problem solvers look around and become alert to situations in need of improvement. They realize that something should be done and make a decision to work for improvement. They first are divergent, considering a variety of possible challenges. They then are convergent, selecting one challenge upon which to focus that is small enough to be solved in the time allowed.

Stage 2: Fact Finding

At the fact-finding stage, problem solvers start divergently, asking questions and collecting and recording data on what is and is not happening with regard to the situation for the purpose of improving their understanding of the situation. It is important to point out here that two people may have contradictory perceptions about the same event. If so, both facts are considered true, as they represent the "personally true" experience of each individual involved. Fact finding ends with problem solvers engaging in convergent thinking by sorting and organizing the facts that are most relevant to the challenge at hand.

Stage 3: Problem Finding

At the problem-finding stage, Awareness Plan 9 (i.e., define a goal in different ways) and Awareness Plan 10 (i.e., break the problem into subproblems) are activated to consider different ways of viewing the problem. Using the "In what ways might we. . . ?" starter phrase, subproblems are identified and written as problem statements. This is done until a bite-sized problem is teased out, which is the convergent closing of this stage.

Stage 4: Idea Finding

This stage of the CPS process engages the rules of brainstorming to generate many possible solutions to the problem. These rules are outlined in Awareness Plan 5 and include stating and recording far-out ideas and deferring any evaluation of ideas. Here, the facts that were recorded at Stage 2 can be used to jog ideas by asking questions such as "How might this fact be reversed (i.e., Awareness Plan 3: Reverse goal or idea.), made smaller or larger, eliminated, or altered to improve the situation?" Note that some ideas will be unusable. This is okay, as the process of generating wild and crazy ideas loosens up thinking, the point of Stage 4.

Stage 5: Solution Finding

Judging ideas occurs at Stage 5. First, many criteria for evaluating ideas are identified, refined, and finally selected for use in judging and selecting the most promising of the ideas generated at Stage 4. Among evaluation criteria that might be chosen are the following:

1. Is the proposed solution feasible?

2. Is it time efficient and cost-effective?

3. Does the user (e.g., student, teacher) like the idea?

4. Is the idea consistent with the values of the organization (e.g., the school) and those who will have to implement it (e.g., the teachers, students)?

Problem solvers then become convergent as they apply the selected criteria to potential action options. This can be done in a freewheeling fashion where criteria are held in the back of each problem solver's mind and collectively applied to each solution. Alternatively, the process can be more formal and systematic, using a matrix in which ideas are listed along one axis and criteria are listed along the other. A plus/minus or weighted rating system can be used to evaluate ideas, remembering that the matrix method is simply a tool, not a formula for selecting promising solutions.

Stage 6: Acceptance Finding

At the final stage, promising solutions are made ready for use by outlining what needs to be done in order for the solutions to work and be accepted by those involved. Steps to achieving the agreed-upon solutions take the facts (i.e., the perceptions of those involved) into consideration. Stage 6 begins divergently with *who*, *what*, *where*, *when*, *why*, and *how* questions being asked and answered. It ends with problem solvers thinking convergently to develop a step-by-step plan of action.

Using Three Variations of the CPS Process With Students

CPS is a generic process anyone can use to solve almost any problem. Since this book is about empowering students, we feature the SODAS and the "Quick Brainstorm With the Kids" applications, variations that students can readily and easily use to solve their own problems. The CPS process also can be used by students and their teachers to deal with the instructional, assessment, and discipline mismatches that inevitably occur in diverse classrooms. This application of CPS has been referred to as the *retrofit approach to differentiated instruction* (Thousand et al., 2007). The retrofit variation is described first, as it employs all of the steps of the CPS process.

Using CPS as a Retrofit Approach to Differentiated Instruction

One approach to differentiating instruction in today's diverse classrooms is known as the retrofit approach (Thousand et al., 2007). In the retrofit approach, teachers and/or students notice that a challenge exists for one or more students in instruction, discipline, or some aspect of schooling and, after the fact, try to do something to remedy the situation. In the retrofit differentiation approach, noticing and acknowledging the challenge is the equivalent of Stage 1, the Challenge Finding stage, of the CPS process.

To retrofit successfully requires delving deep into Fact Finding, the second stage of CPS. Two sets of facts must be closely examined. One concerns the student of concern and his or her strengths, learning styles, preferences and interests, and challenges. The second is classroom and curriculum facts, particularly expectations that are causing concern. Student and classroom facts then are compared, and mismatches between student characteristics and environmental and task demands are identified. This is equivalent to Problem Finding, the third stage of CPS.

The next retrofit step involves examining each of the mismatches and generating several ideas to remediate it. This is the Idea Finding (CPS Stage 4) step of retrofit. Criteria for judging ideas then are generated and applied to select solutions to the mismatches that are acceptable to the student and teacher. This is the Solution Finding (CPS Stage 5) step of retrofit. When the solution-finding team members try out the agreed-upon solutions, this is the Acceptance Finding (CPS Stage 6) step of the retrofit process. In the following chapter, Chapter 6, we provide examples of students and teachers working together to use the retrofit approach to correct curriculum, instructional, and discipline mismatches. Be sure to look at these examples, as they bring the steps summarized here alive and will provide ideas to use in your own efforts to correct mismatches through the retrofit differentiation approach.

The SODAS IF Application of CPS

SODAS IF (Hazel, Schumaker, Sherman, & Sheldon, 1995) is a variation of the CPS process that has been used successfully with students for years. SODAS is an acronym for Situation-Options-Disadvantages-Advantages-Solution. A template for the SODAS IF process, shown in Table 5.1, identifies the stages of CPS that parallel the SODAS IF steps. Specifically,

S—the Situation of the SODAS process parallels Stage 3: Problem Finding of CPS. Here, a specific problem is identified.

O—the Options in the SODAS process parallels Stage 4: Idea Finding of the CPS process. Here multiple options are generated for the situation.

D—Disadvantages and

A—Advantages in the SODAS process parallel the criterion-finding dimension of Stage 5: Solution Finding of CPS.

S—Solution in the SODAS process parallels the convergent aspect of the Stage 5: Solution Finding of the CPS process.

IF—IF in the SODAS process parallels the Stage 6: Acceptance stage of CPS.

As an illustration of a teacher using SODAS IF with students, imagine Ms. Cordova, a third-grade classroom teacher, randomly drawing from the class

Table 5.1 The SODAS IF Problem-Solving Template With Parallel CPS Stages

SITUATION (Stage 3: Problem Finding):

_____

_____

_____

_____

OPTIONS (Stage 4: Idea Finding):

1. _____ 2. _____ 3. _____

DISADVANTAGES (Stage 5: Solution Finding):

a. _____   a. _____   a. _____
b. _____   b. _____   b. _____
c. _____   c. _____   c. _____
d. _____   d. _____   d. _____

ADVANTAGES (Stage 5: Solution Finding):

a. _____   a. _____   a. _____
b. _____   b. _____   b. _____
c. _____   c. _____   c. _____
d. _____   d. _____   d. _____

SOLUTION:

IF you agree to a solution, MAKE A PLAN (Stage 6: Acceptance Finding).
(Who will do what, when? How you know if the plan is working?)

meeting suggestion box this problem: "A student calls another student's sister a name, and the students get into a shouting match in the hallway." Ms. Cordova displays the SODAS problem-solving template with the document projector, as she asks the students to identify the problem situation. Ms. Cordova calls on a student who correctly identifies the problem situation and writes the identified situation on the template form. She then asks students to identify some options for solving this problem and samples students' ideas. Five options are generated, the teacher adds a sixth, and all are recorded on the template.

The next step involves identifying disadvantages for each of the options. Ms. Cordova models an example of a disadvantage of the first option and records the disadvantages on the template. Then she asks the students to turn to their neighbors and discuss possible disadvantages of the second option. After a minute, she calls on various learners and records the disadvantages shared by the students. She repeats this process for the remaining options, calling on students and recording.

Ms. Cordova repeats the process for the advantages. This time, she tallies responses and puts a circle around the advantages with the most votes. She directs the students to turn to different partners to identify the possible solution(s) that would achieve the best advantages and avoid the worst disadvantages. After a few minutes, she asks the students to report out and tallies the results. She explains that if the scenario were real, the two students who had fought would be expected to use SODAS to come up with an alternate response to fighting if a problem like this were to occur again.

Ms. Cordova asks students how the SODAS problem-solving process might help them solve problems on the playground, in class, and at home. She closes the lesson by having each student share an example of how they might use SODAS in their personal lives and telling the students that they will practice using SODAS to solve problems throughout the year.

The "Quick Brainstorm With the Kids" CPS Variation

The "Quick Brainstorm With the Kids" CPS variation, derived from Giangreco and colleagues (2002), focuses students' creative thinking upon the brainstorming of ideas (i.e., the Stage 4: Idea Finding dimension of CPS) to improve their own situations. As an illustration of this variation, consider a class of first graders who are challenged to think of ways to welcome a new classmate, Michelle, a student with multiple disabilities. When challenged by their teacher to think of wild and crazy ideas in three minutes or less, the class came up with more than 60 ideas, the majority of which could be turned into feasible ideas. During the brainstorming, one student suggested, "We could all go to the beach at the ocean." The next student piggybacked on the idea by saying, "I can show her how to play in our sandbox at recess." This student made the mental connection with the similarities between the beach and the playground and came up with a doable modification of the "go to the ocean" idea!

In summary, the key to the CPS variations, both Quick Brainstorming With the Kids and SODAS IF, is to trust that students have lots of good ideas that these creative solution-finding processes can tap. You are sure to be amazed at their creativity.

THINKING FOR COLLABORATIVE PROBLEM SOLVING: FOCUSING UPON WHAT YOU CAN DO

"A fair idea put to use is better than a good idea kept on the polishing wheel."

—Alex Osborn (as cited in Parnes, 1992a, p. 38)

An important disposition shared by creative problem solvers is that they take action on what can be attempted. In other words, rather than taking a "ready, *aim*, fire" stance, where everything has to be perfectly organized and ordered before one steps out and attempts something, effective problem solvers take a "ready, *fire*, aim" stance and give ideas a try.

Now that you have read this chapter, what do you know about blocks to creative thinking and ways to overcome these blocks? How do you plan to engage yourself and students in creative thinking and problem-solving processes? Which awareness plans have you tried or will try yourself? Which will you try with students to increase their inventiveness and enjoyment? How might you use the Obsorn-Parnes Creative Problem Solving process and its variations to expand options for collaborating with students to meet their needs and to solve everyday problems at school and elsewhere? The key is to act and engage others, particularly students, in action as well.

To delve deeper into ways in which to infuse creativity into students' daily work, be aware of the various resources devoted to promoting creativity in students and adults. Following are some examples.

Web Sites

Creative Education Foundation: www.creativeeducationfoundation.org

Creative Think (Roger van Oech): www.creativethink.com/whack/

The de Bono Group: www.debonogroup.com

Publishing Companies

Scroll through the books and manuals available from publishers, such as Prufrock Press (www.prufrock.com)

Lessons and Instructional Techniques

Adapt creative, curriculum-based lessons and instructional techniques, such as those developed by these authors:

Dianne Draze, *Creative problem solving for kids: Grades 5–8*, 2005

Joel McIntosh & April Meacham, *Creative problem solving in the classroom*, 1992

Donald Treffinger, Scott Isaksen, & K. Brian Stead-Dorval, *Creative problem solving: An introduction*, 2006

Students as **6** Instructional Decision Makers

Although special courses on creative thinking have proved beneficial, our whole educational system can be of greater help by giving more attention to this subject. There is abundant opportunity to teach almost any subject in ways that call for productive thinking.

—John Guilford (as cited in Sennett, 2004, p. 63)

After reading the first five chapters of this book, are you wondering if there are other forms of student collaboration that tap the resources of children in delivering the school community's agreed-upon curriculum? In this chapter, you will discover additional forms of student collaboration by examining how students can be partially to fully involved in various aspects of the teaching and learning cycle. Some of your questions might include these:

1. How can students collaborate about determining the content they will learn?

2. How can students collaborate about deciding what instructional processes might help them learn?

3. How will students collaborate in developing the methods they will use to demonstrate what they have learned?

4. How might students collaborate with their teachers to differentiate instruction for themselves and for classmates who may be struggling to learn?

Increasing active learning and responsibility on the part of students is a long-standing and ongoing educational recommendation (Duke & Pearson, 2002; Fisher & Frey, 2008; Johnson & Johnson, 2002; Thousand, Villa, & Nevin, 2002; Villa & Thousand, 1992). Active learning involves students participating in all aspects of the learning process—empowering students to determine what they will learn, how they will learn, and how they will demonstrate what they have learned.

Pearson and Gallagher (1983) advocated a model of instruction in which there is a gradual release of responsibility from teacher to student. They advocated that the cognitive load gradually shift from the teacher-as-model, to joint responsibility of the teacher and students for educational decision making, to independent practice and application by the students. Gradually releasing responsibility for learning to students facilitates students becoming increasingly self-directed, competent individuals who can problem-solve; seek, find, and use information; and communicate what they have learned. The process results in the development of lifelong learners who are better able to thrive in the complex, diverse, information-rich, and technologically driven 21st century.

Guskey and Anderman (2008) believe that "students can learn to act responsibly by practicing meaningful decision making in school" (p. 8). Teachers can collaborate with their students to allow students to (a) choose work locations, (b) use rubrics to evaluate their work, (c) participate in student-led conferences with their parents, and (d) set classroom discipline procedures. Combining advice from Guskey and Anderman and the gradual release of responsibility to the student described above, Douglas Fisher and Nancy Frey (2008), professors of literacy at San Diego State University—California, described how to use literacy strategies to gradually transfer responsibility for learning from the teacher to the learner. In addition to teacher modeling, several other strategies can be used to teach students how to be responsible for their own comprehension when reading text material, as well as how to be responsible for independently solving word problems.

Perhaps the most important reason for involving students in actively deciding what and how they learn is described by Popham (2008). He wrote, "Student ownership of learning requires that students understand the evidence used to signify whether learning is taking place" (p. 81). When teachers collaborate with their students in actively generating their goals, learning processes, learning products, and evaluation systems, students are much more likely to recognize that they have learned!

How can students learn to act responsibly by practicing meaningful decision making in school? What follows in the next two sections of this chapter are examples of students actively engaged and sharing responsibility for their own and classmates' learning. First, we follow Mr. Bandera's students being guided through the process of determining what they will learn, how they will learn it, and how they will show what they have learned in many different ways. Then, we experience two groups of students—elementary and middle level students—as they brainstorm solutions to mismatches between the facts about particular students and the curriculum demands of their classrooms. As you read these examples, reflect upon how collaborating with students is leading to the Circle of Courage outcomes described in Chapter 1. How do these practices and active student involvement and decision making about their own and one another's education lead to the desired Circle of Courage outcomes of belonging, mastery, independence, and generosity?

COLLABORATING WITH STUDENTS TO DETERMINE THE PRODUCT OF LEARNING

It is the first day of a new unit of study in a high school social studies class. The classroom teacher, Mr. Bandera, starts the class by sharing that learning outcomes for the lesson are based on six important standards[1] set by their state, namely the following:

1. Trace the origin and geopolitical consequences (domestic and foreign) of the Cold War and the containment of Communism (e.g., Vietnam War).

2. Organize people and events according to chronology, geography, and theme to analyze similarities, differences, and relationships.

3. Use cause-and-effect arguments to demonstrate how significant events have influenced the past and present in the United States.

4. Identify significant events, people, and documents in major eras of U.S. history.

5. Evaluate, take, and defend positions on the influence of the media on U.S. political life.

6. Formulate questions about and defend analyses of tensions within a democracy (e.g., civil disobedience and the rule of law).

To access students' prior knowledge and engage them in determining the direction that they would take in their learning, Mr. Bandera engaged students in a modified K-W-L strategy (Carr & Ogle, 1987). With a typical K-W-L format, *K* represents what students already **k**now, *W* represents **w**hat students want to learn, and *L* represents what students **l**earned as a consequence of instruction. Mr. Bandera modified the K-W-L format to a K-W-H format by asking students, "What do you *know* about the Vietnam War? What do you *want* to learn about the Vietnam War? *How* do you want to *show* me what you learned about the Vietnam War?" Mr. Bandera organized the class into triads and gave each group a three-column graphic organizer on which members recorded what they currently knew about the subject, what they hoped to learn, and how they preferred to demonstrate their knowledge.

While the groups worked, Mr. Bandera eavesdropped and monitored the conversations, allowing him to discover some gaps in his students' knowledge base. He then assigned them a short passage about the Vietnam War to read and asked them to continue thinking about the K-W-H questions for homework. He also directed students to interview their parents, relatives, and neighbors about the Vietnam War. On the following day, the students reconvened in their triads to update their graphic organizers before sharing as a whole class. Mr. Bandera compiled the groups' K-W-H responses. The results of the whole-class sharing are shown in Table 6.1.

[1] Standard 2: How the Cold War and conflicts in Korea and Vietnam influenced domestic and international politics. 2A: The student understands the international origins and domestic consequences of the Cold War (www.sscnet.ucla.edu/nchs/standards/era9-5-12.html; see also Standard 11.9.3 at http://score.rims.k12.ca.us/standards/grades/?g=11).

Table 6.1 K-W-H Strategy to Determine Collaboratively the Focus of the Unit Content

Student Generated Ideas	Teacher Additions
• Why did we fight the war? • When did the war start? • How long did it take us to win the war? • Why didn't we win the war? • How many people died? • What kinds of weapons were used? • What was the effect of the war on their society and ours? • What role did music play, if any? • Why were so many people opposed to the war? • What happened to people who refused to fight in the war? • How did the war end? • When did the war end? • Which countries were our allies, and which were our enemies? • What is communism? Why was it considered so bad? • What is nationalism? • What kind of government does Vietnam have now? • What was it like to fight there? • What is Agent Orange? • How many other wars has Vietnam fought? Has it won all of them?	• Was the war limited to Vietnam? • How were people selected to fight in the war (e.g., fiscal, human loss, effect on other social initiatives in the United States)? • What role did the media play? Should they have done anything differently? • In what ways did we dehumanize the Vietnamese? • What effect, if any, did the Vietnam War have on subsequent U.S. military involvement? • How did the war affect U.S. and Vietnamese society? • What kind of a relationship does the United States have with the Vietnamese government today? Are there any unresolved issues? • In what ways was the Vietnam War similar to the War in Iraq? • In what ways was the Vietnam War different from the War in Iraq? • What dimensions of comparison are relevant? • How were veterans treated then as compared to now?
Sources or Materials to Learn This Information	**Teacher Additions to Sources or Materials**
• History texts • Interview of relatives (written and person-to-person contacts) • Content from the Internet, newspapers, books, political cartoons • Newspapers, magazines, documentaries, and movies from that time period (e.g., *Deer Hunter, Good Morning Vietnam*).	• Books (e.g., *Pentagon Papers*) • Biographies (e.g., John McCain)

Using the information that emerged from the K-W-H opening exercise, Mr. Bandera developed a menu from which each student could choose options to convey content knowledge at the end of the unit. The menu for student product choices appears in Table 6.2. A blank copy of the menu, which can serve as a template for teachers and students to individualize their instruction, appears as Resource E in the Resources section.

At the beginning of the school year, Mr. Bandera had taught his students about Bloom's cognitive taxonomy (Bloom et al., 1956) and Gardner's (1983)

Table 6.2   Product Options by Levels of Bloom's Taxonomy and Dimensions of Multiple Intelligences

Knowledge	Comprehension	Application	Analysis	Synthesis	Evaluation
		Dimension: Verbal/Linguistic			
Following pre-assessment of knowledge of related vocabulary terms, develop a dictionary of key terms not previously understood. Include at least 20 terms and their definitions.	Describe in your own words how the United States became involved in the Vietnam War. Interview people alive at the time of the Vietnam War. Try to find people who supported the war as well as people opposed to it. Write a report presenting their major points.		Compare and contrast, either by writing or by giving an oral presentation, the Vietnam War and the War in Iraq. Debate an issue associated with the Vietnam War (e.g., Should we have entered the war? Should the draft have been used?).	Predict what might be the result of U.S. intervention in Iraq, Afghanistan, and/or Pakistan.	Write an essay of at least 1,000 words explaining your position on one of the following topics: Should we have used Agent Orange in Vietnam? Should the United States have continued to fight in Vietnam?
		Dimension: Visual/Spatial			
			Review political cartoons, news magazines, and/or films from this era and identify their potential impact on those who read or saw them. Compare and contrast capitalism and communism through a poster or PowerPoint presentation.		Design a visual display to represent the qualities that an effective military leader would possess or the successful outcomes of a military conflict.

(Continued)

Dimension: Logical/Mathematical

	Develop a time line of significant events in the Vietnam War, starting with the Gulf of Tonkin Resolution.	Compare and contrast in tables or charts the United States and Vietnam at the time of the war (e.g., economic structure, GDP, allies, resources, diversity of population, geography, military resources, religions, imports and exports, political system).

Dimension: Naturalist

	Describe the impact of Agent Orange on the environment of Vietnam.	Write a letter to one of your congressional representatives or the president explaining how better to preserve and share the earth's resources so that wars are not fought over natural resources.	Compare and contrast the fighting of a war in two diverse ecosystems (e.g., Vietnam and Iraq).

Dimension: Musical

	Compare and contrast pro- and anti-war songs during the Vietnam War.	Develop a rap, poem, or song about the Cold War. Be prepared to perform your poem, rap, or song in front of the class.

(Continued)

Dimension: Bodily Kinesthetic

Create and perform a commercial designed to attract civilians to enlist in the military to fight a war.		Choreograph and perform an interpretive dance about an aspect of the Vietnam War. Create a board game to assess knowledge and comprehension of information about the Vietnam War. Be sure to include the rules for playing the game.

Dimension: Intrapersonal

Identify 10 ways that the War in Iraq affects your life and/or the lives of your family and neighbors. Be imaginative in how you present the information (e.g., PowerPoint, poster, diary or journal entry, letter to a friend living in another country).		Assume the persona of a soldier fighting a war and either write 5 letters home to family and friends or create 10 diary entries to describe what you see, experience, and feel as you fight the war.

Dimension: Interpersonal

In a cooperative group of two to four, write and perform four TV news scripts depicting major events of the Cold War.		Pick and research a candidate for or against the Vietnam War. Pretend you are a TV journalist at the time. Develop interview questions and predict how your candidate would answer them.

theory of multiple intelligences (MI). He explained to the students that these tools would help him organize the menu of product options and allow them to have fun while they learned and demonstrated their learning. Students completed an MI assessment to clarify for themselves and Mr. Bandera their own multiple intelligence profiles.

At the end of the unit, Mr. Bandera told students they each needed to select three ways to show what they had learned about the Vietnam War. During individual conferences, Mr. Bandera and each student reviewed the curriculum standards and the class-generated lists of questions of interest to select a focus of learning for each student. Each student could choose only one product option from the lowest levels of Bloom's taxonomy—the knowledge and comprehension levels. Thus, each student selected two product options from the higher levels of the taxonomy (i.e., application, analysis, synthesis, and evaluation). Also, students were to complete one activity alone and one activity with a partner or small group. For the third activity, students could choose whether or not to work alone, with a partner, or in a small group of no more than four students.

How did Mr. Bandura engage his students as instructional decision makers? Through the K-W-H exercise, students had a hand in deciding which product options were most relevant to them. By having choice among the options, they were empowered to select options to show their knowing in ways that capitalized upon their preferences and strengths according to their multiple intelligences. By being required to make at least two of three choices at higher levels of Bloom's cognitive taxonomy, they were stretched to use higher thinking skills, but still with a range of choices. Finally, by being required to work alone and with a partner, they were further stretched to work both independently and to engage their small-group interpersonal skills, thus developing their collaborative-teaming and collaborative-learning skills. Mr. Bandura masterfully and collaboratively released responsibility to his class to determine and execute each student's self-assessment of what he or she had learned in this unit.

COLLABORATING WITH STUDENTS TO DIFFERENTIATE INSTRUCTION FOR STRUGGLING LEARNERS

There is no denying that today's increasingly inclusive classrooms are filled with diverse and complex students, many of whom have unique learning needs. It is easy to image any teacher, at times, feeling overwhelmed about what to do differently to meet student needs or being tempted to think about referring particular students to alternative programs, such as alternative special education or gifted and talented programs. Immediate help for teachers confronted with differentiating instruction is available if students are brought into the differentiation problem-solving process.

In the authors' experience, students often have developed fewer barriers to creativity than adults and are a source of novel, relevant, and student-friendly ideas. We know preschoolers and kindergarteners who have assisted educators in developing accommodations and modifications to support a struggling class-mate. To illustrate, Michael Giangreco and colleagues (2002) described what happened when first graders, working in groups, were provided with an overview of how their teacher typically taught an upcoming literacy lesson. The first graders were asked to help the teacher brainstorm ways in which the lesson could be changed so that all learners in the class, including Molly (a new student to the class who was deaf and blind), could meaningfully participate. At the end of 10 minutes, the six-year-olds had generated nearly 70 possible options! Subsequently, the teacher noted that at least 60 ideas could work to include Molly in this lesson, as well as future activities. She recognized that many of the students' ideas not only allowed Molly's active engagement but worked to help other students access the curriculum.

In a more recent experience, Richard Villa facilitated a student assembly in which 650 middle-level students were introduced to facts about various learn-ers and classroom demands. They were asked to identify the mismatches between the learner characteristics and the classroom demands and then to generate a minimum of three possible solutions for each mismatch. For each scenario presented, Richard stopped students after five minutes of brainstorm-ing and sampled their ideas. His favorite part of the assembly was watching the expressions of surprise and pleasure on the faces in the adult audience members as the students shared their ideas.

After the assembly, several teachers who had been in the audience revealed that some of the students who had shared the best ideas were considered to be struggling learners in their classes. The teachers smartly concluded that they needed to collaborate with these struggling learners to identify potential solu-tions to the mismatches that existed between them and the demands of their classrooms. We encourage the readers of this book to react similarly whenever they encounter students struggling in their classrooms.

Professional discretion is required when sharing with students information about a struggling learner. Such information must be shared in a respectful manner, and confidentiality concerns must be addressed. Focus learners and their parents should be made aware of any plans to share information with peers. If a focus learner is receiving special education services, it is best to obtain written parental permission prior to the sharing of any information. In our experience, parents rarely deny this permission once they understand that information will be presented from a strengths-based perspective and is intended to support their child's school success and well-being. Focus learners also should be given the opportunity to determine what information is shared and whether or not they wish to participate in peer problem solving on their behalf. Often focus learners prefer a small number of classmates whom they select rather than an entire class to engage in problem solving.

There are many ways to engage students in addressing mismatches between a classmate's characteristics and classroom demands. Some teachers first model the process by explaining they are "challenged" by how they currently are teach-ing and need student input about how to diversify their typical way of instruct-ing. They explain that they want to be better teachers by matching their instruction to how their students learn. Then, particular mismatches are addressed for particular students. Sometimes, teachers create a composite profile of several students and engage the class in brainstorming for this profile before focusing on an actual student. Teachers also have changed the name of the focus learner and engaged students unfamiliar with the learner to examine facts and brainstorm solutions, as was done for the Albuquerque example that follows.

A Template for Addressing Mismatches Between Student Characteristics and Classroom Demands

When attempting to adapt instruction for a student, it is easy to downplay information about what the student does well and under what conditions he or she performs best. Yet it is the strength-based information that identifies how to support, motivate, and establish a relationship with a struggling learner. A strengths-based approach begins with gathering information about a student's interests, learning preferences and styles, strengths related to multiple intelligences, as well as the classroom demands. Tables 6.3–6.5 offer a template that students and teachers can use to gather information and discover and address mismatches between a student's characteristics and typical classroom demands. (A blank template appears as Resource F in the Resource section at the end of the book.) The far left column of the template prompts identification of *positive* student information, as well as specific student goals and needs. The next column prompts an examination of the content, product/assessment, and process/instructional demands of the lesson, class, or classroom. Using this template to gather "facts" about a student and the classroom is a first step in determining how to develop adaptations that use and build upon student characteristics and strengths.

The next step in the process of crafting adaptations is to compare the student and class or task information to identify mismatches between the two and identify those mismatches in the third column of the template. A mismatch between how the student accesses content and the typical materials used (i.e., content demands) may be discovered. For example, a seventh-grade student reading at a fourth-grade level may have only seventh-grade-level textbooks available in the classroom. This represents a materials mismatch. Alternatively, there may be a mismatch between how classmates best show what they know and how achievement is typically assessed. This is a product mismatch. Or there may be a mismatch between how the classmate best acquires knowledge or skills and how instruction typically has occurred. This would be a process mismatch.

Armed with identified mismatches, students, with teacher guidance, can collaboratively consider possible ways to provide support or change the content and material (content demands), how the student is asked to show what he or she knows (product demands), and/or what is done during instruction (process demands). When generating potential solutions, it is important to avoid solutions that might stigmatize. Thus, we suggest first considering as possible solutions those that could be available to and benefit other students. When prioritizing solutions to mismatches, we suggest selecting solutions that are

- least intrusive; that is, least likely to disrupt what happens with the other students.

- only as special as necessary; that is, not oversupportive of a student.
- the most natural (e.g., natural classmate support, use of already existing technology).

To provide practice using the mismatch-finding and solution-finding template, we describe student profiles for three students—Demetri, Samuel, and Shamonique—together with the content, process, and product demands of these students' classrooms (shown in Tables 6.3, 6.4, and 6.5).

As you examine each student's characteristics and the classroom demands each faces, do you see and can you identify the mismatches? What would you do to adjust the content, process, and product demands of the classroom and use students' characteristics and strengths to eliminate the mismatches you find? Brainstorm solutions to these mismatches with a colleague! What did you come up with for potential solutions? Did your brainstormed list of ideas include any of those actually generated by students in Tables 6.6, 6.7, and 6.8?

Table 6.3   Facts About Demetri and Demands of an Elementary Science Classroom

Facts About Demetri	Facts About the Elementary Science Class Demands	Mismatches	Potential Solutions
<ul><li>Recently arrived from the country of Georgia.</li><li>Is a non-English speaker who is learning English.</li><li>Interested in anything mechanical; can solve technological problems by taking things apart.</li><li>Readily approaches others in a friendly and cooperative manner.</li><li>Draws pictures to communicate.</li><li>Demonstrates understanding through photography and graphic arts.</li><li>Is passionate about environmental issues.</li></ul>	<ul><li>Students are studying food webs.</li><li>A grade-level science textbook is used, and the teacher shows a video.</li><li>Students only work together with a partner to review content prior to quizzes and tests.</li><li>Students must write a report and do a class presentation.</li></ul>		

Table 6.4 Facts About Samuel and Demands of a Middle School Language Arts Classroom

Facts About Samuel	Facts About the Middle School Language Arts Classroom Demands	Mismatches	Potential Solutions
• Is excellent at drawing. • Enjoys discussions. • Doodles in class. • Enjoys making or hearing oral presentations. • Dislikes writing in general. • Does not have a computer at home. • Significant difference exists between oral and written vocabulary. • Makes frequent spelling errors. • When writing, uses short sentences with frequent grammatical errors.	• In-class interactive journaling is required a minimum of 100 words three times per week. • Lecture and note taking occur daily. • No computer is available in class. • Monthly three-page book report is required. • Assessments include short essays, with emphasis on grammar, vocabulary, creativity, and spelling.		

Table 6.5 Facts About Shamonique and Demands of a High School Social Studies Classroom

Facts About Shamonique	Facts About the High School Social Studies Classroom Demands	Mismatches	Potential Solutions
• Has an evident sense of humor. • Is happy and enthusiastic about school and life (energetic). • Is very social. • Gains information from conversations and visual presentations. • Is very empathetic. • Is very interested in music, musicians, and movie stars. • Reads with a sight word approach.	• Grade-level text is assigned. • Teacher lectures while students take notes. • Teacher is very interested in the subject matter and has a vast amount of information to share. • Teacher occasionally gets off-topic and goes on tangents. • Teacher makes limited use of whiteboard during lecture.		

Facts About Shamonique	Facts About the High School Social Studies Classroom Demands	Mismatches	Potential Solutions
• Has a sight word vocabulary of 100 words. IEP goals include the following: ☑ Actively engaging in class activities by making relevant comments or asking questions ☑ Acquiring an additional 100 sight words ☑ Improving enunciation ☑ Transitioning between classes in a timely manner by following her schedule ☑ Learning a minimum of 10 core curriculum facts per month in each academic class ☑ Creating, dictating, and editing a school-related story each week for the school newspaper ☑ Participating in cocurricular activities of her choice ☑ Developing work skills by engaging in community job placements ☑ Traveling independently in the community by walking or riding the bus to and from destinations.	• Nightly homework is assigned, which students start in class the day before toward the end of the class period. • Students are randomly called upon at the start of each class to check whether homework has been read and understood. • Assessment includes frequent quizzes. • Assessment includes weekly tests, which can be on any of the information presented by the teacher in class or in the text.		

Tables 6.6–6.8 show the solutions suggested by 12 students, 6 of whom had IEPs, of an inclusive middle school in Albuquerque, New Mexico, for Demetri, Samuel, and Shamonique. How do their solutions compare with the possible solutions you and your colleagues generated? When we have shared these student-generated solutions with educators, they are astounded by how practical, pedagogically sound, sensitive, and creative the student-generated solutions are in comparison to the ones they generated. The proof is in the solutions!

Table 6.6 Ideas to Address Mismatches for Demetri

Potential Solutions

- Have teacher or peer draw while teacher lectures.
- Increase partner and group work. Put him with students who know how to cooperate.
- Have him draw a picture and have his partner describe what he has drawn.
- He could take pictures of tide pools and describe various environmental impacts on tide pools.
- Class could create a model of a tide pool.
- He could develop a PowerPoint presentation that includes pictures of animals in a food web.
- Demetri writes the scientific name of the animal, and his partner writes the English name of each animal in the food web.
- Get pictures of animals and color-code them (e.g., with a blue border). Write the English name on a card that is also color-coded so he can match pictures of animals with their names in English.
- Change homework to an observation and drawing of something in nature.
- Provide him with picture books.
- Have him classify pictures related to food webs that are environmentally friendly or not environmentally friendly (e.g., trash, oil spills).
- Present a slide show of his pictures.
- Assign him a cross-age peer tutor.
- Reduce his frustration; teach him to control his temper.

Table 6.7 Ideas to Address Mismatches for Samuel

Potential Solutions

- For journal activities, have pictures count for words.
- Make a Rebus—combination of words and pictures.
- For note taking, Samuel could draw a picture of what is happening and write a short sentence to describe the picture.
- Get a peer tutor to write what Samuel thinks.
- Have Samuel dictate to a friend.
- Do mini writes with spelling challenges.
- Make vocabulary/spelling flash cards for him to practice with.
- Introduce drawing letters (e.g., calligraphy) so he wants to write.
- He could use doodles as his notes.
- Have him practice writing letters (e.g., 10 a day).
- Find an activity that he likes and have him write about that.
- Start slow with the writing and then increase the amount.
- Have more group discussion and less writing.
- Have him doodle about words.
- Repeatedly teach him words.
- Let him use a computer.
- For his presentation, he can describe his drawings.
- Have him draw the word and then try to spell it.
- Test him orally.

Table 6.8 Ideas to Address Mismatches for Shamonique

Potential Solutions

- Teacher needs to stay on-topic.
- Teacher develops PowerPoint presentations to use along with lecture. (This also will help him stay on-topic.)
- Have class develop a short song about the people or event they are studying.
- Give Shamonique fill-in-the-blank or multiple-choice tests.
- Change her homework by giving her a word of the day to practice (e.g., Pilgrim).
- Ask parents to help her practice new vocabulary.
- Use lower-level vocabulary for her assignments.
- Provide books on the topics being studied with lower reading levels.
- Develop jingles to help her remember what has been studied. Shamonique or other students can develop the jingles.
- Teach her easy words and review them frequently.
- Do not count her weekly quiz scores toward her grade.
- Select words about music or movie stars for her to learn.
- Challenge her to improve her spelling—have her keep trying to find correct spelling before moving on.
- She can do homework on a computer. She can use spelling and grammar check.
- Use educational songs.
- Stop at times during the lecture and let students discuss what they have heard.
- Encourage conversation after the lecture.
- Debate frequently.
- Begin class with volunteers and then randomly select students to highlight key points after they have heard them from a classmate.
- Let Shamonique make up jokes about the people being studied.
- Use graphic organizers and lecture guides.

SUMMARY

In this chapter, we explored additional ways to engage students in educational decision making. We peeked into Mr. Bandera's class and learned how his students participate in determining the content they will learn, the way in which they will learn it, and the ways in which they will demonstrate what they have learned. We explored how to identify and generate solutions to mismatches for several learners and the demands of their classrooms. We learned about and perhaps marveled at the ideas generated by middle school students to address mismatches for three very different learners.

As you reflect about what you have learned in this chapter, to what extent do you find yourself thinking about ways in which you might gradually release responsibility to your students for their own education? To what extent do you find yourself thinking about how you might meaningfully collaborate with students to find ways to improve and adapt instruction for their classmates who might otherwise struggle? We encourage you to turn your thinking into action and enjoy the collaboration, creativity, fun, and educational success that can result!

Students as Designers of Their Own Learning 7

Person-Centered Education

Surely it is an obligation in a democracy to empower the young to become members of the public, to participate and play articulate roles in the public place.

—Maxine Greene (1988)

In this chapter, we ask the following questions:

1. What would happen in a classroom if students explained how they wanted to plan their education for their own futures?

2. How would you change the way you teach if you listened to what your students want to learn?

We focus on collaborating with students to do what Maxine Greene (1988) is chiding us to do—to empower students to become self-determined. We believe that, although some students become self-determined seemingly on their own, most students need careful guidance and coaching. We believe that some students need more explicit instruction and support than others.

We begin this chapter by defining *self-determination* in the context of the goals of education first explained in Chapter 1 (belonging, mastery, independence, and generosity). We then offer three ways to nurture self-determination: (a) using the Making Action Plans (MAPs) futures-planning process, (b) teaching students who are eligible for special education to lead their own Individual Education Program planning process, and (c) implementing personal learning plans for all students (Fox, 1995).

DEFINING AND NURTURING SELF-DETERMINATION

What is self-determination? Self-determination has been characterized as a basic human right involving respect, dignity, and choice. A powerful combination of skills, knowledge, and beliefs, self-determination allows people to engage in goal-directed independent actions (Malian & Nevin, 2002). Self-determination incorporates a basic understanding of one's strengths and limitations together with a belief in oneself as capable and effective (Field, Martin, Miller, Ward, & Wehmeyer, 1998). Self-determined individuals are more likely to experience a more satisfying quality of life. In fact, the self-determined individual is able to balance mastery, independence, generosity, and belonging—all aspects of the Circle of Courage described as part of the goals of education.

Self-determination is a valuable skill. The research suggests that students who are self-determined become adults who can enjoy an enhanced quality of life, because they have an increased likelihood of being able to manage, advocate for, and receive services as an adult (Barrie & McDonald, 2002; Hammer, 2004; Hapner & Imel, 2002; Keyes & Owens-Johnson, 2003; Konrad & Test, 2004; Martin et al., 2006; Mason, McGahee-Kovac, Johnson, & Stillerman, 2002; Trainor, 2005, 2007). What this means for teachers is that all students (even those at risk for school failure and those with disabilities) should be given the opportunity to learn and use self-determination behaviors while they are in school. Beneficial life outcomes can be anticipated for a greater number of students if they participate in managing their own school program (i.e., they are self-determined) before graduating from high school. In their lesson planning and implementation, teachers can promote self-determination of their students by including skills such as (a) choice and decision making, (b) goal setting and attainment, (c) problem solving, (d) self-evaluation and management, (e) self-advocacy, (f) planning for their futures, (g) responsible relations with others, and (h) self-awareness.

Teachers can promote student self-determination when using carefully developed curricula such as *Steps to Self-Determination: A Curriculum to Help Adolescents Learn to Achieve Their Goals* (Hoffman & Field, 2005; see Table 7.1 for a description). Programs such as these coach teachers to (a) guide students to make carefully selected choices, (b) encourage students to express interests and needs, (c) help students practice dealing with objections to a desired activity or direction in which they want to go, and (d) role-play scenarios that allow assessment of possible courses of action.

MAKING ACTION PLANS (MAPs) AS A TOOL TO ACTUALIZE SELF-DETERMINATION

Making Action Plans or MAPs (Falvey et al., 2002) is a person-centered futures-planning process for engaging a group of people who have various relationships with an individual (e.g., parents, siblings, neighbors, friends,

Table 7.1 Resources for Teaching Self-Determination Skills

Field, S., & Hoffman, A. (1996). *Steps to Self-Determination curriculum.* Austin, TX: Pro-Ed.

An 18-session curriculum with five major components: Know Yourself, Value Yourself, Plan, Act, and Experience Outcomes and Learn. In this experientially based curriculum, students establish and work toward goals as they learn self-determination knowledge and skills. Teachers and students model the steps, reflect on their progress, and gradually assume more and more responsibilities for learning outcomes. The curriculum covers the areas of discovering options, setting and reaching goals, asking for help, and negotiation and conflict resolution. These skills, very often lacking in students with and without disabilities, are needed throughout life. (Note: The Step to Self-Determination curriculum requires a fifth-grade reading level; the curriculum includes knowledge-based tests and an observation tool, which provide pretesting and posttesting opportunities.)

Wehmeyer, M., Agran, M., & Hughes, C. (1998). *Teaching self-determination to students with disabilities: Basic skills for successful transition.* Alexandria, VA: Council for Exceptional Children.

A teacher's guide to helping students achieve the goal of education—preparing youth to become self-determined adults. The authors have crafted practical, user-friendly lessons in four sections: Promoting Autonomous Behavior (teaching independence, risk taking, and safety skills; identifying preferences and making choices; social problem-solving and decision-making skills), Promoting Self-Regulated Behavior (self-monitoring, self-evaluation, self-reinforcement strategies; self-instruction skills; goal setting and task performance), Promoting Self-Advocacy and Leadership Skills (assertiveness and effective communication skills, leadership and teamwork skills, self-advocacy through student involvement), and Promoting Self-Realization and Psychological Empowerment (self-awareness and self-knowledge, positive perceptions of control in the classroom, self-efficacy and outcome expectations).

Wood, W., Karvonen, M., Test, D., Browder, D., & Algozzine, B. (2004). Promoting student self-determination skills in IEP planning. *Teaching Exceptional Children, 36*(3), 8–16. Available November 16, 2009, at http://www.transitiontocollege.net/percpubs/SelfDeterminationArticle.pdf

A helpful overview of several self-determination curricula, including examples of how specific students have benefited.

teachers, classmates, administrators) to highlight what they know about that person's strengths; interests; and other learning, social, and emotional characteristics to plan creatively for the future.

A MAPs gathering can be held anywhere—in a living room, backyard, classroom, office, restaurant—that is comfortable for the focus person and those who are invited by that person. The person on whom that meeting is focused determines the guest list for the MAPs session. A neutral facilitator welcomes attendees, explains the process, and guides the group through a series of eight questions, shown in Table 7.2. The order of questions is flexible and can be altered to accommodate the dynamics of the group and the flow of contributions.

A public record of contributions at each step of the process is displayed for all to see, using flip chart paper, a whiteboard, an overhead transparency, or a

---

Table 7.2 The Eight Key MAPs Questions

---

1. What is a MAP?

A *map* is designed to assist people to get from where they are to where they want to be (goals). At a MAPs meeting, participants are asked what a MAP means to them.

2. What is the person's history or story?

The person and the family are asked to describe their history or story.

3. What is the dream?

This is in many ways the most important step of the process because it identifies the goal(s) for which you will develop a plan of action. Again, the person and family members speak first, and then others in attendance may add to the list of goals. The facilitator must be nonjudgmental in both words and body language.

4. What is the nightmare?

This question helps those in attendance to understand the fears and concerns of the focus student and family—the things they want to avoid. At times, this step elicits emotions and reactions that are strong and/or sad. The information is critical because the entire point of the process is to achieve the dream while avoiding the nightmare.

5. Who is the person?

In this step, participants brainstorm and generate a list of words that describe the person for whom the MAP is being held. The facilitator often groups descriptors into themes. The focus person is asked to describe him- or herself and pick out three favorite words from the list.

6. What are the person's gifts, strengths, and talents?

Here particular emphasis is placed upon the learner's "giftedness." The focus is not solely academic but designed to acknowledge the learner's strengths and interests.

7. What does the person need?

Participants consider what resources and supports will be needed to assist the learner to reach the dream and avoid the nightmare. Those assembled may need to consider academic, communication, behavioral, biological, health, safety, and security needs of the person.

8. What is the plan of action?

The final step is the development of a plan that includes the who, the what, and the when of actualizing the dreams and avoiding the nightmares.

---

computer connected to an LCD projector. At each step, the focus person and those closest to that person, such as family members and friends, speak before any professionals who attend the meeting.

For school-aged students, the MAPs process is a forum for the voices of a student and those who personally know best and care most about the student to be expressly solicited and heard. For a student's teachers, the process offers valuable information about a student that could not be obtained by a standardized test or academic assessment. MAPs can be used with any student. Many teachers have developed a mini version of a MAPs for every child in their classroom as part of student-parent-teacher conferences. Some states have incorporated components of MAPs as part of the Individual Education Program (IEP) planning process for students eligible for special education.

High school educators (Villalobos, Eshilian, & Moyer, 2002) have used the MAPs process as a framework to empower secondary students to take the lead in their schools to promote advocacy, inclusion, and social justice. These students develop a school-based plan for change to increase inclusion, tolerance, respect, belonging, kindness, friendship, and so forth. The plan is developed by going through the MAPs process of examining the school's history, strengths, and other characteristics; identifying the students' dreams for and nightmares of the school; and then laying out goals and a plan of action for change. The authors of this book have also used MAPs with organizations that are seeking new direction or focus. MAPs, then, is an all-purpose self-determination vehicle for anyone, including students of all ages—kindergarten through college—for "giving direction, pointing out landmarks, showing routes and directions, and detours or things to 'get around'" (personal communication, Evan at his MAPs meeting, January 8, 2009).

Evan's MAPs Meeting

The following is a brief example of using MAPs to identify issues and steps in transitioning from high school to postschool life for Evan, a 17-year-old high school senior with autism. Evan's MAPs was facilitated by a high school educator who had known Evan since he was a freshman. Evan has strong values with regard to environmental issues and what is "right and wrong." At times, these values put him in compromising positions. For example, when he observes people who litter, smoke, or otherwise disrupt the environment, he is offended and takes a strong stand against them. Evan requested a MAPs meeting to plan his options postgraduation. Evan invited a number of people, including his mother and his behavior support person.

What was discovered and planned as a consequence of Evan's MAPs meeting? See Figure 7.1 for a photograph of the summarized notes for each step of Evan's MAPs.

• *What is the person's history or story?* In terms of his personal history, Evan had been fully included in general education classes throughout his high school years and was a very successful student. He had the credits to receive a diploma and had passed the high school exit exam. Things were good at home with his parents, brother, and two dogs.

• *What is the dream?* Dreams for Evan were to continue his education, perhaps at a multi-use campus where smoking is prohibited. Continuing to develop his drawing talent and being involved in community activities (e.g., an organization concerned with environmental issues, a recycling center, advocacy group) were priority dreams, as well as enjoying local entertainment venues (Disneyland, Knott's Berry Farm, casinos once he turned 21), working around animals, and getting a job at age 25 or older that was "busy, but not hectic" and "challenging but rewarding."

• *What is the nightmare?* Nightmares, frustrations, and concerns included time pressure and deadlines, workload in college and work, nagging, classmates who did not really work, getting along with college peers and dorm roommates, needing supported living services to live away from home, and relaxing with others (especially girls).

Figure 7.1 Visual Summary of Evan's MAPs Meeting

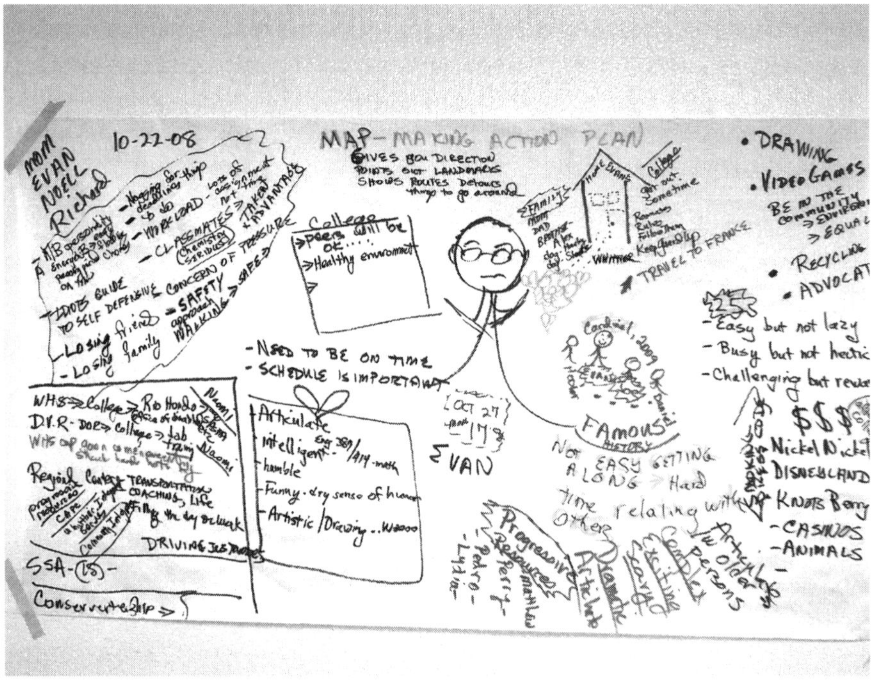

SOURCE: Photographer: Richard Rosenberg

- *Who is the person? What are the person's gifts, strengths, and talents?* All those at the meeting provided their responses to the questions *Who is Evan?* and *What are Evan's gifts?* They agreed that Evan has a dry sense of humor, enjoys video games, and likes to draw and be around animals. He is articulate, intelligent, interested in going to community college, humble, funny, and an environmental advocate intolerant of smoking and littering.

- *What does the person need? What is the plan of action?* With the history, dreams, nightmares, and Evan's "Who is?" and gifts sections of the MAPs in mind, needs and a plan of action steps were identified. A long list of needs and actions were generated and prioritized. The list included a range of items:

  - Agreeing to engage in senior activities and attend commencement in order to shake the principal's hand
  - Connecting with the Department of Vocational Rehabilitation for employment preparation and to take steps to reach employment goals
  - Visiting local community college campuses to explore enrollment, as well as supports available from the Office of Disabled Students
  - Considering the pros and cons of conservatorship
  - Revisiting progress on the plan of action developed at this MAPs meeting on a regular basis with Evan, his mother, and Dr. Rosenberg (see Figure 7.2 showing Evan and Dr. Rosenberg).

Figure 7.2   Evan and Mr. Rosenberg, His MAPs Facilitator

SOURCE: Photographer: Jacqueline Thousand.

For Evan, the MAPs meeting was an important step in the development of his self-awareness about his strengths and post–high school dreams, as well as his understanding of the complex maze of supports and services he might want or need to access to realize those dreams. The MAPs set the stage for identifying a network of people and community services to help Evan execute a plan to address expected challenges and concerns (nightmares). It is critical to emphasize here that MAPs provides a starting rather than an ending point. The reality of the process is in the implementation and follow-up; thus, success requires time and the commitment of a team working together for the common goals and dreams of an individual.

STUDENT-LED INDIVIDUAL EDUCATION PROGRAMS: A TOOL FOR STUDENTS WITH DISABILITIES TO PRACTICE SELF-DETERMINATION

When teachers think about self-determination as part of the curriculum for all students, it is a natural next step to include self-determination goals as part of the process of teaching students with disabilities. From 10 to 15 percent of students in any classroom have an IEP to help them achieve their educational goals. In fact, advocacy efforts spearheaded by individuals with disabilities led to the incorporation of self-determination as part of federal special education legislation. Namely, the Individuals with Disabilities Education Improvement Act of 2004 (IDEIA) increases the likelihood that students will be more self-determined: at the age of 18, students sign their own IEPs, and at age 16, students participate in developing an Individualized Transition Plan, which charts the course of activities during their school years to help them to achieve their goals and plans for post-school life.

Student-led IEPs provide a powerful tool for students who have an IEP as part of their educational experience not only to actively and meaningfully engage in the development of their IEP goals but also to develop self-determination skills (e.g., Hammer, 2004; Mason et al., 2002; Mason, McGahee-Kovac, & Johnson, 2004). Outcomes reveal that students who learn to lead their own IEPs become more confident in exercising self-determination across settings by advocating for themselves as they negotiate their life paths. Mason et al. (2004) also found that students who were involved in their own IEPs were more inclined to meet their goals. Further, rather than being a static document, the IEP becomes a dynamic process and vehicle for students to secure a future that realizes their full potential. In fact, students who have graduated report that because they have practiced asking for accommodations and talking to others about their disability, they find it easier to apply self-advocacy skills in college or on the job (Mason et al., 2004, p. 22).

Who can lead his or her own IEP meeting? Students of elementary, middle, and high school age have successfully learned to direct their own IEP meetings (e.g., Barrie & McDonald, 2002; Hapner & Imel, 2002, Konrad & Test, 2004; Schumaker, 2006; Test, Browder, Karvonen, Wood, & Algozzine, 2002), as have students with all types and degrees of learning and behavioral challenges. Students with moderate and severe disabilities can and have taken leading roles in directing their own IEPs, with the support of their classmates' voices and ideas, teacher coaching, and alternatives to verbal direction of a meeting (i.e., PowerPoint presentation of photos, icons, or descriptive words about a student) (e.g., Barton, 2003; Brown & Dean, 2009).

Table 7.3 identifies easily accessible resources teachers can use to learn how to teach and support students to lead their own IEP meetings. Instructing and coaching students to develop their own educational programs can be very comprehensive, or it can be simplified and focus on key points a student wants to communicate to his or her IEP planning team. In a comprehensive approach (e.g., McGahee-Kovac, 2002), students learn about (a) their strengths and own disability and its impact on their learning, (b) the regulations and safeguards that regulate their IEP under IDEIA, (c) the components of an IEP, and (d) the steps of an IEP meeting. Students also learn valuable skills, such as determining their present levels of performance in academic and social domains, identifying their needs, setting goals, monitoring their own progress, practicing skills to communicate effectively (e.g., active listening; volume, clarity, and pacing of speech; giving and receiving positive and constructive negative feedback), and running an effective meeting.

Table 7.4 shows an abbreviated version of a "Checklist for Individual Educational Plan (IEP) Presentation" developed by Erica Dean to assist high school students in leading their own IEP meetings (Brown & Dean, 2009). The student agenda is identical to any IEP agenda, except there are prompt statements

Table 7.3 Resources for Student-Led Individual Education Plans

Küpper, L. (2002). Helping students develop their IEPs (2nd ed.). *Technical Assistance Guide.* Washington, DC: National Information Center for Children and Youth with Disabilities. Retrieved November 16, 2009, from http://www.nichcy.org/InformationResources/ Documents/NICHCY%20PUBS/ta2.pdf

This technical assistance guide describes how parents, teachers, and school administrators can help students with disabilities become active participants in their own IEP meetings. The guide is designed to be used in combination with *A Student's Guide to the IEP* (see below) and comes with an accompanying audiotape featuring students with disabilities, parents, and school staff discussing their experiences with student participation in the IEP process. Detailed suggestions are given for teaching students about the purpose and contents of IEPs and how to discuss their disabilities, learning styles, and accommodation needs.

McGahee-Kovac, M. (2002). *A student's guide to the IEP* (2nd ed.). Washington, DC: National Information Center for Children and Youth with Disabilities. Retrieved November 16, 2009, from http://www.nichcy.org/InformationResources/Documents/NICHCY%20PUBS/st1.pdf

This student's guide set will help students develop their own IEPs. The audio portion for students features several students talking about their experiences as active participants on their IEP teams. Supporting materials include a student booklet to guide students through the IEP process (12 pages); a Technical Assistance Guide (20 pages) to assist individuals who would like to help students be involved in their IEP meetings; and another audio program for parents, transition specialists, and teachers. The audio portion is available on CD or audiotape.

Ripley, S. (Project Director), Küpper, L. (Editor), Ellis, A. (Writer/Producer), & Edwards, M. (Narrator). (1995). *Audio script for* A Student's Guide to the IEP. Retrieved November 16, 2009, from http://www.nichcy.org/InformationResources/Documents/NICHCY%20PUBS/ st1scrpt.htm

This document is the script of the audiocassette program that accompanies NICHCY's publication *A Student's Guide to the IEP* (see above). The audio program is designed especially for students with disabilities who are becoming involved in the IEP process. The program features the experiences, suggestions, and observations of students with disabilities who have written their own IEPs and, in many cases, led the IEP meeting, as well as the observations of administrators, teachers, and parents who have worked with these students. While listening to the audio program is not essential to students becoming a part of their IEP team, it's a fun program and both informational and motivational.

(e.g., "Thank team members for coming.") or prompt questions (e.g., "What transition activities do I need to reach my life goals?") for the student at each step. Patricia Brown (Brown & Dean) developed a simplified agenda for her middle-level students with more intensive educational challenges who are planning for transition to high school. After introductions, students present (or display via PowerPoint slides) information they have written to explain topics such as "A Little About Me," "Successes this Year," "What I Liked About School This Year," "What I've Learned," "Things I Do Well," "Things I Need Help With," "What I Need to Be Successful at High School," "My Current Goals and Progress on Goals," and "My Future When I Finish School." Rehearsal for the actual IEP meeting is a key pre-IEP meeting activity.

Marcy McGahee-Kovac (2002), a pioneer in the student-led IEP movement, offered the following start-up tips to teachers. Realize that supporting students to be self-determined by leading their own IEPs takes time. So start early in the year, devote time each week to some aspect of the process, and never underestimate students' capabilities. Mason et al. (2004) encouraged teachers and students to be flexible by adopting different levels of student participation. At Level 1, the student presents information about or reads from a transition plan for the future. At Level 2, the student explains his or her disability, shares information on individual strengths and weaknesses (present levels of performance), and explains the accommodations needed. The student also presents Level 1 information and may suggest new IEP goals. At Level 3, the student leads the IEP conference, including Level 1 and Level 2 responsibilities, introductions, and closing.

Table 7.4   Checklist for Student-Led Individual Education Plan Meeting

_____ Introductions of People Present

_____ Meeting Agenda

- Review **IEP Front Page**
  Is the information about me correct?
  What is my identified "disability"?
  Why do I qualify for special education services?

- Review Present Levels of Performance
  How am I doing? What do my teachers say about my achievement?

- Review **Assessment Data/Special Factors**
  What are my test scores? Do I need any special supports?

- Review **Goals**
  What do I need to do to be successful in classes and move toward my future goals? What do I need to graduate?

- Review **Accommodations/Modifications**
  What helps me in classes? How and where will I take my state standardized tests? Will tests have accommodations or modifications?

- Review **Services** and **Educational Setting**
  What special education services do I receive?
  Where and how often do I get these services?
  What does my entire educational program look like?

- Review (if 16 or older) **Transition Services and Individualized Transition Plan**
  What am I doing inside and outside of school to prepare for adulthood? What transition activities do I need to reach my life goals?
  What am I doing to work toward passing the high school exit exam?
  What classes do I need to receive a diploma?

_____ Take questions and feedback from team members.

_____ Note parent concerns.

   Now that my parents have heard all about my plans and achievement, is there anything else they want addressed?

_____ Propose class schedule for next semester or next year.

_____ Read meeting notes and have teachers and parents review the notes.

   Make any needed additions or modifications.

_____ Get signatures and approval from IEP team members.

_____ Thank team members for coming.

_____ Pat myself on the back! I did a great job!

SOURCE: From Brown, P., & Dean, E. (2009), July. _Listen to the voice of students: Student-led IEPs and slef-advocacy._ Paper presented at the 11th Annual San Diego Summer Leadership Institute, San Diego, CA.

PERSONAL LEARNING PLANS AS A TOOL TO TEACH SELF-DETERMINATION

Personal Learning Plans expand the practice of having an Individualized Education Program for students eligible for special education to having an individualized plan for learning for all students. They were originated in Vermont (Fox, 1995) in the late 1990s, when that state lead the nation in inclusive education—the practice of welcoming, valuing, and educating all students, including students with significant learning challenges, in general education. Personal Learning Plans are intended to build upon already excellent classroom strategies that support diverse learners (e.g., cooperative learning, integrated curriculum projects, authentic assessment, class meetings that emphasize collaboration, discipline models that emphasize personal responsibility and social skills instruction). Personal Learning Plans also are intended to bring the school, community, and home together to ignite a student's interests in a coordinated fashion.

What Is a Personal Learning Plan, and How Is It Developed?

A Personal Learning Plan, when developed by a student, gives the student a stake in his or her education, gives the student's family increased opportunities to be involved in their child's education, and creates a "contract" by which a student takes responsibility for engaging in and documenting his or her own learning. As Figure 7.3 illustrates, a Personal Learning Plan channels a student's strengths and personal learning priorities into a directed project or set of activities; this leads to personal development in areas selected by a student, which is supported by the student's teacher and family and connects to the core curriculum.

The process of developing a Personal Learning Plan involves collaborating with a student to identify

1. strengths and interests (e.g., using the MAPs process, described in the previous section of this chapter, as a vehicle for identifying strengths);

2. high-priority skills or knowledge to be addressed during the school year;

3. projects and learning activities through which the student can address his or her priorities that build on strengths and capitalize upon interests;

4. supports (e.g., teacher, peer, parent, community connections) the student needs to benefit from the plan and opportunities for family involvement; and

5. methods to assess progress in completing the activities set forth in the plan.

Figure 7.3   Personal Learning Plan Project Development Cycle

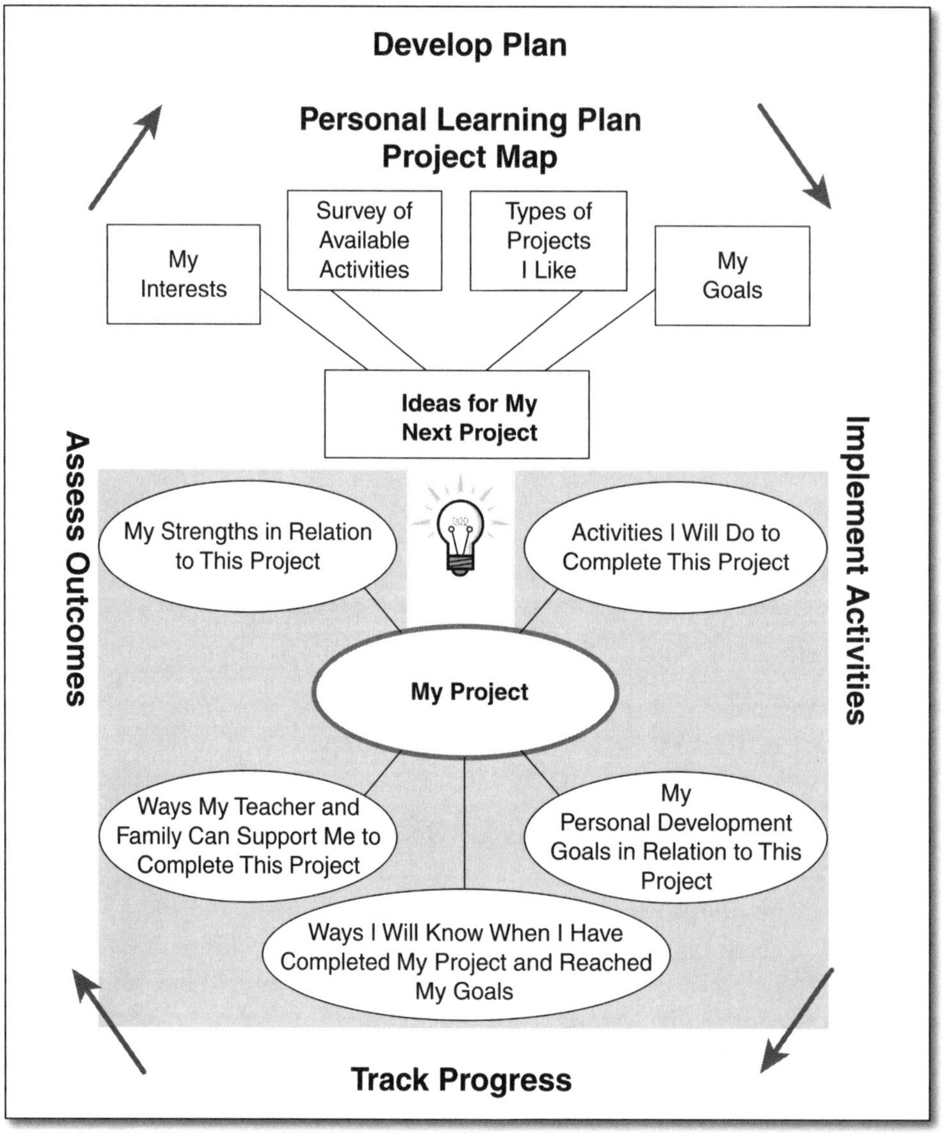

SOURCE: From Fox, T. (1995). Student-centered education: Creating a collaborative school climate through Personal Learning Plans. Progress report prepared for the Vermont Statewide Systems Change Project. Burlington, VT: University of Vermont; reprinted with permission.

After a Personal Learning Plan has been developed (usually in the first few weeks of each school year), the student meets periodically with a classroom teacher (and, if possible, parents) to monitor, adjust, and assess the outcomes of the projects and activities included in the plan.

Advantages of Personal Learning Plans

An essential element of self-determination is the development of personal responsibility. Personal Learning Plans provide opportunities for students to have personal responsibility for and investment in targeted areas of their own education. Because the plan lays out experiences tailored to students' skills and interests, students know that some aspect of each school day is intended to be meaningful and exciting. The process of developing, implementing, and assessing progress in a Personal Learning Plan provides a vehicle for students (with teachers' and parents' guidance) to learn and practice numerous communication, collaboration, and problem-solving skills, as well as the skill of setting and evaluating goals—core curriculum standards in most states.

Personal Learning Plans also represent a vehicle for readily adding supports for a student, if that support is needed. If the student's individual needs become more complicated or intensive, a student's support team can be expanded from the student's teacher(s) and family to include additional school and community support persons (e.g., paraprofessional, special educator, counselor, physical therapist, psychologist, community service provider).

WHAT DO STUDENTS SAY ABOUT SELF-DETERMINATION?

In Tolleson, Arizona, where Hapner and Imel (2002) spearheaded student-led IEPs, junior high and high school students were quite vocal about their taking charge of their educational programs. Jason, an 18-year-old with learning disabilities, noted,

> *I used to think IEP meetings weren't needed. . . . Now I just can't wait to have them. I'm telling what I need, not my teachers.*

Raul, a student with language challenges, stated, with a smile,

> *Teachers started to listen and show respect.*

Juan added,

> *I graduated eighth grade feeling proud of myself for working hard on how I can improve [even with] my disability. (Hapner & Imel, p. 126)*

Stephen Hinkle, a college graduate with autism who has become an accomplished self-advocate and keynote speaker due to his consistent participation in his own educational program planning, emphasizes the power of person-centered processes in a person's life. He is very clear about self-determination in his following advice to teachers:

> *After all, it is my life. . . . Let me choose the path. . . . [Then] respect and guide and assist me on taking it. (Nevin, 2004, p. 102)*

What else is there to say?

SUMMARY

Take a moment to reflect on the options for collaborating with students discussed in this chapter. What option is most appealing to you? Which options might you already have incorporated into your classroom teaching? Which are you willing to practice now? Now, please return to the questions posed at the beginning of the chapter. How would you change the way you teach if you used the options to help you hear what your students want to learn? Finally, consider how your classroom climate might change if all your students gained the self-determination skills described in this chapter. Are you feeling more empowered to help students become more self-determined or, as Maxine Greene suggested, *to become members of the public, to participate and play articulate roles in the public place?*

Students as Mediators of Conflict and Controversy

8

What we learn in the daily reciprocity of caring goes far deeper than test results.

—Nel Noddings (2005, "In Conclusion")

In this chapter, you will develop your own answers to these questions:

1. Do you see examples of caring exchanges among the students in your classrooms, or do you lament the many conflicts, fights, and arguments that abound in your classrooms every day?

2. Do you wonder how to teach your students to manage intellectual controversies and classroom or playground conflicts?

3. Do you know that young children, elementary students, and middle and senior high school students can effectively and successfully mediate conflicts among their peers?

In this chapter, we explain various ways to understand origins and responses to conflicts in classrooms and schools. We briefly outline the scientific evidence for peer mediation and conflict resolution programs. In the midst of the conflicts that teachers and students face in 21st-century classrooms, Nel Noddings's (2005) encouraging statement sometimes seems to be a lofty and unattainable, yet highly valued, ideal. The purpose of this chapter is to showcase how teachers and students can work together to learn and practice conflict resolution skills so that the reciprocity of caring can be demonstrated in your classrooms every day. By learning how to resolve both interpersonal conflicts and cognitive controversies, students can attain the Circle of Courage goals of education. They increase mastery of the content they are learning, become more independent learners, become aware of belonging within a classroom or school community, and practice their skills in giving back to their communities.

We begin with descriptions of the everyday conflicts students face; then we describe a way of understanding conflict, and we provide an example of a class-wide or schoolwide peer mediation program (especially helpful when implementing bullying prevention programs). We then describe a lesson plan in which students learn a specific social skill (how to disagree without being disagreeable). We end the chapter with a brief summary and a reflection of what was learned.

EXAMPLES OF EVERYDAY SCHOOL CONFLICTS

Students, no matter how young or how old, are involved in conflicts every day. The question is not "Will I have a conflict today?" but "How can I avoid or handle it?" Students can be bullied, "dissed," harassed, or treated as outcasts. Boys and girls alike are exposed to name-calling (e.g., "Re-tard." "D-uh!" "You slut!" "Fag!") or threats (e.g., "I'll get you after school, just wait.") When students bring these conflicts to their teachers or parents, they are often told, "Just ignore it," or "Walk away." When students ask their friends, they are often told, "Get 'em back!" And when the students' conflicts reach the principal's desk, the consequences often are detention or suspension for all involved. None of these responses help students get the conflicts resolved, nor do these responses help students develop conflict resolution skills. Thus, conflicts continue and often escalate.[1]

UNDERSTANDING CONFLICT

What do we mean by conflict, controversy, and peer mediation? A *conflict* is a disagreement between people. A *controversy* is a disagreement of opinion or ideas. *Peer mediation programs* rely on peers, not just teachers or administrators, to resolve conflicts that occur in classrooms, on playgrounds or school buses, and in the community.

---

[1] A general search on any search engine can reveal decreases in school violence but also a concern that it is not accurately reported (see McGreevy, 2005). Also, not many current reports exist. However, in a recent research report issued by CASEL (Collaborative for Academic, Social, and Emotional Learning), a meta-analysis of 207 research studies found that social and emotional learning programs have a positive impact on a wide range of student measures including achievement tests and grades (Durlak, Weissberg, Taylor, Dymnicki, & Schellinger, 2008). The analysis found that a wide array of social and learning programs produced gains in achievement test scores (11 percent); improvement in social and emotional skills (23 percent); improvement in attitudes about self, others, and school (9 percent); improved school and classroom behavior (9 percent); decreases in conduct problems (9 percent); and decreases in emotional distress, such as anxiety and depression (10 percent).

Everyone can name examples of conflicts in school: teasing, put-downs, bullying, being excluded, rumormongering, lost or damaged property, threats, and aggression. Some schools have more conflicts than others, often due to how the faculty and administration handle conflicts in and out of the classroom or how the families in the neighborhood handle conflicts at home.

Students often must handle (a) conflicts of interest over limited resources, (b) controversies over ideas and opinions as they learn new material, and (c) interpersonal clashes as they learn to form and maintain friendships. For example, Glasser (1986, 1990) suggested that conflicts arise when students cannot satisfy their four basic needs: (a) the need to belong (loving, sharing, and cooperating), (b) the need for power (being recognized and respected, achieving), (c) the need for freedom (making choices in their school activities), and (d) the need for fun (laughing and playing). When students feel excluded or discriminated against, are unrecognized, have no freedom to make classroom decisions, or stop having fun, there will be more conflicts in the classroom. Limited resources, such as sharing scarce materials or equipment or getting the teacher's attention for assistance, can be a source of school conflict.

Conflicts can arise because of different values, beliefs, priorities, and principles. Concepts of honesty, equality, and fairness vary widely across different cultures. Prejudices and cross-cultural stereotypes often contribute to such conflicts. Thus, an important first step in conflict resolution is to become aware of the sources of conflict and the different responses to conflict.

Schrumpf and Janson (2002) distinguished between hard and soft responses to conflict. Hard responses include confrontation, threats, aggression, and anger. Avoidance, on the other hand, is a soft response and can include withdrawal, ignoring, or denying a conflict. However, neither the hard nor the soft response to conflict is likely to result in resolution but in fact can escalate to vengeance or smoldering resentment. As shown in Table 8.1, Schrumpf and colleagues summarized the origins of conflict, the responses to conflict, and the outcomes of conflict in a way that helps everyone remember the options. An alternative to hard or soft responses to conflict is the *principled response* to conflict resolution, which includes understanding, respect, and resolution, principles explicated by Fisher, Ury, and Patton (1991).

These responses to conflict are echoed by the research of David and Roger Johnson, University of Minnesota gurus for cooperative group learning techniques, who conducted a comprehensive review of the literature on conflict resolution and peer mediation training programs developed by researchers in the field of conflict resolution, advocates of nonviolence, anti–nuclear war activists, and members of the legal professions. Five important findings emerged from their review (Johnson & Johnson, 1996a, p. 506):

1. conflicts among students occur frequently but rarely result in injury;

2. untrained students use strategies that create destructive outcomes that ignore ongoing relationships;

3. conflict resolution and peer mediation programs can be effective ways to teach students to negotiate and mediate conflicts;

4. after training, students tend to use these conflict strategies, which generally lead to constructive outcomes; and

5. students' success in resolving their conflicts constructively tends to result in reducing the numbers of student-student conflicts referred to teachers and administrators, which, in turn, tends to reduce suspensions.

Table 8.1 Understanding Conflict

Origins of Conflict	Responses to Conflict	Outcomes of Conflict
Limited Resources (time, money, property)	Soft (withdrawing, ignoring, denying, giving in)	Both parties lose. OR One party loses, other wins.
Unmet Basic Needs (belonging, power, freedom, fun)	Hard (threatening, pushing, hitting, yelling)	Both parties lose. OR One party wins, other loses.
Different Values (beliefs, priorities, principles)	Principled (listening, understanding, respecting, resolving)	Both parties win.

SOURCE: From *Creating the peaceable school: A comprehensive program for teaching conflict resolution* (p. 92) by Richard Bodine, Donna Crawford, and Fred Schrumpf, 1994, Champaign, IL: Research Press. Copyright 1994 by Bodine, R., Crawford, D., and Schrumpf, F. Adapted by permission.

In the 21st century, there is an even more urgent need for peer mediation and conflict resolution programs. Johnson and Johnson (1995a) followed up their literature review by developing and field-testing their curriculum to teach K–12 children how to be peacemakers. A schoolwide program on constructive conflict resolution, the peacemaker curriculum integrates negotiation and mediation procedures with academic learning in a way that enhances subject matter understanding. Summarizing more than 16 studies conducted in two countries, Johnson and Johnson (2004) reported, "The evidence indicates that without training, children and adolescents tend to manage their conflicts in destructive ways. When given training, however, they learn how to engage in integrative negotiations and how to mediate their schoolmates' conflicts" (p. 68). In fact, the participating students maintained their skills months after the training had ended. The researchers also found evidence that students applied the learned procedures to actual conflicts in the classroom, school, and family settings.

In addition, other researchers have confirmed that conflict and negotiation skills can be integrated into academic curriculum. Stevahn (2004) described a practical and effective approach to curriculum-integrated conflict resolution training to resolve diverse conflicts found in subject matter. According to Stevahn, "Research results indicate that this approach to conflict training not only enables students to learn, use, and develop more positive attitudes toward conflict resolution, it also enhances academic achievement" (p. 58).

However, there are cautions. Casella (2000) reported the benefits of peer mediation in the context of urban schools while discovering who benefits the most and what types of conflict are not easily addressed by peer mediators. In a study of a high school peer mediation program, Casella examined the training of student mediators, the curriculum, the dynamics of actual mediation sessions, and the comments of the mediators and trainers. However, Casella noted that peer mediation defines conflict in a way that prevents examination of certain conflict issues, such as those related to inequity and prejudice. The mediators themselves benefited most, rather than the disputants. On the other hand, Cremin (2002) showed that when young people themselves became active participants in a peer mediation program in Birmingham, England, primary schools, their active participation led to improvements in discipline and school climate.

Bullying in schools has long been recognized as a problem and a challenge for educators to address. Olweus (1993) found that approximately 15 percent of students reported that they had been bullied regularly. And two-thirds of the students in a recent poll reported that fights at their schools are a "very big" or "fairly big" problem (Gallup Organization, 2000). Noting the occurrences of girl-on-girl bullying in schools, Garii and SooHoo (2008) described the invisibility of bullying among females; unlike boy bullying, it is typically not physical and therefore more difficult to see. They referred to a study by the American Association of University Women, which revealed a strong relationship between hostile school environments and (a) lack of self-confidence, (b) absence of attachment to school, and (c) diminished academic outcomes for girls. In other words, bullying, whether among boys or girls, requires systematic attention from school personnel. The bottom line is that when teachers collaborate with their students to learn peer mediation skills, bullying prevention programs can become more effective.

Bullying prevention programs have been studied worldwide in the last two decades. Many such programs have been implemented in U.S. schools. According to *School-wide Prevention of Bullying*, a pamphlet published in 2001 by Education Northwest, when deciding which program to adopt, educators should gain agreement on key questions, such as whether or not the program has research-based evidence of effectiveness, includes specific lesson plans, is cost-efficient, is teacher-friendly, and includes community members and parents. Perhaps the most important question is whether or not the program is enjoyed by and useful to students themselves. The bottom line for successful bullying prevention programs is consistent implementation of the policies, direct teaching of social skills to confront and stop bullying, and frequent evaluation and redesign of the program (Educational Northwest, 2001). Table 8.2 lists some examples of curricula that have yielded evidenced-based research showing decreased bullying and increased school safety.

Cowie and Hutson (2005) critiqued the research on peer support strategies that help bystanders challenge school bullying. Peer support included such activities as (a) befriending, (b) peer counseling, (c) conflict resolution or mediation, and (d) intervening in bullying situations. They analyzed studies with

Table 8.2 A Sampler of Effective Bullying Prevention Programs

Teaching Students to Be Peacemakers by D. W. Johnson & R. T. Johnson at the University of Minnesota—Minneapolis/St. Paul (2004; www.acrnet.org/about/crejohnson.htm) is a 12-year spiral program in which each year, students acquire and practice more and more sophisticated negotiation and mediation procedures. Evidence of effectiveness is based on 12 years of research with diverse participants in elementary, middle, and high schools in two countries and under a variety of controlled conditions. The curriculum is versatile and robust, as evidenced by its adoption in North America and in schools in Central and South America, Europe, the Middle East, Asia, and the Pacific Rim. The curriculum is available in five languages.

The Bullying Prevention Handbook: A Guide for Principals, Teachers, and Counselors by John Hoover and Ronald Oliver (2008) provides a comprehensive, step-by-step bullying-intervention model for understanding, preventing, and reducing the day-to-day teasing and harassment attributed to bullying. Chapters focus on cyberbullying; bullying of gay, lesbian, bisexual, and transgender students; and the importance of bringing a multicultural perspective to antibullying interventions. Includes a CD with reproducible survey instruments, screening checklists, and handouts.

The *Olweus* [pronounced Ol-VEY-us] *Bullying Prevention Program* (www.olweus.org) is a comprehensive, schoolwide program designed for use in elementary, middle, and junior high schools to reduce and prevent bullying problems among schoolchildren and to improve peer relations at school. The program has been found to reduce bullying among children; improve the social climate of classrooms; and reduce related antisocial behaviors, such as vandalism and truancy. The Olweus Program has been implemented in more than a dozen countries around the world.

respect to their relevance to bystander behavior. Effectiveness was related to the wider context of the developing role of peer support available to students while they are in school. This means that administrators and teachers must (a) emphasize the benefits to peer supporters, (b) be flexible in monitoring peer support, and (c) be aware of the needs of the students who need peer support. Karan (2004) cited six factors inhibiting the use of peer mediation in a junior high school: (a) students' attitudes, feelings, and behaviors regarding mediation; (b) students' methods of dealing with conflict; (c) students' attitudes, feelings, and behavior in school; (d) school climate; (e) structure of the mediation program (such as whether the program is located in the guidance office or the principal's disciplinary office); and (f) societal issues. In summary, we can agree that there is a need for conflict resolution and controversy management and for creative methods to deal with the limitations of peer mediation programs that have been identified by researchers and practitioners.

AN EXAMPLE OF A CLASSWIDE OR SCHOOLWIDE PEER MEDIATION PROGRAM

In this section, we describe two types of programs that (a) empower students to confront and manage conflict and controversy and (b) address important societal needs. One involves a classwide or schoolwide peer mediation program to resolve conflicts, and the other showcases a classroom student-specific program to resolve disagreements without being disagreeable. First, we describe how to get started, how a peer mediation process works, how to avoid pitfalls, and how to implement guidelines for a successful peer mediation program. You can apply this information to your classroom, work with a cadre of teachers at your grade level to implement it at your school, or encourage your school district guidance and administrative personnel to implement programs in all schools in your district.

Getting Started

When a peer mediation program is implemented, students are selected and trained in the process. They then are available during the school day to conduct mediations, which can be requested by teachers, principals, or students themselves. Sometimes mediators are assigned to be available in specific areas of the school site, such as the playground or the cafeteria, so as to settle disputes on the spot. Teaching the mediation skills that are necessary to a good peer mediation program can be incorporated as part of the curriculum, integrated into various classroom content areas (e.g., science, social studies, language arts, or health). Mediators learn the nature of conflict, communication skills to express their points of view and their understanding of others' points of view, problem solving, and the negotiation and mediation steps.

As an example of program effectiveness, Johnson, Johnson, Dudley, and Burnett (1992) found an 80 percent reduction of conflicts that teachers had to manage. In addition, the number of referrals to the principal was reduced to zero. Jones (1998) reported the effectiveness of peer mediation in 27 elementary, middle, and high schools in three sites across the nation involving a total of 430 peer mediators. The data showed that peer mediation resulted in "significant benefits in developing constructive social and conflict resolution behavior" and decreases in "aggressiveness" and increases in "perspective taking and conflict competence" (Jones, p 18).

Successes like these influenced Schrumpf and colleagues (Schrumpf, Crawford, & Bodine, 1997; Schrumpf, Crawford, & Usadel, 1991) to develop and implement a peer mediation program, which resulted in high success rates. For example, 26 percent of requests for peer mediation involved name-calling, which were resolved at a 98 percent success rate; 23 percent of requests involved rumors, which were resolved at a 100 percent success rate; 16 percent involved hitting or fighting, which were resolved at a 100 percent success rate; and 35 percent involved lost or damaged property, relationship problems, and other issues, which were resolved at a 93 percent success rate. During the subsequent years of the program, the number of requests for peer mediation increased approximately 25 percent over previous years, suggesting increased support for the program.

To initiate the program, Schrumpf and colleagues (1997) disseminated to all teachers and students in the school district a brochure describing the program. The information in the brochure briefly defined typical conflicts, mediation, student mediators, the rules for mediation, the procedures to access mediation, and reasons why students should try mediation. The brochure, shown in Table 8.3, served as an important tool to gain support for the use of the program and had an unintentional side effect of gaining volunteers.

Table 8.3 Sample Brochure for a Peer Mediation Program

Are you having a conflict?

- Has someone made fun of you or teased you?
- Did someone say, "I'll get you after school . . ." in a threatening tone?
- Is there a rumor about you going around the school?

What is mediation?

Mediation gives you a chance to sit face-to-face and talk, uninterrupted, so each side of the conflict is heard. After the problem is defined, solutions are created and evaluated. When an agreement is reached by all involved, it is written and signed.

Who is a student mediator?

A student mediator is one of your peers who has been trained to conduct the mediation meeting. The mediator makes sure the meeting is helpful and fair. Your mediator was selected to help you resolve your differences because he or she might better understand your point of view.

Are there rules to peer mediation? Yes.

- Mediation is a process that both students involved in the conflict choose.
- Everything said during the meeting stays in the room; it is kept confidential.
- Students take turns talking, and no one can interrupt.
- The peer mediator does not take sides.

If you have a conflict, how do you get it mediated?

- It is easy!
- Pick up a mediation request form from a counselor or the principal's office.
- Take 2 minutes to fill it out and return it.
- Within a day, you will be told the time and place for the mediation meeting.
- Mediations are scheduled so the least amount of class time is missed.

Why should I use peer mediation?

- It's fun, and it's effective.
- Conflicts that don't get resolved often end in fights, and then suspension.
- Conflicts that do not get resolved often hurt feelings, causing you to lose friends.
- You will learn a peaceful, responsible way to solve your own problems without adults doing it for you!
- Mediation helps develop mutual respect and clear communication.
- Mediation makes the school a more positive place to be!

SOURCE: From *Peer mediation: Conflict resolution in schools* (p. 277) by Fred Schrumpf, Donna Crawford, and Richard Bodine, 1997, Champaign, IL: Research Press. Copyright 1997 by Schrumpf, F., Crawford, D., and Bodine, R. Adapted by permission.

The Peer Mediation Process

What happens during a peer mediation session? Peer mediators are taught how to implement a simple problem-solving strategy that involves setting the ground rules, fact finding, interest finding, idea or option finding, and solution finding. You may recognize these steps as a variation of the Osborn-Parnes Creative Problem Solving process described in Chapter 5 of this book. Table 8.4 shows an agenda for a peer mediation session that students have found to be useful and easy to implement.

Table 8.4 Sample Peer Mediation Session Agenda

Step 1. Opening and Setting Critical Rules

- Make introductions.
- State the ground rules:
    1. Mediators are neutral (they do not take sides).
    2. Everything said is confidential (stays in this room).
    3. No interruptions.
    4. Agree to solve the conflict.
- Get commitment to the ground rules.

Step 2. Fact Finding

- Ask each person, "Please tell me what happened."
  (Listen and then summarize.)
- Ask each person, "Do you want to add anything?"
  (Listen, summarize, and clarify with questions.)
- Repeat until the problem is understood.
  (Summarize the problem.)

Step 3. Interest Finding

- Determine interests. Ask each person,
  "What do you really want? Why?"
  "What might happen if you do not reach an agreement?"
  "What do each of you have in common?"
  (Listen, summarize, and question.)
- Summarize shared interests.
- State what disputants have in common.

Step 4. Idea/Option Finding

- Brainstorm solutions. Ask disputants,
  "What could be done to resolve the problem?"

Step 5. Solution Finding

- Evaluate options and decide on a solution.
- Ask each person,
  "Which of these options are you willing to do?"
- Restate: "You both agree to . . . [list all they agree to do]."

Step 6. Write an Agreement and Close the Session

- Write an agreement and sign it.
- Shake hands.

SOURCE: From *Creativity and collaborative learning: A practical guide to empowering students, teachers, and families* (2nd ed., p. 293) by J.S. Thousand, R.A. Villa, & A.I. Nevin, 2002, Baltimore, MD: Paul H. Brookes Publishing. Copyright 2002 by Thousand, J.S., Villa, R.A. and Nevin, A.I. Adapted by permission.

Step 1: Opening and Setting Critical Rules (Ground Rules). The peer mediator demonstrates three steps in active listening. The mediator makes eye contact with the speaker, sits slightly forward to show interest, keeps a friendly yet neutral facial expression, and keeps gestures at a minimum. He or she summarizes by restating the facts and reflecting the feelings expressed by the speaker. The mediator clarifies by using open-ended questions or statements. Each disputant is asked to take a turn in expressing his or her responses to the questions posed by the peer mediator. Each disputant talks to the peer mediator, not to the other disputant. Once the disputants agree to the ground rules, the session continues. If the disputants do not agree to the ground rules, the peer mediator closes the session respectfully and the dispute is referred to an adult.

Step 2: Fact Finding. The peer mediator uses active listening while posing questions to discover the "story" from each disputant's point of view. Sometimes the peer mediator may pose other questions for clarification, such as "Is this a recent problem?" "Were you friends before?" "Is there a difference in your beliefs?" The mediator finishes this step by restating the problem.

Step 3: Interest Finding. The peer mediator asks what each disputant wants to happen so that the conflict will be resolved. The peer mediator is trying to find common ground with respect to the disputants? shared interests, showing them that they may have a lot in common. If students are having difficulty identifying shared interest in resolving the conflict, the peer mediator may motivate them to resolve the conflict by asking them each to identify what they lose by continuing the conflict (e.g., friendship, privileges imposed by adults) and what they gain (e.g., feel safer at school) by resolving the conflict.

Step 4: Idea/Option Finding. The mediator asks the disputants to work together to list as many ideas as possible to solve the conflict. All ideas are valued and will be evaluated only later. The intent of the process is to generate a list of new possibilities. Each disputant is encouraged to think of at least three possible solutions. The peer mediator refrains from making suggestions so that the disputants will "own" the solutions, as well as the problem itself.

Step 5: Solution Finding. The peer mediator asks the disputants to review the list of solutions and to name those solutions that are acceptable. Often disputants will say what they want the other person to do. The peer mediator points out that each person must say what he or she is willing to do rather than what the other person should do. Agreed-upon options should be mutually satisfactory to both disputants because a balanced agreement is important to a lasting resolution. The peer mediator may ask, "Does this help the interests of everyone involved?" "Can this solution be implemented?" and, "What will be the results?"

Step 6: Agreement and Closure. The peer mediator summarizes the agreements in writing and asks participants to sign the document. Then the peer mediator shakes hands with each disputant and encourages the disputants to shake hands with each other. Sometimes an agreement can not be reached during the session. The peer mediator may suggest that the disputants agree to a truce and come back for a follow-up session the next day. If an impasse is reached, the peer mediator may talk with each disputant separately; this is called *caucusing* and has the same ground rules as the peer mediation session. If the caucused person agrees to share the outcomes, the peer mediator takes the results to the other disputant, and the session continues until an agreement is reached.

Cautions and Guidelines for Successful Peer Mediation Programs

Peer mediation programs must be implemented with *eyes wide open*, as there are several cautions. In addition to the cautions listed in the previous section, there is a potential student barrier. When implementing a schoolwide peer mediation program, teachers, administrators, and peer mediators must be aware that it takes time for students to develop trust in the peer mediation program itself. Karan's (2004) comprehensive study of a peer mediation program revealed that how a student typically resolves conflict likely influences whether that student will seek mediation. The mediation program that was the focus of this study was based in a junior high school (Grades 7 through 9) in a city of approximately 35,000 in southern New England. The 1,000 junior high school students had attended 6 elementary schools in the school district and represented 21 different national origins. In the program, selected students were trained as peer mediators to help students in conflict find nonviolent, mutually agreeable ways to resolve their differences. Although almost 95 percent of the school's students reported that they knew about the mediation program, only 12 percent reported that they or people they know had used it to resolve conflicts. The study set out to learn why so few students had turned to the mediation program.

Among students surveyed, 31.03 percent thought that the usual ways in which students resolved conflicts were not conducive to mediation. When asked how they resolved conflict, 79.31 percent of students surveyed said they ignored it, and 55.17 percent said they avoided it. These responses, as well as backing off, submitting, and being nice, are passive responses. Because mediation requires active acknowledgment of conflict and willingness to work it out with the other person, passive responses were not likely to lead to mediation.

In contrast, a small proportion, 22.41 percent, of students surveyed mentioned aggressive responses of threatening and name-calling as ways that they and people they knew responded to conflict; 27.59 percent reported that they or people they knew resolved conflicts through physical or verbal attack. The researchers found that students relied more on their peers than on adults to help resolve their conflicts. Only 13.79 percent of students said that they sought adult help. Rather, 50 percent said that friends helped them work out their conflicts, with 41.38 percent saying they "talked out" their conflicts. Although reliance on friends might appear to support peer mediation, it may be that this informal reliance on peers, outside of the formal peer mediation program, in effect sets up a competing peer structure for resolving conflict.

What do the results of this study suggest in terms of how to promote the use and success of formal peer mediation programs? For one, in order for students to adopt a peer-mediated confrontation and problem-solving approach to dealing with conflict, promoters of the process must attend to developing students' trust that the peer mediation program can and will be effective to help them deal with rather than avoid the real conflicts they face. Namely, once a peer mediation program has been in effect for a period of time, it is important for success stories to be disseminated to students in any way that gains their attention (e.g., stories, DVD, student advertisements, testimonials by high-status peers using the process). Of course, this means ensuring that these success stories represent a range of real examples, including some of the types of altercations that otherwise would lead to more aggressive verbal and physical responses. This is really part of the process of changing the culture of a school with regard to bullying, diversity appreciation, race relations, and views regarding personal responsibility for one's own actions.

A LESSON PLAN EXAMPLE: LEARNING FRIENDLY DISAGREEMENT SKILLS

Why is it important to learn how to disagree? Where does friendly disagreeing fit into the social skills that students use when they manage the conflicts and controversies that arise each day? Students face many types of conflicts, as described above, throughout their school day. Academic controversies are conflicts that are often structured by teachers to help students learn more than one side to a controversial issue. This type of controversy exists whenever one person's ideas, opinions, information, theories, or conclusions are incompatible with those of another and the two seek agreement (Johnson & Johnson, 1995b). There are many ways to resolve academic controversy, such as deliberate discourse, creative problem solving, and debate. In all of these approaches, students typically engage in the following steps (Johnson & Johnson, 1995b).

1. *Prepare a position:* Students conduct research in the library; learn from instruction, films, or interviews; organize their ideas into a persuasive agreement; and plan how to advocate for the position.

2. *Present and advocate the position:* Students state their reasons to make sure that their listeners receive a fair and complete picture.

3. *Discuss the positions:* Students participate in spirited disagreements while they argue for their position, critically analyze and refute the opposing position, and rebut or provide counterarguments for their position.

4. *Reverse positions:* Students reverse their perspectives and present the best case for the opposing position. (This step increases each person's investment in understanding the other side.)

5. *Synthesize positions:* Students work together to drop all advocacy for "their" positions. They summarize the best evidence and reasoning from both sides, integrate it into a joint position, and then report the team synthesis to others.

As you can see, these steps are similar to the creative problem solving steps described above that students learn when they practice peer mediation (Fact

Finding, Interest Finding, Idea/Option Finding, and Solution Finding). Within academic controversies, teachers not only teach academic content (math, social studies, language arts, science, health, etc.) but the academic controversy skills that are required to help students gain the skills to argue persuasively. For example, in language arts, students learn how to write persuasive arguments (see fifth-grade teacher Jack Wilde's [n.d.] "Teaching Persuasive Writing" unit). In science classes, students learn how scientists have argued about key breakthroughs (see University of California—Berkeley and University of Washington scientists Lachtermacher-Truinfol & Hines's [2002] Science Controversies: Online Partnerships in Education [SCOPE] program).

Through the peer mediation steps and the academic controversy processes outlined above, teachers and students alike can experience the synergistic outcomes of successful conflict and controversy management (Leff et al., 2002). They can experience firsthand how to focus on satisfying the underlying needs of those involved in the conflict and on finding a big enough or exciting enough goal or reason for cooperating that stimulates disputants to set aside their positions to embrace the new position.

Figure 8.1 shows a template that teachers can use to design lesson plans to teach the required skills for peers to learn how to mediate conflicts.

As shown, the lesson plan format includes essential information about who will teach the lesson, when the lesson will occur, what academic and social skills learning objectives will be included, materials, and instruction. The lesson sequence includes an anticipatory set to gain student attention and awareness of the purpose of the lesson, how the teacher will instruct, modeling and guided practice, evaluation, and closure. A special feature of this lesson plan template is the inclusion of a transfer or generalization component.

To illustrate how the template can be used, Figure 8.2 shows how Cathy Conn-Powers (1988) structured a lesson to teach students how to disagree without being disagreeable, a skill that her students could then incorporate in the controversy management process, as well as in the peer mediation process.

Figure 8.1   Lesson Plan Template for Teaching Social Skills to Resolve Conflicts and Controversies

Teachers (Names):

Grade Level(s):

Time Frame:

Social Skill Lesson Title:

Content Area(s):

Class and Student Descriptions: *What is the general background (challenges and prior learning) of students in relationship to the social skill? What are differentiation needs for students with unique learning characteristics?*

Materials *(books, forms, worksheets, curriculum):*

(Continued)

(Continued)

Social Learning Objective and Content Standards: *State the objective in 4 parts—(1) conditions or givens, (2) learners, (3) observable measureable behavior, and (4) performance criteria. Be sure to use small steps of behaviors that can be task analyzed or described in a "T" chart—looks like/sounds like.*

Which state-adopted content standard or item from Health Frameworks does this social skill address?

Lesson Sequence

Anticipatory Set: *How will you have the students discover WHY this is an important social skill for them to learn?*

Input: *How will you clarify what the social skill looks like and sounds like and feels like?*

Model: *Ask students to role-play what the skill should look like and sound like. Check for understanding.*

Group Practice: *How will the students practice? In small groups? Or in pairs? How will the teacher monitor performance? Will students record and monitor the practice? If so, how?*

Evaluate: *How will you provide feedback to the pairs or groups? How will you have the students evaluate each other?*

Closure: *Close the lesson by having the students share "round-robin" what they liked about the lesson.*

Transfer: *After the skill is taught and practiced, what follow-up activities will you schedule inside and outside the classroom (e.g., playground, cafeteria)? Make sure your students continue to practice in real-life contexts.*

Figure 8.2 Lesson Plan for Teaching Social Skills to Resolve Conflicts and Controversies: Teaching Friendly Disagreeing Skills

---

Teachers (Names): C. Conn-Powers and Ms. B, sixth-grade teacher

Grade Level(s): 4–6

Time Frame: 45-minute math class

Social Skill Lesson Title: *"Learn how to disagree without being disagreeable."*

Content Area(s): Mathematics Problem Solving (reasoning), Social/Communication: Maintain friendly relationships

Class and Student Descriptions:

A total of 28 students attended math class with Ms. B every day. Reading comprehension skills ranged from 1.5 to 8.5 grade equivalent. Approximately 14 students came from linguistically diverse families who spoke languages other than English, such as Spanish, Bosnian, Russian, or Vietnamese. Four students had Individual Education Plans to increase reading and math skills, two students were receiving English as a Second Language instruction, and four others had trouble getting along on the playground and in the classroom.

Materials:

Teacher-prepared worksheet with at least four math problems to solve that (a) require up to fifth-grade computational skills and (b) can be solved two or more different ways. Poster paper and magic markers for students to show their solutions. Friendly Disagreeing Skills Checklist with spaces for students to tally their participation.

Social Learning Objective and Content Standards:[1]

Given four opportunities to resolve four different math problems that include controversial or different processes to solve, students will practice four of the five friendly disagreeing skills at least three times per 45-minute class period. Given four different math problems with two or more different solutions, students will solve the problem and explain the reasoning for at least three of the four problems within a 45-minute class period.

> 1. Vermont's Framework of Standards and Learning Opportunities: Mathematical Problem Solving and Reasoning (p. 7.4): (b) Create and use a variety of approaches, and understand and evaluate the approaches that others use; determine how to break down a complex problem into simpler parts (http://education.vermont .gov/new/pdfdoc/pubs/framework.pdf).

Lesson Sequence

Anticipatory Set: Think about what YOU do when you disagree with a classmate! How do you feel when you hear words such as "I don't agree with you," said in a friendly tone with a smile or an unfriendly tone with a frown.

Teacher demonstrates and acknowledges students' responses, elicits comments by probing questions such as "Do you think you'll feel like talking more if you hear a friendly or an unfriendly tone?"

Input: Ask students to practice saying, "I don't agree with you," with a smile and friendly tone, then with a frown and unfriendly tone.

"Now we know what you look like and sound like! In today's lesson, we will practice disagreeing with a friendly tone and smile. There are at least five ways to do this. In the math lesson today, you will use your reasoning skills to determine which math operation (addition, subtraction, multiplication, or division) to use to solve the problems. I'll be looking for how many DIFFERENT ways you can solve the same problem—you must come up with at least two different ways. Your group will make a poster to show the different ways to reason out the solution. If your group solves all problems and you show all solutions, you each earn an A for the day's work. If your group has three problems with three solutions, you earn a B. If your group has two problems and two alternative solutions, then you earn a C. If you have no alternative solutions, then you will have a chance to work with me at recess."

Model: Teacher takes the students through an example. Asks the students to use at least one of the five friendly disagreeing skills to practice.

Group Practice: Students work in groups of four; teacher visits each group to make sure they are (a) coming up with alternative solutions and (b) tallying their use of friendly disagreeing skills.

Evaluate: Approximately 10 minutes before the end of class, the teacher asks students to showcase their posters, creating a class gallery. The teacher randomly selects one student from each group to explain one of the questions and their group's solutions. Then the teacher randomly selects another group spokesperson to summarize the tallies for each friendly disagreeing skill.

Closure: Teacher comments on creativity and the use of friendly disagreeing skills.

Transfer: The teacher asks the students if they think that the third graders next door might be interested in their posters. If the students agree, then the third graders are invited to come to their classroom the next day and visit each group, who will explain the group's poster and solutions to the third graders.

In this lesson, students learn and practice the five ways to disagree in a friendly way shown in Table 8.5. Developed by Cathy Conn-Powers (1988) and a sixth-grade teacher, the goal was to teach sixth graders how to manage the conflicts they faced when solving math problems that could be solved in multiple formats. The students learned to describe their reasoning skills, and they practiced interpersonal skills of maintaining friendly relationships with their study group partners at the same time as stating their differing opinions.

The prerequisite skills for the lesson involved computational skills through fractions and reading skills at the fifth-grade level to decode the math story problems. The academic objective was to solve math story problems that required reasoning and basic computational skills. Students could check their answers with calculators. They were to demonstrate their skills by making statements such as "I think we should go about solving the problem this way because. . . ." If the study group of four students developed and rationalized multiple ways to solve all four problems, each student earned an A on the assignment; if they solved three problems, they each earned a B; if they solved two problems, they earned a C. Those groups that solved less

Table 8.5 Five Ways to Disagree in a Friendly Way

Skill	Examples of What to Say
Ask others for different opinions.	"Why do you think that's best?" "What is your opinion?" "What is your answer to the problem?"
Ask others to explain why.	"Can you show me how that works?" "How do you think that will solve the problem?" "Explain that last part."
Add onto or modify others' ideas.	"Could we expand on your answer?" "How about if we added this?"
Offer alternatives.	"What do you think about this idea?" "Would this work too?" "Here is a different way to look at things."
State the disagreement	"I have a different idea." "My answer is different. Here is why I think that way."

than two problems were encouraged to eavesdrop on their classmates to discover alternative ways to resolve conflicts of opinions and different ways to solve the problems.

Study groups of four were formed heterogeneously on the basis of students' academic rankings: one high-achieving student, one low-achieving student, and two average-achieving students. They had a chance to practice the controversy management skills prior to the math assignment. For example, they were asked, "How do you feel when you hear the words 'I don't agree with you,' said in a friendly tone with a smile versus an unfriendly tone with a frown?" Two students volunteered to role-play for their classmates. Students chorused, "Yes!" enthusiastically when asked, "Do you think you'll feel like talking more if you hear a friendly tone?"

During the lesson, students monitored their use of the ways to disagree in a friendly way by using a simple checklist. When students used one of the skills, the study group monitor placed a tally mark by that particular skill. In addition, the teacher monitored the groups systematically, strategically eavesdropping so as to verify the accuracy of the monitoring process. When necessary, the teacher encouraged the study groups to practice a specific skill that had not yet earned a check mark. For example, the teacher might have said, "I notice that one of you is doing all the writing on the poster. Does that feel fair? Remember that creating the poster showing your group's work is a task to be shared by each member of the study group."

At the end of the study group work time, the teacher asked the student groups to present their findings. In addition to discussing the solutions to their math story problems, the students also described how they used the friendly disagreeing skills. As part of the debriefing of the lesson, the teacher asked the students if they knew of any famous mathematician who disagreed with an accepted solution and came up with a better way. Students then could search the Internet for examples of controversial mathematicians who challenged the status quo (e.g., Blaise Pascal, www.maths.tcd.ie/pub/HistMath/People/Pascal/RouseBall/RB_Pascal.html). Understanding that mathematicians argue and have conflicts can help students realize two important facts about conflicts. First, conflicts and controversies exist no matter how "accurate" the content seems to be. Second, conflicts and controversies do not disappear in childhood but persist throughout all phases of one's life. R. Buckminster Fuller (1991), the inventor of the geodesic dome and many other novel creations, once said,

> What is common to all humans in history are problems, problems, and more problems. If you are good at problem solving, you do not eventually arrive at Utopia; you get ever more difficult, more comprehensive, more incisively stated problems to solve. (p. 25)

SUMMARY

Take a moment to reflect on the conflict resolution and controversy management options discussed in this chapter. What is appealing to you? Which options might you already have incorporated into your classroom teaching? Which are you willing to practice now?

Now, please return to the questions posed at the beginning of the chapter: Do you understand the origins and responses to conflicts in classrooms and schools? Can you outline the scientific evidence for peer mediation and conflict resolution programs? Can you describe the steps involved in teaching peer mediation skills? Is the lesson plan template for teaching social skills helpful to you? Can you detect ways in which your students are applying their newly developed conflict resolution skills to academic controversies? Being able to handle conflicts of ideas and controversies is important in academic subjects such as science, social studies, and literature, in which students often are faced with the challenge of weighing the merits of the arguments for and against the facts described.

Finally, consider how your classroom climate might change if all your students gained the peer mediation and controversy management skills described in this chapter. Do you think that your students might be in a better position to showcase Nel Noddings's (2005) ideal; namely, that *what we learn in the daily reciprocity of caring goes far deeper than test results* [emphasis added].

Students as Collaborators in Responsibility 9

Our students will not care how much we know, until they know how much we care.

—Craig & Gould (2007, p. 112)

In this chapter, we ask you to consider the following questions:

1. How do you define the concept of "responsibility"?

2. How does the Self-Discipline Pyramid help students develop responsibility?

3. How do students develop "controls from within"?

A CIRCLE OF COURAGE DEFINITION OF RESPONSIBILITY

In Chapter 1, we introduced a Circle of Courage conceptualization of the desired outcome of education; that is, courageous youth whose sense of self-worth is strong due to their basic needs for belonging, mastery, independence, and generosity being met through the guidance of and collaboration with adults. The purpose of this chapter is to focus attention on achieving the Circle of Courage education outcome of *independence* or responsibility through adults collaborating with students to foster the learning and use of responsible behavior.

Do you agree that there are two dimensions of responsibility? The first dimension is *flexibility*—an ability to respond or to exhibit "response-ability." Van Bockern and colleagues (2000), who elegantly described the Native American Circle of Courage framework, identified a few of the flexible behaviors of courageous and resilient youth: "social competence, problem-solving skills, autonomy, and a sense of purpose and of the future"(p. 60). The second dimension of responsibility is *accountability*—a sense of personal ownership or internal self-discipline. Again, Van Bockern and colleagues elaborated, directing educators to construct experiences that "seek the child's inner control, a self-efficacy that allows the child to do the right thing when he or she is not under surveillance" (p. 71). This inner control and self-efficacy also is known as self-discipline.

Given this two-dimensional definition of responsibility, then as educators, it becomes our responsibility to be flexible and accountable in order to increase children's behavioral flexibility and accountability or self-discipline. What are ways educators can collaborate with students to develop responsibility and self-discipline?

THE SELF-DISCIPLINE PYRAMID

Developing student responsibility is no less demanding a task than teaching any other curriculum area: it requires educators to think carefully and reflect, provide complex instruction throughout the school years, and have patience. The authors conceptualize an effective system for collaborating with students to develop responsibility or self-discipline as a five-level pyramid, shown as Figure 9.1. The strength of the self-discipline pyramid is its base, where the focus is upon developing a classroom climate of caring and positive interdependence. The second level of the pyramid includes recovery methods that maintain student dignity and engage student reflection when class expectations are violated. The third level of the pyramid represents long-terms supports, which include the teaching of social skills and problem-solving methods as well as activating extra supports, such as personal contracts, for students who need them. The fourth level represents a "somewhere else" place where students can go on a short-term basis when they are unable to resolve a conflict or issue at the classroom level. The pinnacle of the pyramid involves assembling a support team of caring individuals to develop a plan with a student that will result in long-term behavior change.

What follows are descriptions of strategies, structures, and procedures for supporting the development of student responsibility at each of the five levels of the self-discipline pyramid. It should be noted that the five-level pyramid conceptualization presented in this chapter is different from the three-tiered Response to Intervention (RTI) and schoolwide Positive Behavior Support (PBS) approaches to behavioral intervention.[1] The five-level pyramid described in this chapter is meant to be an idea jogger for educators collaborating with students to develop responsibility and self-discipline (Villa, Udis, & Thousand, 2002). In contrast, RTI and PBS are systematic approaches for problem-solving inappropriate behavior through interventions at different levels (tiers) of intensity.

Some RTI and PBS strategies useful in supporting students experiencing behavioral problems are more about altering teacher behavior (e.g., using differentiated instruction techniques, greeting students at the door, knowing the multiple intelligence strengths of students) or instituting systems of motivation (e.g., token economies with contingent rewards and privileges) than teacher

---

[1] For more details about Positive Behavior Supports (PBS), Response to Intervention (RTI), and the PBS-RTI interface, see the Web site maintained by the U. S. Office of Special Education Programs Technical Assistance Center, www.pbis.org, and Sandomierski, Kincaid, and Algozzine (2007).

Figure 9.1 Self-Discipline Pyramid

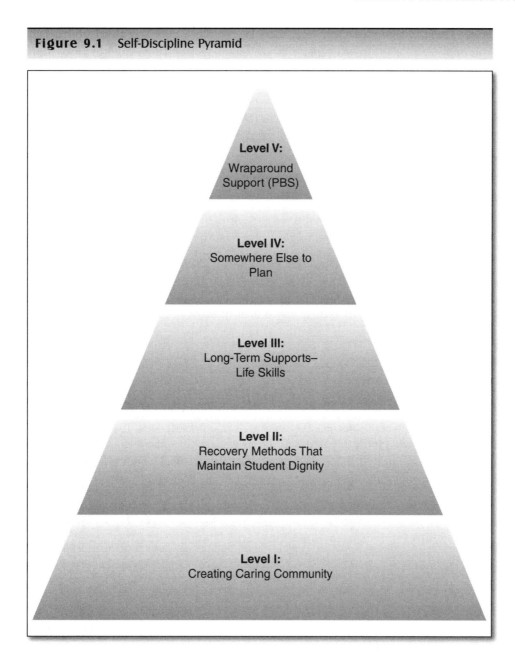

and student collaboration. These strategies, although important and useful, are outside the scope of this chapter.

Also, the authors wish to acknowledge in advance that many of the concepts or approaches represented in the next five sections of this chapter are expanded in the writings of esteemed colleagues Richard Curwin and Allen Mendler. Their book *Discipline with Dignity* (Curwin, Mendler, & Mendler, 2008) is an important resource in guiding teachers to affirm approaches to managing the classroom that promote respect for self and others. Additionally, literally hundreds of strategies and structures for developing student responsibility and dealing with every type of discipline issue can be found in the *Win-Win Discipline* text (Kagan, Kyle, & Scott, 2004), which is primarily authored by the renowned cooperative group learning author, Steven Kagan. We strongly recommend that readers interested in effective classroom discipline procedures and additional ways in which to promote responsible student behavior extend their reading of these authors.

Creating a Caring Community: The Base of the Self-Discipline Pyramid

It is within the context of a caring relationship that the concept of responsibility acquires meaning. Central to the learning of responsibility is that students perceive the adults in the school as caring about them. Stated otherwise, if students are to acquire values, attitudes, and behaviors that are "response-able" (flexible and accountable), the adults in their lives (i.e., teachers) need to have a systematic approach for developing relationships with and among their students. Collaborating with students to develop responsibility starts with engaging students in co-creating a caring classroom community. A teacher can do this in many ways, and many of these already have been examined in this text. For example, collaborating in instruction by having students work in cooperative group learning structures (see Chapter 2) or as actual co-teachers (see Chapter 4) are obvious ways that students take responsibility for their own learning and the learning of classmates. When teachers collaborate with stable, heterogeneous base teams (see Chapter 2) to accomplish morning and end-of-day routines (e.g., clarifying assignments, updating absent members, giving feedback on papers, checking homework) or supporting teammates to prepare for upcoming tests, students are taking responsibility by being individually accountable to teammates for ongoing support. When students are expected to use previously taught small-group interpersonal social skills in their cooperative groups, they have the opportunity to develop responsibility—practice accountability and flexibility—in the use of social skills that will serve them a lifetime.

At the base of the pyramid are three additional major ways to develop responsibility; namely, engaging students in (1) collaboratively developing the classroom social contract; (2) learning and using predictable procedures, routines, and signals; and (3) using class meetings to check in on the social contract, plan, make decisions, and problem solve as a community.

Collaborative Development of the Social Contract

Equity among students and adults in educational decision making is more likely to promote active student participation and a climate of mutual respect than a situation in which adults make the decisions alone. One area of great importance to student life is student accountability for behaving within the limits of agreed-upon behavioral and social norms established by the school community. *Social contract* is the term that Curwin and colleagues (2008) used for the process of teachers and students jointly developing and implementing the values, norms or expectations, and consequences of classroom behavior. Social contracts should reflect the democratic decision-making process of government. Further, teachers want students to buy into and own the social contract. Therefore, active involvement of students in developing norms, logical consequences that teach and remind students about accountable behavior and the values upon which it is based (e.g., do onto others as you would have them do onto you, all who come in will be safe and will learn), is key to the ultimate success of the social contract.

Steps to develop the social contract. Kagan and colleagues (2004) described a process used by high school teachers for generating norms, which we have modified based upon a video example of norm development shown in the *Ways We Want Our Class to Be* video series produced by the Developmental Studies Center (1996). Consider this or a variation of this sequence of steps as one way to collaborate with students to develop the social contract.

Step 1. Have students develop classroom values by having them close their eyes and leading them through a guided visualization of all of the parts of the day. Ask them to picture what an ideal school day would look and sound like and how people would treat one another and things.

Step 2. Students individually brainstorm what behaviors represent this ideal school. They then share with partners and jointly write their ideas on slips of paper.

Step 3. Students post their ideas on the board or wall and are asked if they see any categories of ideas that belong together. Categorical labels (no more than four or five) are written on the board. Students then stand and categorize their initial ideas.

Step 4. Students in groups examine each category and come up with two or three positively stated behaviors or expectations that operationalize these values. We use the term *expectations* rather than *rules*. The term *rules* often connotes for students external control, whereas the term *expectations* can represent personal expectations or expectations for one another in a community. To illustrate, if the value is "Everyone feels safe," an expectation might be "When upset, we tell someone how we feel and try to solve the problem."

Step 5. Expectation statements are posted under the category in which they belong, and students are asked if a "good teacher" list would be different or similar. The expectations are then combined or modified, and the class is asked if they can live with the list. By then, they usually have ownership and "vote" yes.

Step 6. The list is memorialized in writing and sent home as a social contract for the parents and student to sign.

Step 7. The values and list of expectations are posted and referred to regularly when a discussion is needed about whether a given behavior falls within or outside of the boundaries of the expectations and what is the best way to help a student to stay within the class's social contract.

Curwin and colleagues (2008) suggested that to demonstrate equity, students develop at least a couple of expectations for their teacher. For example, an expectation might be that the teacher does not drink coffee in class if students cannot drink sodas or, stated positively, the beverage students and teachers drink in class is water. These authors also recommend testing students on the content of the social contract so they cannot claim ignorance of expectations. Further, to increase collaboration on the part of those students who have difficulty staying within the boundaries of the social contract, they suggest following the lead of a suburban middle school in which

- a "student council of poor achievers" and "in-trouble students" (different labels were used) was created to help set school policy [and]
- students who served detention were given the job of commenting on how school climate could be improved. (Curwin et al., 2008, p. 26)

Predictable Procedures, Routines, and Signals

In addition to the social contract and expectations, procedures, routines, and signals assist students with becoming accountable for their learning and behavior by offering them known, predictable, and practical ways of participating in the classroom community. *Procedures* are practiced steps of behaviors that reoccur in the classroom. Potential classroom procedures range from how to enter a classroom; transition from individual desks to cooperative groups; ask for help; or respond to an earthquake, tornado, or fire. As with the learning of any task or a social skill, the teacher collaborates with students to help them discover why this procedure is important and what it looks and sounds like through modeling, guided practiced, and reinforced distributed practice. Once a procedure is learned, it can be strung together with others to create a *routine* that allows students to be self-directed or flexible in taking ownership for the way the class operates. A typical beginning-of-the-day routine might be for students to enter the class, greet the teacher, pick up personalized file folders in which homework and teacher-read work are exchanged, engage in a three-minute "bell work" transition task, and listen to the morning announcements read by a classmate on a predetermined rotating basis.

Signals are nonverbal or brief verbal cues taught and rehearsed that save transition time. Signals are for both the teacher and students. For example, the authors use the "signal on" quiet signal when wanting our students or audiences to transition from collaborative conversation or work. This signal's procedure is as follows: (1) the instructor raises his or her hand, saying, "Signal on"; (2) learners stop conversation, raise one hand, and turn their attention to the instructor; and (3) learners prompt others who have not heard or seen the signal. In our experience, this has reduced transitions to five seconds or less. Of course, the signal can be varied, and students surely can suggest signals. In a variation that uses a "call–response" format, the teacher calls out, "Goodness gracious!" and students respond with "Great balls of fire."

Student signals include traditional ones, such as raising a hand to ask a question or request to speak or giving a thumbs-up to indicate being finished. Other hand signals or gestures can be created to indicate the need for more think time (e.g., pointing to the side of the head) or that the information is "over my head" (e.g. waving a hand over the top of the head). For teams, the "three before me" signal indicates that members have conferred with at least three classmates and still have an unanswered question. The procedures are described as follows:

> If an individual student has a question, he/she is not to hold up a hand and interrupt the teacher. Rather, the student is to . . . ask his/her shoulder partner [person seated adjacent to him/her]. If the shoulder partner cannot answer the question, then the two students have a pair question and they are to ask their face partners. If all four students . . . cannot answer the question, then they have a Team Question. They signal the teacher . . . by each holding up a hand. Four hands up is the signal to the teacher that the team has exhausted their resources. (Kagan et al., 2004, p. 18, 19)

To hold team members accountable for trying to answer the question, when the teacher comes over, anyone may be asked to state the question.

Class Meetings

John Dewey (cited in P. Fairfield, 2008) noted,

> Democracy is much broader than a method for conducting government. . . . [It is] a way of life. . . . Its foundation is faith that each individual has something to contribute. . . . The interactive participation of all individuals is the keynote of democracy as a way of life. (p. 82)

Class meetings are interactive forums for students to listen to and take the perspective of others, have their voice elicited and heard, and participate in democratic decision making about things that matter to them. Class meetings can range from a few minutes to 30 or more minutes, depending upon the students' age, complexity of the topic, and the students' interest level. Regularly scheduled (daily, weekly) class meetings allow students to develop "moral" habits in behavior, feelings, and judgment under teacher guidance but without teacher-imposed solutions. Regularly scheduled meetings also let students know their issues will be brought up and addressed.

There are three types of class meeting items. The first type is planning and decision-making items, such as planning for how to support a substitute teacher or making decisions as to what to include in the class social contract. Another type is check-in items, such as checking in on how well the class did to support the substitute teacher or periodically assessing how well the class is following the class expectations. Consciousness-raising activities, the third type of agenda item, are those where the class examines a community problem (e.g., teasing, bullying on the playground, name-calling) and rather than blaming culprits, focuses upon using problem-solving strategies, such as those presented in Chapter 5, to generate and agree upon solutions.

Class meetings also are a time for students to build community by appreciating one another's demonstration of responsible behaviors. Appreciations can be structured into the meeting agenda by using strategies such as those used for group processing in cooperative groups presented in Table 2.4. Celebrations of individual and group successes also should be structured into class meeting agendas. For example, after being taught the SODAS IF problem-solving script (see Chapter 5), two students who had stepped in and mediated a conflict on the playground using the SODAS IF script might report out how they used the script successfully to come up with an agreeable solution.

Recovery With Accountability: Level Two of the Self-Discipline Pyramid

When a student or students step outside of the boundaries of norms and expectations, recovery methods can be engaged to remind students of expectations and get them back on track. We deliberately use the term *recovery* versus *disciplinary response* to emphasize that the goal here is not to blame or shame students but to engage supports to maintain or re-engage responsible involvement in instruction and learning. Typical low-level recovery strategies that do not break the flow of instruction include proximity or "management by walking around"; eye contact or "the look"; and expectation reminder signals, such as pointing to the class norms and expectations poster. Recovery strategies that momentarily break the flow of instruction and, at the same time, maintain student dignity are verbal reminders or reteaching of expectations (e.g., "Remember, the expectation is. . . ." or "Let's take a moment to review how we want our class to be.") and redirection (e.g., Right now, you are/feel. . . . That's fine, *and* what you need to do is. . . .").

For recovery strategies to be most effective and truly build student "response-ability," some type of follow up is advised. Scheduling a follow-up conversation, either as an individual conversation or a consciousness-raising problem-solving agenda item for a class meeting, promotes future accountability and flexibility by having students reflect upon a behavior and find a more responsible alternative.

Peer mediation, described in Chapter 8, is an additional recovery method whereby students collaboratively engage with classmates as supports to defuse anger and redirect students to productive solution finding. When students disrupt or disengage because they are unsure of what to do or when the curriculum is too difficult or too easy, extra supports, such as informal momentary peer tutoring or natural peer supports such as classroom buddies, can be engaged to help clarify content, model responsible choices for a classmate, and guide the classmate to make those choices. Students also can be engaged as instructional decision makers, developing accommodations and modifications for others or themselves. Chapter 3 describes how to set up peer tutoring and partner learning systems. Chapter 6 provides processes and examples for students to use in supporting one another in instructional decision making.

In summary, at this second level of the self-discipline pyramid, the teacher and students prompt and support one another to recover instructional involvement. The recovery strategy often involves using established structures (e.g., peer tutoring, conflict mediation), the social skills and problem-solving and self-control scripts, and the cooldown procedures that are taught as long-term life skills at the next, third level of the pyramid.

Long-Term Supports—Life Skills: Level Three of the Self-Discipline Pyramid

The third level of the self-discipline pyramid represents a host of skills and procedures that are long-term supports for success in and outside of school. Long-term supports include students learning, practicing, and using social skills, problem-solving methods, and self-control scripts; establishing and using a cooldown procedure; and activating extra supports, such as personal contracts, for students who need additional structure.

Teaching Social Skills

None of us are born with social skills; instead, social skills are learned. All of the collaborative structures and arrangements described in this text work only if students have and use a repertoire of interpersonal, academic, and small-group social skills. We often hear teachers, pressured to cover the requisite academic standards, resist teaching and then holding students accountable for using social skills, claiming that it takes too much time away from the real curriculum. We would argue that teachers cannot afford *not* to teach social skills. These skills enable students to abide by the classroom and social contract and live by the values underlying this contract. They are skills that contribute to students' current and future quality of life. Further, they are skills identified as essential to the vast majority of jobs today, which involve some sort of on-site or interdependent global teamwork.

It is beyond the scope of this chapter to construct a curriculum on social skills. Many well-established programs are available (e.g., Goldstein, 1999). However, Chapter 2 identifies some essential social skills for the small-group interpersonal collaboration required for effective cooperative group learning. Curwin and colleagues (2008) also identified essential social skills often lacking among students who get in trouble; namely, greeting others, making eye contact, making a request, getting someone's attention, following instructions, accepting criticism, and resisting peer pressure. Kagan et al. (2004) identified nearly 200 resources for developing not only social skills but other life skills in the personal (self-knowledge, goal setting, organization), affective (expressing feelings, relaxation), motivational (learned optimism, self-talk), cognitive (e.g., memory, moral reasoning), and physical (nutrition, play) domains.

Similarly to developing classroom procedures, the teacher collaborates with students so that they (a) learn, (b) see a model, (c) practice what the social skill looks like and sounds like, and (d) understand why a particular social skill is important to learn and use now and in the future. Posters explaining the steps involved in using the learned skills serve as reminders to students of what they know and can do interpersonally and can be used to prompt recovery at the second level of the pyramid.

Teaching Problem-Solving and Self-Control Scripts

For students to have flexibility and accountability in problem solving at any level of the self-discipline pyramid, they must have familiar problem-solving and self-control procedures or scripts that they can activate for themselves or others, when needed or requested. Chapter 5 offers a host of tools students can use in problem solving. It describes 12 awareness plans that enhance problem solving; the generic Osborn-Parnes Creative Problem Solving (CPS) process, which can be adapted for almost any challenging situation; the simplified SODAS IF variation; and a Quick Brainstorm With the Kids variation that focuses students' creative thinking upon the brainstorming of ideas to improve their own situations. Chapter 6 provides examples of students and teachers working together to use CPS to correct curriculum, instructional, and discipline mismatches.

The "What are you doing?" helping script is specifically designed for adults to collaborate with students to help them take ownership of their behavior when it does not conform to the classroom or school social contract and expectations. Ideally, all students and adults in a school learn, rehearse, and systematically use the script to interrupt behaviors outside of the norms. This script leads to a plan and a commitment for engaging in alternative behaviors in the future that fall within the boundaries of the agreed-upon expectations. Systematic use of this script turns violations of norms into learning opportunities for students, as well as opportunities to get back into alignment with social contract expectations. The ultimate goal of learning and using the script systematically is for students to stop and think before acting and realize that it is easier to make a good (i.e., expectation-following) choice rather than having to go through the script with an adult if they make a bad (i.e., expectation-violating) choice. The script goes as follows:

1. What are you doing?

2. Is it helping? OR
   Does it comply with expectations? (If not, which expectation does it violate?)

3. How will you solve the problem? OR
   What could you do instead (that falls within expectations)?

4. Is this something you can really do?
   (Optional: Do you need help or a reminder to do this? What would help?)

5. When will you start? For how long can you do this?

6. What will you get out of following this plan?

7. Congratulations, you made a good plan/choice/decision!

We particularly like the script known as STAR—**S**top, **T**hink, **A**ct, **R**eview—which is a variation of the "What are you doing?" script. The STAR script is easy for students to complete at their desks or in a cooldown area, described in the next section. See the script in Figure 9.2 and notice the addition of the affective questions at the beginning and end of the script (i.e., "Right now I am feeling . . . ," "Now I am feeling . . . ."), which acknowledge and honor the emotions students experience when they are in distress and make poor choices. The addition of these affective questions helps students to recognize that making a better choice can lead to feeling happier and less frustrated, angry, worried, sad, or bored. Students can feel more deeply respected when teachers ask, "Is there anything else you would like to say?"

A *self-control* script is a problem-solving script in which a student engages in self-talk to exert self-control. For example, if you reword the "What are you doing?" script above so that *you* is changed to *I*, the script now is a "What am I doing?" self-control script, which a student can think through alone and even memorialize as a written commitment to action.

Scripts can use acronyms to assist recall of the steps. Recall the SODAS IF problem-solving script described in Chapter 5 and consider the following three self-control scripts. The first two, STOMA and WIN, were described by Curwin

Figure 9.2 STAR Review Plan Script

STAR Review Plan

Student _____
Teacher _____
Date _____

Right now I am feeling: (circle one)

happy   OK   frustrated   angry   worried   sad   bored

Stop	What did I do? What happened because of what I did? What expectations (rule[s]) did I forget? What else could I have done? 1. 2. 3.
Think	What might have happened if I acted differently? 1. 2. 3.
Act	What do you plan to do the next time?
Review	Is there anything else you would like to say? Now I am feeling: (circle one) happy OK frustrated angry worried sad bored

and colleagues (2008, p. 151); the third script, POP, is used by preschool and primary school teachers in Nebraska (Personal communication, Richard Villa, April 17, 2009).

STOMA

Stop before you do anything.

Take a breath; think about what happened and what you want to do.

Options: What are the consequences of each choice?

Move on it (make a choice).

Appreciate yourself (for not losing control and doing your best).

WIN

What is the problem?

Identify possible solutions.

Narrow it down to the best choice.

POP

Problem?

Options?

Plan?

Cooldown and Planning Procedure

Kagan and Kagan (2008) described a simple cooldown procedure for intervening when students' emotions begin to "warm up." It can be used with an entire class or individual students. Teaching the cooldown procedure is a Level Three intervention; implementing it is a Level Two recovery action. As with all procedures and social skills, the procedure is described, modeled, and rehearsed, and the rationale for needing a cooldown time and place in order to regain composure is discussed. Students can collaboratively agree on the place, duration, and activity options (e.g., draw, journal, read, practice deep breathing) for cooldown. A nonverbal signal or a physical cue (e.g., a miniature fan or plastic ice cream bar) is agreed upon to signal that a student is to go to the cooldown area. If the entire class is asked to cool down, a verbal signal is used. For example the verbal cue might sound like "Ladies and gentlemen, we all need to use a two-minute cooldown. Everyone [e.g., close your eyes, rest your head on your desk] while I play our calming music."

Implementing cooldown begins with a reminder. For the class, it might sound like "Emotions feel like they are warming up. I believe we can calm down without using our cooldown procedure." For an individual, the reminder would be private and in the form of a signal, a short note, or a quick conversation, which might sound like this: "Rich, I believe you can manage your feelings so we don't need to cool down."

When implementing cooldown for an individual student, that student may be asked to use any of the problem-solving scripts described above to reflect upon what occurred and later confer with the teacher to make a plan. Cooldown does not excuse a student from work missed while in cooldown. Accountability for work is part of this procedure.

Personal Contracts

Individual teacher-student contracts are an excellent example of student-teacher collaboration for responsibility. Contracts assist a student with learning to keep commitments and follow through on agreements and plans. As with problem-solving and self-control scripts, the basic steps of contract development are to identify a problem and explore solutions, options, and results in a commitment to arriving at a solution. To motivate student participation, it also is important to communicate, up front, that the contract is being created out of the teacher's care and concern for the student and articulate how abiding by the contract will benefit the student in the short and long term. The student and teacher also discuss and agree upon a payoff or incentive that motivates the student to follow through and a logical consequence (inclusive of revisiting the plan and examining the temptations that led to breaking of the contract). Finally, a timeline and monitoring or data collection system is agreed upon. This all is recorded in a written agreement signed by both parties and, perhaps, the family. Figure 9.3 shows a contract and recording system developed by Jan Israel, an educational psychologist, and a student named Rich. Notice how simple this contract and self-monitoring system is. As you can see, Rich was successful in achieving his contracted goal within the time frame set out by his contract. Contracts, when crafted collaboratively in concrete, student language and with teacher validation of student input and suggestions, are powerful tools for promoting student self-control.

Somewhere Else to Plan—The Planning Room: Level Four of the Self-Discipline Pyramid

The fourth level of the pyramid represents a "somewhere else" place for students to go when they are not able to calm down or resolve a conflict or issue within the classroom. Virtually every classroom social contract and the accompanying expectations articulate in some way that students and teachers have a right to be safe, free from threat and disruption from learning. When a student refuses or is emotionally too out of control to use the in-class cooldown procedure or engage in planning using a problem-solving script, the solution is not to expel the student from the class and school but to create an opportunity for calming, thinking, planning, and committing to a plan to move forward. When a student disrupts the learning process in the classroom, he or she is invited to deal with the distress in a safe, controlled physical space staffed by adults knowledgeable about the school's chosen planning script (e.g., "What are you doing?" script). This space is referred to as the Planning Room, because the goal is for a student to (a) come to an emotional state where rational thinking can occur and (b) through a planning process under adult guidance, craft a written plan

Figure 9.3 Sample Behavior Contract and Recording System

Behavior Contract

I _Rich_ understand I have a problem with:

Not doing what I am asked to do the first time I am asked.

I _Rich_ understand I do this on an average of:

Five times a day

I _Rich_ understand that if by _October 27th (in 3 weeks)_,

I average not more than _two times a day_,

I will earn the following reward:

A $10.00 gift certificate for Jamba Juice™

Rich Villa
Student Signature
Jan Israel
Teacher Signature

Recording System

Week	Monday	Tuesday	Wednesday	Thursday	Friday
Week 1	0	///	0	///	0
Week 2	/	0	/	/	/
Week 3	/	/	0	//	0

Key: **/ =** each incident of not doing what is asked the first time asked.

Results: 13 incidents/14 days = 0.9 incidents/day (which is a lot fewer than 2/day!)

SUCCESS! Enjoy Jamba Juice™ with your friends!

for re-entering the classroom in a "response-able" way (i.e., being _accountable_ for the disruption and choosing a better way of dealing with the situation in the future).

Table 9.1 suggests gatekeeping procedures for entering and exiting the Planning Room. There may be variations of these procedures, depending upon the policies and practices of a school (e.g., a student might first see a designated administrator or guidance person to determine if the Planning Room is the appropriate option). However, what remains constant is that students get a chance to take responsibility for their own behavior, practice using planning and problem-solving tools they can use the rest of their lives, re-enter the classroom with dignity maintained, be acknowledged for taking responsibility, and experience pride in working through to a solution.

It is absolutely essential not to mix functions of the Planning Room (e.g., study hall, time-out, detention, resource room) to ensure that the room does

Table 9.1 Planning Room Gatekeeping Procedures

Step 1. The decision to send a student to the Planning Room

Sending a student to the planning room is last-resort response after all other interventions (i.e., reminder, warning, calming in cooldown, planning in cooldown) have been unsuccessful at helping a student to re-engage. If a student does *not* agree to plan or if a student's behavior clearly indicates an inability (e.g., too emotionally distressed) to think clearly at the moment or an unwillingness to plan, say, "Jon, I am unable to plan with you. I need you to go to the Planning Room. Thank you."

Step 2. Getting a student to the Planning Room

The sending teacher fills out a form indicating the student's behavior. In schools where students change classes, the teacher also indicates a good time to return the student to class or a good time to meet with the student to review the plan, (e.g., "Send back ASAP." "Send back 5 minutes before class ends." "Please have the student see me at [time and place within 24 hours] so we can schedule a meeting to review the plan." If a student needs to be accompanied to the Planning Room, follow the procedure that was agreed upon to ensure the student makes it to the Planning Room.

Step 3. Getting a student back to class

Any plan developed by a student ultimately must be approved by the referring teacher, although the Planning Room teacher gives first approval. After a student writes a plan judged satisfactory by the planning room teacher, the student returns to the classroom with the plan and either returns to his or her desk or the cooldown area to wait for the teacher to review the plan. It is understood that the teacher will review the plan as quickly as possible (i.e., within 10 minutes). If the plan is acceptable to the referring teacher, the teacher signs it, and the student rejoins classroom activities. If the plan is not acceptable, the teacher has three choices: (1) have the student return to the Planning Room to revise the plan, (2) have the student stay at the desk or in the cooldown area and revise the plan, or (3) schedule a time to work with the student to revise the plan. In some schools, the Planning Room teacher goes with the student to the classroom.

Step 4. Increasing support to repeat visitors

After a student has been in the Planning Room two or three times during a marking period, a letter is sent to the parents explaining this, with a request to take some time to talk with their child about how school is going and how they might offer support.

After four or five visits to the Planning Room, a meeting is called, inviting the student, the referring teacher(s), a peer or two, the Planning Room teacher, and a designated administrator to engage in developing a more comprehensive support plan with and for this student. The purpose of this meeting is *not* to identify punishments or make threats! The purpose is to identify underlying causes and find solutions.

not become a dumping ground, place of punishment, or a place that stigmatizes students. A space is needed for the Planning Room. Ideally, it should be removed from the main traffic of the school and have enough room to accommodate at least three to four students at a time. The Planning Room also needs to be "staffed" with a trained adult throughout the day. In one of the author's schools with no budget for staff, the teachers considered the Planning Room so important, they rotated spending a planning period a week as the Planning Room teacher. Whether one person or several people staff the room, whoever is staffing should be trained and proficient in problem solving, anger management, social skills instruction, and guiding a student through the steps of the "What are you doing?" planning script or whatever planning script is used.

A Planning Room is *not* magic; it is *not* a quick fix; it does *not* work for all students all of the time. It *is* a place for developing short-term solutions that build a student's sense of self-control. For this reason, the authors are very strong advocates of the Planning Room being an essential component of any school's system for promoting student responsibility.

Unfortunately, in the current zero-tolerance and "three strikes, you're out" climate fostered by federal, state, and local policies, this fourth-level "safety net" segment of the self-discipline pyramid has been overlooked. In most schools, it is completely missing as a way to teach and hold students accountable for socially responsible behavior. The authors suggest that rather than *zero tolerance,* what is needed to promote student responsibility is *zero indifference* to the students whose behaviors can make classrooms uncomfortable and sometimes unsafe. A Planning Room and the planning and problem-solving processes that occur there represent and signal zero indifference rather than zero tolerance to the very students who need the most support to behave within the boundaries of classroom and societal norms.

Individualized Wraparound Support: Level Five of the Self-Discipline Pyramid

Every student is entitled to a free and appropriate public education (FAPE). This implies that the educational experience is one in which students experience academic and social/emotional growth. Consequently, any behavior that interferes with a student's learning process needs to be addressed for the benefit of the student, as well as his classmates and the learning environment. The fifth and top level of the self-discipline pyramid involves processes for collaborating with an individual student for whom responsible behavior is an issue and an area in need of intensive support. The process for increasing support to repeat visitors to the Planning Room described in Step 4 of Table 9.1 is an example of intensive, individualized wraparound support.

Uniquely useful at the top of the pyramid is the process for developing a Positive Behavior Support plan. For a student eligible for special education, the federal Individuals with Disabilities Education Improvement Act (IDEIA) requires a student's Individual Education Program (IEP) team to address any behavior that interferes with the student's learning or the learning of others by developing a Positive Behavior Support (PBS) plan (Bombara & Kern, 2004). A PBS plan should be developed for any student for whom behavior impedes learning. However, it is mandatory for a student with an IEP who exhibits difficult behavior.

To develop a PBS plan requires a team inclusive of the student to assemble to try to detect and understand what the function of a behavior is for the student; that is, why a chronic difficult behavior is occurring. The process of researching and hypothesizing the function of the behavior is referred to as a functional behavioral assessment (Steege & Watson, 2009). A student may or may not be aware of the function of his or her behavior. Therefore, the first step involves gathering information to determine what need a student is trying to fulfill through the behavior. Is the student trying to gain attention? Does the behavior indicate boredom or a need to expend energy? Is the behavior an attempt to avoid or escape a situation. Is it related to impulsivity and self-regulation?

Based upon observations of and interviews with the student, as well as interviews with others—teachers, parents, peers—who know the student in multiple contexts, a function of the behavior is hypothesized and agreed upon. Then an individualized PBS plan is developed and implemented. Essentially, a PBS plan is a teaching plan that specifies what the student will do and what teachers and family members will do to alter the environment and teach and reinforce behaviors to replace the behaviors of concern. For more information on the specifics of positive behavior interventions, see the *Journal of Positive Behavior Interventions,* available online at http://pbi.sagepub.com.

The Making Action Plans (MAPs) futures-planning process and the student-led IEP procedures described in Chapter 7 also are examples of self-determination processes in which a support team of caring individuals assembles to develop a plan with a student intended to result in long-term educational gains. If behavioral change is a targeted educational outcome, then both of these processes can serve as powerful wraparound supports for a student with behavioral challenges.

SUMMARY

In the powerful environments of schools or other group settings, relationally-oriented practices enable children and youth to develop "controls from within."

—VanderVen & Brendtro (2009, p. 3).

This assertion, made by the coeditors of an issue of *Reclaiming Children and Youth* entirely devoted to examining ways in which to develop controls from within, is based upon the concepts of Fritz Redl who, in the 1940s and 1950s, pioneered strengths-based, caring, and collaborative versus coercive approaches for working with troubled and troubling youth (Redl & Wineman, 1952). We endorse and support their statement, particularly when thinking about how to foster responsibility—flexibility and accountability—as controls from within for children and youth.

Do you see the approaches included in the self-discipline pyramid (see Figure 9.1) as relationally oriented and collaborative? Can you picture how you might work with other teachers and students in your school to promote student flexibility in and accountability for their behavior through teacher-student collaboration rather than more traditional, externally imposed discipline procedures? How might you use the self-discipline pyramid conceptualization of developing controls from within to approach your administration or school board about ways to improve student behavior? How might you engage students to experiment with some of the structures and strategies described in this and other chapters to develop responsibility? What do you do that goes beyond the ideas presented in this chapter and expands one or more of the five levels of the self-discipline pyramid?

In closing, we remind the reader that this chapter in no way is meant to be a comprehensive treatment of discipline procedures but rather an idea jogger to just what the title says—collaborate with students to develop responsibility. We hope it does just that!

Epilogue

Beyond Benevolence to Befriending and Advocacy

What the world needs now is less benevolence and more social justice!

—Norman Kunc and Emma Van der Klift
(Personal communication, 2008)

What is involved in befriending and advocacy? Why should teachers help their students become advocates? What core values must students show when they become advocates? Can you agree that when students become advocates, they show that they can take action on behalf of themselves and others? What happens when students gain experiences that show them how to make their own social worlds?

In this Epilogue, we invite readers to extend their work in collaborating with students to examine ways that students can develop collaboration, creativity, and self-advocacy skills to employ in advocacy for themselves and other members of the student body. How can students consciously build and maintain friendships? The notion of "befriending" captures all of the goals of education—independence, mastery, generosity, and belonging—in ways that make room for social justice in students lives. We include how-to strategies, resource tools, and real-life vignettes depicting the strategies in operation. We begin with cautions about how to use and not abuse these best-practice strategies and procedures.

As described in Chapter 1, the goals of education clearly call for advocacy skills. For example, we described four educational objectives or components of self-esteem—belonging, mastery, independence, and generosity (first articulated by Brendtro et al., 2002). When asked what are the goals of education for their children, Villa and Thousand (2005) noted that teachers, parents, administrators, professors, and students agree that generosity is a goal that is important to them. Generosity is described in many and varied ways—"being a contributing member of society, valuing diversity, being empathetic, offering compassion and caring and support to others, being a responsible citizen, exercising global stewardship" (Villa & Thousand, p. 42).

Teachers and educational administrators can be assured that there is a sound theoretical and research base on which to build their programs for advocacy. The theoretical framework is derived from social emotional learning theory. Students who become advocates acquire important social-emotional skills, especially when teachers use a cooperative group learning approach to teach advocacy skills. According to Zins, Bloodworth, Weissberg, and Wahlberg (2007), students not only develop important skills in negotiation and conflict resolution but also a peer culture for supporting academic achievement.

Social-emotional instruction can produce significant improvements in school attitude, school behavior, and school performance; in fact, a meta-analysis of 165 studies of school-based prevention activities found interventions with social competency instruction decreased rates of student dropout and increased attendance (Elias, Gara, Schuyler, Branden-Muller, & Sayette, 1991). Research has also shown that social-emotional learning develops important bonds among students, which can be a protective factor against many problem behaviors. In addition, students' positive attitudes and commitment to school significantly increase, as well as the grades and standardized achievement scores of male students (Hawkins, Guo, Hill, Battin-Pearson, & Abbott, 2001).

Teachers and administrators can be assured that many of the same goals that are embedded in character education are also achieved when students become advocates. Because social-emotional learning is an important aspect of character education programs, many effective programs rely on implementation of social-emotional programs that use varied instructional procedures (Elias et al., 1991). *Character education*, broadly defined, encompasses all aspects of schooling, including "responsibility and advocacy for common welfare" (Berkowitz & Simmons, 2003, p. 118).

The authors also are aware of the potential negative aspects of advocacy. Teachers and students must be hyperconscious of what Van der Klift and Kunc (2002) described as "the politics of help" (p. 21), reminding us that "our society still perceives those with disabilities as constant receivers of help. Descriptors such as 'less fortunate' and 'needy' and telethons and tear jerker journalism all continue to perpetuate this view" (p. 21). Students in the advocacy role must guard against this attitudinal barrier to full participation of their partners in the advocacy relationship. Several ways to get around this attitudinal barrier are shown in Table E.1.

The bottom line is that everyone will need to go beyond benevolent helping relationships. We hope you agree with Norman Kunc and Emma Van der Klift who say, "What the world needs now is less benevolence and more social justice!" (Personal communication, San Diego 10th Annual Leadership Conference, San Marcos, CA, July 22, 2008).

Table E.1   How Advocates Go Beyond Benevolence

Do not make advocacy a big deal.	When children and youth take on an advocacy role, it should be with equality and reciprocity among the receivers and the givers.
Respect personal boundaries.	Some children and youth may not want to be advocated to . . . the advocacy process must be mutually acceptable to the giver and the receiver.
Model valuing behavior.	Children and youth must see their teachers behaving in exemplary advocacy roles. If interactions between the teacher and other children are respectful, then they are more likely to believe that it is okay to behave respectfully towards all children in the class.
Share information.	Ask children and youth to share their opinions and observations. What social injustices are perhaps being perpetuated in the classroom that only the children can really experience? How might these social injustices be corrected?
Acknowledge reciprocity and contribution.	Behave as though reciprocity is really possible, even when there are clear power differences. For example, a teacher cannot ignore individual differences in children's intellectual and emotional growth. However, the teacher can demonstrate reciprocity and show value for children's contributions by simply asking, "What if you were in my shoes? What would you do? What can we do together to solve this problem?"
Merge help and respect.	Remember that too much helping, too much advocating, can be debilitating. Offering choices and emphasizing self-determination are ways to avoid overhelping. Ask before advocating!
Appeal to empathy and social justice.	Children and youth have an innate sense of what is fair. They observe acts of unfairness in their daily lives in and out of school. They are also aware of being powerless, and they know what it is like to be ignored, or silenced. They want to and can learn how to correct these acts of unfairness through advocacy experiences for themselves and others.

SOURCE: From *Creativity and collaborative learning: A practical guide to empowering students, teachers, and families* (2nd ed., pp. 25–28) by J.S. Thousand, R.A. Villa, & A.I. Nevin, 2002, Baltimore, MD: Paul H. Brookes Publishing Co. Adapted by permission.

Glossary

accommodation: Physical, environmental, instructional supports or services that align with a student's learning style and preferences so that the presence of the student's disability does not unnecessarily affect learning.

active learning: This term refers to any process that involves students in doing things and thinking about the things they are doing. Active learning might include a spectrum of activities, from a modified lecture format to role-playing, simulation, games, project work, cooperative problem solving, collaborative research, partner learning, service learning, and teaching others.

collaboration: Collaboration is a process in which people "work jointly with others or together esp[ecially] in an intellectual endeavor" (*Merriam Websters Collegiate Dictionary*, 2003, s.v. "collaborate"). In the context of this book, students, teachers, para-educators, and others collaborate to increase the effectiveness of instruction for students in diverse classrooms.

components of self-determined behavior: "choice-making skills, decision-making skills, problem-solving skills, goal-setting and attainment skills, independence, risk-taking and safety skills, self-observation, evaluation, and reinforcement skills, self-instruction skills, self-advocacy and leadership skills, internal locus of control, positive attributions of efficacy and outcome expectancy, self-awareness, self-knowledge" (Wehmeyer, 2007, p. 8).

cooperative process: The cooperative process is an essential element of successful co-teaching and includes face-to-face interaction, positive interdependence, interpersonal skills, monitoring the progress of the co-teachers, and individual accountability.

cooperative learning: Cooperative learning is an instructional structure in which students work together toward mutual goals while simultaneously maintaining positive relationships with group members so as to achieve individual and collective goals.

co-teaching: Co-teaching is two or more people sharing responsibility for teaching the same group of learners.

DI: DI is an acronym for *differentiated instruction,* which is defined as a way for teachers to recognize and react responsively to their students' varying background knowledge, readiness, languages, learning preferences, and interests (Hall, 2002).

ELL: ELL is an acronym for *English language learner.* Teachers of English language learners assist these students either through in-classroom support or resource room support. Instruction of English language learners is sometimes referred to as English as a foreign language (EFL) or English for speakers of other languages (ESOL).

IDEIA: IDEIA is an acronym for the *Individuals with Disabilities Education Improvement Act,* the 2004 reauthorization of the federal legislation that guarantees students with disabilities a free and appropriate education in the least restrictive possible environment. This latest reauthorization emphasizes the importance of students with disabilities having access to the core general education curriculum through highly qualified teachers and providing early learning support for struggling learners through a Response to Intervention (RTI) approach.

MAPs (Making Action Plans): MAPs is a person-centered planning process to lay out a road map for working toward and achieving goals for the focus person. MAPs identifies where the person currently is, what the goal is, and how others will assist the individual in reaching the goal. The framework establishes a person's history, identity, dreams, nightmares, strengths, gifts, needs, and action strategies.

monitoring: Monitoring student progress toward learning goals occurs on a regular basis.

NCLB: NCLB is the acronym for the *No Child Left Behind Act* of 2001, a federal mandate for ensuring that schools and teachers are accountable for the academic progress of all students in public schools.

peer tutoring/partner learning: Cross-age and peer tutoring are methods of instruction in which learners help each other and, in turn, learn by teaching. Peer tutoring is the process by which a competent student, with minimal training and with a teacher's guidance, helps one or more students at the same grade level learn a skill or concept. Cross-age tutors are students in higher grade levels who work with younger students.

peer buddy: A peer buddy is a student of the same age who agrees to be a friend with another student to (a) assist the student in moving throughout the school and grounds, (b) introduce the student to other students, and (c) establish a friendly atmosphere.

peer mediator: A peer mediator is a classmate or a slightly older student who has been trained to conduct a mediation meeting. The mediator makes sure that mediation meetings are helpful and fair.

peer mediator program: A peer mediation gives students who experience conflicts at school a chance to sit face-to-face and talk, uninterrupted, so each person involved in the conflict is heard. After the problem is defined, solutions are created and evaluated. When an agreement is reached by all involved, it is written and signed.

RTI: RtI is an acronym for Response to Intervention, which allows professional educators to design and evaluate academic and behavioral interventions for students at increasing levels of intensity, depending on the students' reactions to the intervention. RTI features the following elements: (1) high-quality classroom instruction, (2) research-based instruction, (3) classroom performance measures, (4) universal screening, (5) continuous progress monitoring, (6) research-based interventions, (7) progress monitoring during interventions, and (8) fidelity measures (Graner, Faggella-Luby, & Fritschmann, 2005).

self determination: Individuals who "know how to choose, know what they want and how to get it. From an awareness of personal needs, self-determined individuals choose goals, then doggedly pursue them. This involves asserting an individual's presence, making his or her needs known, evaluating progress toward meeting goals, adjusting performance and creating unique approaches to solve problems" (Martin & Marshall, 1995, p. 147).

stages of co-teacher development: Just as groups experience stages of development, co-teachers should expect to experience and need different communication skills, depending on whether they are just beginning (forming), deciding how they'll work together (functioning), working through the problems they might face (formulating), or managing conflicts of ideas or procedures about what to emphasize or how to teach certain students (fermenting). The social interaction and communication skills they use at each of these stages will facilitate the development of their cohesiveness as a co-teaching team (Villa et al., 2008).

Resources

RESOURCE A. COOPERATIVE GROUP LEARNING LESSON PLAN TEMPLATE

Author(s): _____ **Subject(s):** _____ **Grade Level(s):** _____

Phase I. ACADEMIC AND SOCIAL OBJECTIVES and ORGANIZATIONAL DECISIONS

Academic Objective(s): **Social Skills Objective(s):**

Group Size:

Group Membership:
- ❑ Heterogeneous
- ❑ Homogeneous
- ❑ Other Considerations for Membership: _____

Room Arrangement:
- ❑ Desk Clusters ❑ Chair Clusters
- ❑ Floor Clusters ❑ Tables
- ❑ Other: _____

Materials Needed:

Distribution:
- ❑ Shared
- ❑ Individual
- ❑ Jigsaw

Phase II. OPENING AND SETTING UP THE LESSON

Structuring of Positive Interdependence	Explanation of Steps of Academic Task	Explanation of Success Criteria	Explanation of Individual Accountability	Explanation of Social Skill Expectations
❑ GOAL ❑ INCENTIVE ❑ RESOURCE ❑ ROLE ❑ SIMULATION ❑ SEQUENCE ❑ OUTSIDE FORCE ❑ ENVIRONMENT ❑ IDENTITY ❑ INTERGROUP COOPERATION				

Phase III. MONITORING AND INTERVENING DURING FACE-TO-FACE INTERACTION

Who Monitors:
- ❑ Teacher(s)
- ❑ Teacher(s) & Students

How Students Are Monitored:
- ❑ Informal Notes
- ❑ Formal Observation Sheet

Intervening:
- ❑ What are likely task or social problems?
- ❑ How do you plan to intervene?

Phase IV. EVALUATING ACADEMIC PERFORMANCE AND GROUP PROCESSING OF SOCIAL SKILL PERFORMANCE

Academic Feedback:

(How and when is academic performance evaluated?)

Social Skills Processing: (How do students reflect on social interactions?)

Student Self-Evaluation, by: _____
Small-Group Processing, by: _____
Whole-Class Processing, by: _____

RESOURCE B. PEER TUTOR AND PARTNER LEARNING LESSON PLAN TEMPLATE

Lesson Objectives:

Content Standards:

What is the room arrangement? Will other spaces outside of the classroom be used?

What materials do the peer tutors and partner learners need?

How is student learning assessed?

What specific supports, aids, or services do select students need?

What does the tutor and tutor partner do before, during, and after the lesson?

Tasks	Peer Tutor/Tutee	Peer Tutor/Tutee
Before		
During		
After		

Evaluation: Where and when will lesson be debriefed and evaluated?

RESOURCE C. CO-TEACHING LESSON PLAN TEMPLATE

Lesson Name: Content: State Standard(s):	When one co-teacher does this . . .	Who	The other co-teacher(s) does this . . .	Who
Anticipatory Set *Motivate and focus students.*				
Input *Teach to objectives; model; actively engage all students.*				
Guided Practice *Students practice under co-teacher's guidance. Check for understanding.*				
Closure *Summary of learning by students.*				
Independent Practice/Transfer *Structured opportunities for independent practice and transfer of learning.*				
Reflection *What went well? What changes will we make to improve the next lesson?*				

RESOURCE D. SYLLABUS FOR HIGH SCHOOL COURSE FOR TEACHING STUDENTS TO BE CO-TEACHERS

Course Description & Syllabus Form
School: Etiwanda High School
Date Prepared: March 2008
Course Title: Assistant Teaching I/II

Brief Course Description: This course gives students the opportunity to work in a classroom environment on a daily basis to provide instructional assistance. The course will teach students fundamental principles and skills in teaching. Under the direction and supervision of a classroom teacher, assistant teachers will provide individual and small-group tutoring and, if appropriate, direct instruction as they practice the teaching skills they learn. The student will attend regular seminars conducted by EHS staff and have the opportunity to attend other inservices.

District Department: Miscellaneous   Series/Course No.:

Reviewed by site division or department: Yes   No ✓

Course already offered at: (circle): ALHS CDS CHS COHS CVHS EHS LOHS MHS <u>NEW</u> ✓ OHS RCHS VVHS

Prerequisite: minimum 3.0 GPA and/or teacher approval

Basic Text: *A Guide to Co-Teaching*   Board approval date:

Other Curriculum Resources: AVID tutor training, periodic seminars.
(Check items below where appropriate)

Length of Course: Quarter   Semester   Year ✓

Type of Course: Required   Elective ✓

Descriptor Level: R   B   P   TP   H   SH   ELD   NA   NCLB   Core ✓

May be repeated for credit? Yes ✓ (max. credits 20)   No

Variable credit? Yes   No ✓ Grade Level: 9   10   11 ✓   12 ✓

Experimental? Yes ✓ (report due mo/yr ____)   No

Meets the following graduation requirements: English   Social Studies ✓ Math
Fine Arts   Science   Foreign Language   P.E.

Focus area: Meets U.C./C.S.U. a-g requirement: Yes   No ✓
                 Career Technical Education Course: Yes   No ✓

Meets Computer Studies Graduation Requirement: Yes   No ✓

Year originally adopted: 2008   Year Reviewed:

COURSE OBJECTIVES/OUTCOMES

The student outcomes/goals to be achieved by the end of the course.

1. Students will demonstrate understanding of basic instructional practices.

2. Students will develop and deliver various components of a lesson in a supporting role with the classroom teacher. These components include anticipatory set, presentation of new material, demonstration, and closure.

3. Assistants will help establish and maintain classroom routines and management and develop rapport with students in the classroom.

4. Students will assist and support students in the class via individual and group tutoring.

5. Students will develop skills in the use of various classroom technologies.

6. Students will gain an understanding of various student needs based on such indicators as prior knowledge and multiple intelligences.

7. Students will work with the classroom teacher to write performance objectives, plan units, and examine standards.

8. Students will demonstrate understanding of Bloom's taxonomy, Costa's levels of questioning, AVID methodologies, and Marzano's strategies for increasing student achievement.

9. Students will develop and practice public speaking and presentational skills.

10. Students will practice various approaches to co-teaching: supportive, parallel, complementary, and team teaching.

11. Students will learn about various assessments and assessment practices.

[Syllabus to be written in topic outline form, which will include appropriate references to basic text and/or curriculum resources. Syllabus must be written to reflect each grading period (by week, quarter, etc.). Include suggested homework policy and suggested grading criteria where appropriate. The syllabus should not be a copy of the table of contents.]

COURSE OUTLINE

First Quarter

Student's role
Instructional partner
Cooperative process
Roles and responsibilities
Class observations and practical experience
Lesson planning
Anticipatory set
Objective
Presenting new material
Modeling
Checking for understanding
Guided practice
Closure
Sample lesson plans
Classroom routines and procedures
Purpose
Strategies and techniques
Blackboard configuration (BBC)
Classroom management
Tutor training
Individualized tutoring strategies
AVID tutoring strategies and methodologies
Tutorial skills
Organizational skills
WICR strategies
Cornell note taking
Costa's levels of questioning

Second Quarter

Continue above
Add four approaches to co-teaching:
    Supportive
    Parallel
    Complementary
    Team Teaching

Third Quarter

Continue above
Add effective instructional practices
Performance criteria

Modeling/demonstration
Marzano's strategies
Bloom's taxonomy
Multiple intelligences
Presentational skills
Public speaking
Appearance
Classroom technology
LCD projector
DVD
Computer
PowerPoint
Assessments
Rubrics

Fourth Quarter

Continuing practice and study of above
Add final project

Course Grading Policy

1. Attendance and participation in regular seminars and training

2. Self-assessments

3. Assessments by teacher

4. Classroom surveys

5. Assistant Teaching Portfolio

   The Assistant Teaching Portfolio is a record of the student's experience. The teacher and student will negotiate the contents of the portfolio and the rubric to assess it. The portfolio may include the following:

   - Journal entries and other writing assignments
   - Objectives and goals, lesson/unit plans
   - Self-assessments and reflection
   - Reports on progress of individuals in class
   - Videos
   - Self-analysis of a lesson taught

Homework Policy

Complete homework as assigned by the teacher as needed.

SOURCE: Adapted from materials developed by James Cronin, high school administrator at Etiwanda High School, CA; used with permission.

RESOURCE E. TEMPLATE FOR PRODUCT-ACTIVITY MATRIX INTEGRATING BLOOM'S TAXONOMY AND GARDNER'S MULTIPLE INTELLIGENCE THEORY

	Knowledge	Comprehension	Application	Analysis	Synthesis	Evaluation
Verbal/ Linguistic						
Visual/ Spatial						
Logical/ Mathematical						
Naturalist						
Musical/ Rhythmic						
Bodily/ Kinesthetic						
Intrapersonal						
Interpersonal						

RESOURCE F. TEMPLATE FOR FACTS ABOUT THE LEARNER, CLASSROOM DEMANDS, MISMATCHES, AND POTENTIAL SOLUTIONS

Facts About the Learner	Facts About the Classroom Demands	Mismatches	Potential Solutions

Resource G. Student Collaboration Quiz

Directions: Please circle the rating that best fits your own experience as a student.

1. How often were you expected to support the academic and social learning of other students, as well as be accountable for your own learning, by working in cooperative groups?

   Never   Rarely   Sometimes   Often   Very Often

2. Were you, as a student, given the opportunity and training to serve as an instructor for a peer?

   Never   Rarely   Sometimes   Often   Very Often

3. Were you, as a student, given the opportunity to receive instruction from a trained peer?

   Never   Rarely   Sometimes   Often   Very Often

4. How often were you involved in a discussion of the teaching act with an instructor?

   Never   Rarely   Sometimes   Often   Very Often

5. Were you, as a student, given the opportunity to co-teach a class with an adult?

   Never   Rarely   Sometimes   Often   Very Often

6. How often were you taught creative problem-solving strategies and given an opportunity to employ them to solve academic or behavioral challenges?

   Never   Rarely   Sometimes   Often   Very Often

7. How often were you asked to evaluate your own learning?

   Never   Rarely   Sometimes   Often   Very Often

8. How often were you given the opportunity to assist in determining the educational outcomes for you and your classmates?

   Never   Rarely   Sometimes   Often   Very Often

9. How often were you given the opportunity to advocate for the educational interests of a classmate or asked to assist in determining modifications and accommodations to curriculum?

   Never   Rarely   Sometimes   Often   Very Often

10. How often were you asked to provide your teachers with feedback as to the effectiveness and appropriateness of their instruction and classroom management?

   Never   Rarely   Sometimes   Often   Very Often

11. Were you, as a student, given the opportunity and training to serve as a mediator of conflict between peers?

   Never   Rarely   Sometimes   Often   Very Often

12. How often were you, as a student, encouraged to bring a support person to a difficult meeting to provide you with moral support?

   Never   Rarely   Sometimes   Often   Very Often

13. How often were you provided the opportunity to lead or facilitate meetings that were addressing your academic progress and/or future (e.g., developing personal learning plans, student-parent-teacher conferences, an IEP meeting)?

   Never   Rarely   Sometimes   Often   Very Often

14. How often did you participate as an equal with teachers, administrators, and community members on school committees (e.g., curriculum committee, discipline committee, hiring committee, school board)?

   Never   Rarely   Sometimes   Often   Very Often

15. How often did you, as a student, feel that the school "belonged" to you, that school experiences were structured primarily with student interests in mind?

   Never   Rarely   Sometimes   Often   Very Often

References

Abdel Hamid Soliman, S. (2005). *Systems and creative thinking.* Cairo, Egypt: Center for Advancement of Postgraduate Studies and Research in Engineering Sciences, Faculty of Engineering, Cairo University. Retrieved November 16, 2009, from http://www.pathways.cu.edu.eg/subpages/Creativity-Engine.htm

Adams, J. (2001). *Conceptual blockbusting: A guide to better ideas* (4th ed.). New York: Basic Books.

Alexander, D., Gomezllanos, J., & Sanchez, G. (2008, July). *System kids: From our perspective.* Presentation at the 10th Annual San Diego Summer Leadership Institute, California State University—San Marcos, CA.

Anliker, J. A., Drake, L. T., & Pacholski, J. (1993). Impacts of a multi-layered nutrition program: Teenagers teaching children. *Journal of Nutrition Education, 25,* 140–143.

Apple, M. W., & Beane, J. A. (1995). *Democratic schools.* Alexandria, VA: Association for Supervision and Curriculum Development.

Armstrong, T. (2009). *Multiple intelligences in the classroom* (3rd ed.). Alexandria, VA: Association for Supervision and Curriculum Development.

Barbetta, P. M., Miller, A. D., & Peters, M. T. (1991). Tugmate: A cross-age tutoring program to teach sight vocabulary. *Education and Treatment of Children, 14*(1), 19–37.

Barrie, W., & McDonald, J. (2002). Administrative support for student-led individualized education programs. *Remedial and Special Education, 23*(2), 116–121.

Barton, D. (2003). *Helping students develop their IEPs: Making it accessible to every student.* Unpublished master's thesis, California State University—San Marcos, San Marcos.

Befring, E., Thousand, J., & Nevin, A. (2000). From normalization to enrichment: A retrospective analysis of the transformation of special education principles. In R. A. Villa & J. S. Thousand (Eds.). *Restructuring for caring and effective education: Piecing the puzzle together* (2nd ed., pp. 558–574). Baltimore, MD: Paul H. Brookes.

Benjamin, S. (1989). An ideascape for education: What futurists recommend. *Educational Leadership, 7*(1), 8–14.

Bennett, B., Rolheiser-Bennett, C., & Stevahn, L. (1991). *Cooperative learning: Where heart meets mind.* Toronto, Canada: Educational Connections.

Berkowitz, M. W., & Simmons, P. (2003). Integrating science education and character education. In D. L. Zeidler, *The role of moral reasoning on socioscientific issues and discourse in science education* (pp. 117–138). Norwell, MA: Kluwer Academic.

Block, M. E., Oberweiser, B., & Bain, M. (1995). Using classwide peer tutoring to facilitate inclusions with disabilities in regular physical education. *Physical Educator, 52*(1), 47–56.

Bloom, B. S., Englehart, M. B., Furst, E. J., Hill, W. H., & Krathwohl, D. R. (Eds.). (1956). *Taxonomy of educational objectives: The classification of educational goals; Handbook I. Cognitive domain.* New York: McKay.

Bodine, R., Crawford, D., & Schrumpf, F. (1994). *Creating the peaceable school: A comprehensive program for teaching conflict resolution.* Champaign, IL: Research Press.

Bombara, L., & Kern, L. (2004). *Individual supports for students with problem behavior: Designing positive behavior plans.* New York: Guilford Press.

Brendtro, L. K., Brokenleg, M., & Van Bockern, S. (2002). *Reclaiming youth at risk: Our hope for the future* (Rev. ed.). Bloomington, IN: National Educational Service.

Brown, P., & Dean, E. (2009, July). *Listen to the voice of students: Student-led IEPs and self-advocacy.* Paper presented at the 11th Annual San Diego Summer Leadership Institute, San Diego, CA.

Carr, E. G., & Ogle, D. (1987). K-W-L-plus: A strategy for comprehension and summarization. *Journal of Reading, 21*(8), 684–689.

Carter, C. (1997). Why reciprocal teaching? *Educational Leadership, 54*(6), 64–68.

Casella, R. (2000). The benefits of peer mediation in the context of urban conflict and program status. *Urban Education, 35*(3), 324–355.

Conn-Powers, C. (1988). *Cooperative group lesson plan.* Unpublished manuscript submitted in partial fulfillment of requirements for the Educational Specialist graduate program, Professor J. S. Thousand, University of Vermont, Department of Special Education, College of Education and Social Services.

Costa, A. (2000). *Activating and engaging habits of mind.* Alexandria, VA: Association for Supervision and Curriculum Development.

Cowie, H., & Hutson, N. (2005). Peer support: A strategy to help bystanders challenge school bullying. *Pastoral Care in Education, 23*(2), 40–44.

Craig, W. L., & Gould, P. M. (2007). *The two tasks of the Christian scholar: Redeeming the soul, redeeming the mind.* Wheaton, IL: Crossway Books.

Cremin, H. (2002). Pupils resolving disputes: Successful peer mediation schemes share their secrets. *Support for Learning, 17*(3), 138–143.

Cummings, C., Nelson, C., & Shaw, D. (2002). *Teaching makes a difference.* Edmonds, WA: Teaching.

Curwin, R. L., & Mendler, A. N. (1988). *Discipline with dignity.* Alexandria, VA: Association for Supervision and Curriculum Development.

Curwin, R. L., Mendler, A. N., & Mendler, B. D. (2008). *Discipline with dignity: New challenges, new solutions* (3rd ed.). Alexandria, VA: Association for Supervision and Curriculum Development.

Damon, W., & Phelps, E. (1989). Critical distinctions among three approaches. In N. M. Webb (Ed.), *Peer interaction, problem-solving, and cognition: Multidisciplinary perspectives* (pp. 9–19). New York: Pergamon Press.

Davidson, N. (2002). Cooperative and collaborative learning: An integrative perspective. In J. S. Thousand, R. A. Villa, & A. I. Nevin (Eds.), *Creativity and collaborative learning: The practical guide to empowering students, teachers, and families* (2nd ed., pp. 181–195). Baltimore: Paul H. Brookes.

de Bono, E. (1985). *Six thinking hats.* Boston: Little Brown.

de Bono, E. (1992). *Serious creativity: Using the power of lateral thinking to create new ideas.* New York: Harper Business.

Developmental Studies Center. (1996). *Ways we want our class to be: Class meetings that build commitment to kindness and learning.* Oakland, CA: Author.

Draze, D. (2005). *Creative problem solving for kids: Grades 5–8.* Waco, TX: Prufrock Press.

Duke, N. K., & Pearson, P. D. (2002). Effective practices for developing reading comprehension. In A. E. Farstup & S. J. Samuels (Eds.), *What research has to say about reading instruction* (pp. 205–242). Newark, DE: International Reading Association.

Durlak, J. A., Weissberg, R. P., Taylor, R. D., Dymnicki, A. B., & Schellinger, K. B. (2008). *The positive impact of social and emotional learning for kindergarten to eighth-grade students: Findings from three scientific reviews; Executive summary.* Retrieved November 16, 2009, from http://www.casel.org/downloads/PackardES.pdf

Education Northwest. (2001). *School-wide prevention of bullying.* Portland, OR: Author. Retrieved November 25, 2009, from http://educationnorthwest.org/webfm_send/465

Elbaum, B., Vaughn, S., Hughes, M. T., & Moody, S. W. (2000). How effective are one-to-one tutoring programs in reading for elementary students at risk for reading failure? A meta-analysis of the intervention research. *Journal of Educational Psychology, 92,* 605–619.

Elias, M. J., Gara, M. A., Schuyler, T. F., Branden-Muller, L. R., & Sayette, M. A. (1991). The promotion of social competence: Longitudinal study of a preventive school-based program. *American Journal of Orthopsychiatry, 61,* 409–417.

Fairfield, P. (2008). *Why democracy?* New York: SUNY Press.

Faltis, C. (1993). Critical issues in the use of sheltered content teaching in high school bilingual programs. *Peabody Journal of Education, 69,* 136–151.

Falvey, M. A., Forest, M. S., Pearpoint, J., & Rosenberg, R. L. (2002). Building connections. In J. S. Thousand, R. A. Villa, and A. I. Nevin (Eds.), *Creativity and collaborative learning: The practical guide to empowering teachers, students, and parents* (2nd ed., pp. 29–54). Baltimore: Paul H. Brookes.

Field, S., & Hoffman, A. (1996). *Steps to Self-Determination curriculum.* Austin, TX: Pro-Ed.

Field, S., Martin, J., Miller, R., Ward, M., & Wehmeyer, M. (1998). *A practical guide for teaching self-determination.* Reston, VA: Council for Exceptional Children.

Fisher, D., & Frey, N. (2007). *Checking for understanding: Formative assessment techniques for your classroom.* Alexandria, VA: Association for Supervision and Curriculum Development.

Fisher, D., & Frey, N. (2008). *Better learning through structured teaching: A framework for the gradual release of responsibility.* Alexandria, VA: Association for Supervision and Curriculum Development.

Fisher, R., Ury, W., & Patton, B. (1991). *Getting to yes: Negotiating agreement without giving in.* New York: Penguin.

Fox, T. (1995). *Student-centered education: Creating a collaborative school climate through Personal Learning Plans.* Progress report prepared for the Vermont Statewide Systems Change Project. Burlington, VT: University of Vermont.

Froh, J. J., Kashdan, T. B., Ozimkowski, K. M., & Miller, N. (2009). Who benefits the most from a gratitude intervention in children and adolescents? Examining positive affect as a moderator. *Journal of Positive Psychology, 4*(5), 408–422.

Froh, J. J., Kashdan, T. B., & Yurkewicz, C. (2009). Gratitude and subjective well-being in early adolescence: Examining mechanisms and gender differences. *Journal of Adolescence, 32,* 633–650.

Fuchs, D., Fuchs, L. S., Mathes, P., & Martinez, E. (2002). Preliminary evidence on the social standing of students with learning disabilities in PALS and non-PALS classrooms. *Learning Disabilities Research and Practice, 17,* 205–215.

Fuchs, D., Fuchs, L. S., Thompson, A., Svenson, E., Yen, L., Otaiba, S. A., et al. (2001). Peer-assisted learning strategies in reading. *Remedial and Special Education, 22*(1), 15–21.

Fuchs, L. S., Fuchs, D., Yazdin, L., & Powell, S. R. (2002). Enhancing first-grade children's mathematical development with peer-assisted learning strategies. *School Psychology Review, 31,* 569–583.

Fuller, R. B. (1991). *Critical path.* New York: St. Martin's Press.

Gallup Organization. (2000, October 2). Teens see increase in fighting at school [Press release]. Washington, DC: Gallup News Service.

Gardner, H. (1983). *Frames of mind: The theory of multiple intelligences.* New York: Basic Books.

Garii, B., & SooHoo, S. (2008). Hidden in plain sight: The invisibility of homophobic harassment and girl-on-girl bullying in schools. *Excelsior, 3*(1), 83–101.

Gersten, R., & Baker, S. (2000). What we know about effective instructional practices for English-language learners. *Exceptional Children, 66,* 454–470.

Giangreco, M. F., Cloninger, C. J., Dennis, R. E., & Edelman, S. W. (2002). Problem-solving methods to facilitate inclusive education. In J. S. Thousand, R. A. Villa, & A. I. Nevin (Eds.), *Creativity and collaborative learning: The practical guide to empowering students, teachers, and families* (2nd ed., pp. 111–135). Baltimore: Paul H. Brookes.

Giesecke, D., Cartledge, G., & Gardner, R. (1993). Low-achieving students as successful cross-age tutors. *Preventing School Failure, 37*(3), 34–43.

Glasser, W. (1986). *Control theory in the classroom.* New York: HarperCollins.

Glasser, W. (1990). *The quality school: Managing students without coercion.* New York: HarperCollins.

Glasser, W. (1998). *Choice theory: A new psychology of personal freedom.* New York: Perennial.

Goldstein, A. (1999). *The PREPARE curriculum: Teaching prosocial competencies.* Champaign, IL: Research Press.

Goleman, D., Kaufman, P., & Ray, M. (1993). *The creative spirit* [companion to PBS television series]. New York: PLUME.

Graner, P., Faggella-Luby, M., & Fritschmann, N. (2005). An overview of Responsiveness to Intervention: What practitioners ought to know. *Topics in Language Disorders, 25*(2), 93–105.

Greene, M. (1985). A philosophic look at merit and mastery in education. *Elementary School Journal, 86*(1), 17–26.

Greene, M. (1988). *The dialectic of freedom.* New York: Teachers College, Columbia University.

Guskey, T. R., & Anderman, E. M. (2008). Students at bat. *Educational Leadership, 66*(3), 8–14.

Hall, T. (2002). *Differentiated instruction.* Wakefield, MA: National Center on Accessing the General Curriculum. Retrieved November 16, 2009, from http://www.cast .org/publications/ncac/ncac_diffinstruc.html

Hall, T., & Stegila, A. (2009). *Peer mediated instruction and intervention.* Wakefield, MA: National Center on Accessing the General Curriculum. Retrieved November 16, 2009, from http://www.cast.org/publications/ncac/ncac_peermii.html

Hammer, M. (2004). Using the self-advocacy strategy to increase student participation in IEP conferences. *Intervention in School and Clinic, 39*(5), 295–300.

Hapner, A., & Imel, B. (2002). The students' voices: "Teachers started to listen and show respect." *Remedial and Special Education, 23*(2), 116–121.

Hawkins, J. D., Guo, J., Hill, K. G., Battin-Pearson, S., & Abbott, R. D. (2001). Long-term effects of the Seattle Social Development Intervention on school bonding trajectories. *Applied Developmental Science, 5*(4), 225–236.

Hazel, J. S., Schumaker, J. E., Sherman, J. A., & Sheldon, J. (1995). *ASSET: A social skills program for adolescents* [DVD and book]. Champaign, IL: Research Press.

Hiraga, R., Mizaki, R., & Fujishiro, I. (2002). Performance visualization—A new challenge to music through visualization. In *Proceedings of the 10th ACM International Conference on Multimedia* (pp. 239–242). New York: ACM. Retrieved November 16, 2009, from http://portal.acm.org/citation.cfm?id=641054

Hoffman, A., & Field, S. (2005). *Steps to Self-Determination: A curriculum to help adolescents learn to achieve their goals* (2nd ed.). Austin, TX: Pro-Ed.

Hoover, J., & Oliver, R. (2008). *The bullying prevention handbook: A guide for teachers and counselors* (2nd ed.). Bloomington, IN: Solution Tree.

Jaben, T. H., Treffinger, D. J., Whelan, R. J., Hudson, F. G., Stainback, S. B., & Stainback, W. (1982). Impact of instruction on learning disabled students' creative thinking. *Psychology in Schools, 19*(3), 371–373.

Janssen, J. J., & Sheikh, A. A. (1994). Enhancing athletic performance through imagery: An overview. In A. A. Sheikh & E. R. Korn (Eds.), *Imagery in sports and physical performance* (pp. 1–22). Amityville, NY: Baywood.

Johnson, D. W., & Johnson, R. T. (1989). *Cooperation and competition: Theory and research.* Edina, MN: Interaction Book Company.

Johnson, D. W., & Johnson, R. T. (1994). An overview of cooperative learning. In J. S. Thousand, R. A. Villa, & A. I. Nevin (Eds.), *Creativity and collaborative learning: The practical guide to empowering students, teachers, and families* (pp. 31–44). Baltimore: Paul H. Brookes.

Johnson, D. W., & Johnson, R. T. (1995a). *Teaching students to be peacemakers program* (3rd ed.). Edina, MN: Interaction Book Company.

Johnson, D. W., & Johnson, R. T. (1995b). *Creative controversy: Intellectual challenge in the classroom* (3rd ed.). Edina, MN: Interaction Book Company.

Johnson, D. W., & Johnson, R. T. (1996a). Conflict resolution and peer mediation programs in elementary and secondary schools: A review of the research. *Review of Educational Research, 66*(4), 459–506.

Johnson, D. W., & Johnson, R. T. (1996b). Cooperative learning and traditional American values. *National Association for Secondary School Principals Bulletin, 80*(579), 11–18.

Johnson, D. W., & Johnson, R. T. (1999). *Learning together and alone: Cooperative, competitive, and individualistic learning* (5th ed.). Needham Heights, MA: Allyn & Bacon.

Johnson, D. W., & Johnson, R. T. (2000). Cooperative learning, values, and culturally plural classrooms. In M. Leicester, S. Modgill, & C. Modgill (Eds.), *Classroom issues: Practice, pedagogy, and curriculum; Vol 3. Education, culture, and values* (pp. 15–29). London: Falmer Press.

Johnson, D. W., & Johnson, R. T. (2002). Ensuring diversity is positive: Cooperative community, constructive conflict, and civic values. In J. S. Thousand, R. A. Villa, & A. I. Nevin (Eds.), *Creativity and collaborative learning: The practical guide to empowering students, teachers, and families* (2nd ed., pp. 197–208). Baltimore: Paul H. Brookes.

Johnson, D. W., & Johnson, R. T. (2004). Implementing the "Teaching Students to Be Peacemakers Program." *Theory Into Practice, 43*(1), 68–79.

Johnson, D. W., & Johnson, R. T. (2009). An educational psychology success story: Social interdependence theory and cooperative learning. *Educational Researcher, 38*(5), 365–379.

Johnson, D. W., Johnson, R. T., Dudley, B., & Burnett, R. (1992). Teaching students to be peer mediators. *Educational Leadership, 50*(1), 10–13.

Johnson, D. W., Johnson, R. T., & Johnson Holubec, E. (1994a). *Cooperative learning in the classroom.* Alexandria, VA: Association for Supervision and Curriculum Development.

Johnson, D. W., Johnson, R. T., & Johnson Holubec, E. (1994b). *The new circles of learning: Cooperation in the classroom and school.* Alexandria, VA: Association for Supervision and Curriculum Development.

Johnson, D. W., Johnson, R. T., & Smith, K. (1998). *Active learning: Cooperation in the college classroom* (2nd ed.). Edina, MN: Interaction Book Company.

Johnson-Glenberg, M. (2000). Training reading comprehension in adequate decoders/poor comprehenders: Verbal versus visual strategies. *Journal of Educational Psychology, 92*(4), 772–782.

Jones, T. S. (1998). Research supports effectiveness of peer mediation. *The Fourth R, 82,* 1–25.

Kagan, S., & Kagan, M. (2008). *Kagan cooperative learning.* San Clemente, CA: Kagan Cooperative Learning.

Kagan, S., Kyle, P., & Scott, S. (2004). *Win-win discipline: Strategies for all discipline problems.* San Clemente, CA: Kagan.

Karan, O. C. (2004). Six factors inhibiting the use of peer mediation in a junior high school. *Professional School Counseling, 7*(4), 283–291.

Kesson, K., Koliba, C. J., & Paxton, K. (2002). Democratic education and the creation of a loving and just community. In J. S. Thousand, R. A. Villa, and A. I. Nevin (Eds.), *Creativity and collaborative learning: The practical guide to empowering teachers, students, and parents* (2nd ed., pp. 3–12). Baltimore: Paul H. Brookes.

Keyes, M., & Owens-Johnson, L. (2003). Developing person-centered IEPs. *Intervention in School and Clinic, 38*(3), 145–152.

Konrad, M., & Test, D. (2004). Teaching middle-school students with disabilities to use an IEP template. *Career Development for Exceptional Individuals, 27*(1), 101–124.

Kourea, L., Cartledge, G., & Musti-Rao, S. (2007). Improving the reading skills of urban elementary students through total class peer tutoring. *Remedial and Special Education, 28*(3), 95–107.

Lachtermacher-Truinfol, M., & Hines, P. J. (2002). *Science Controversies: Online Partnerships in Education (SCOPE).* Retrieved November 16, 2009, from the National Institute of Standards and Technology Web site: http://www.nist.gov/public_affairs/Posters/scope.htm

LaPlant, L., & Zane, N. (1994). Partner learning systems. In J. S. Thousand, R. A. Villa, & A. I. Nevin. *Creativity and collaborative learning: A practical guide to empowering students and teachers* (pp. 261–274). Baltimore: Paul H. Brookes.

LaPlant, L., & Zane, N. (2002). Partner learning systems. In J. S. Thousand, R. A. Villa, & A. I. Nevin (Eds.), *Creativity and collaborative learning: A practical guide to empowering students, teachers, and families* (2nd ed., pp. 271–283). Baltimore: Paul H. Brookes.

Leff, H. L. (1984). *Playful perception: Choosing how to experience your world.* Burlington, VT: Waterfront Books.

Leff, H. L., & Nevin, A. I. (1994). *Turning learning inside out.* Tucson, AZ: Zephyr Press.

Leff, H. L., Thousand, J. S., Nevin, A. I., & Quiocho, A. M. L. (2002). Awareness plans for facilitating creative thinking. In J. S. Thousand, R. A. Villa, & A. I. Nevin (Eds.), *Creativity and collaborative learning: The practical guide to empowering students, teachers, and families* (2nd ed., pp. 157–173). Baltimore: Paul H. Brookes.

Longwill, A. W., & Kleinert, H. L. (1998). The unexpected benefits of high school peer tutoring. *Teaching Exceptional Children, 3*(4), 60–65.

Lovitt, T. (1991). *Preventing school dropouts: Tactics for at-risk, remedial, and mildly handicapped adolescents.* Austin, TX: Pro-Ed.

Maheady, L., Sacca, M. K., & Harper, G. F. (1988). Classwide peer tutoring with mildly handicapped high school students. *Exceptional Children, 55*(1), 52–59.

Malian, I., & Nevin, A. I. (2002). A review of self-determination literature: Implications for practitioners. *Remedial and Special Education, 23*(2), 68–74.

Marks, S. U. (2008). Self-determination for students with intellectual disabilities and why I want educators to know what it means. *Phi Delta Kappan, 90*(1), 55–58.

Martin, J. E., & Marshall, L. H. (1995). ChoiceMaker: A comprehensive self-determination transition program. *Intervention in School and Clinic, 30*(3) 147–156.

Martin, J. E., van Dycke, J., Christensen, W. R., Greene, B., Gardner, J. E., & Lovett, D. (2006). Increasing student participation in IEP meetings: Establishing the self-directed IEP as an evidenced-based practice. *Exceptional Children, 72*(3), 299–303.

Marzano, R., Pickering, D., & Pollack, J. (2001). *Classroom instruction that works: Research-based strategies for increasing student achievement.* Alexandria, VA: Association for Supervision and Curriculum Development.

Mason, C., McGahee-Kovac, M., & Johnson, L. (2004). How to help students lead their own IEP meetings. *Teaching Exceptional Children, 36*(3), 18–25.

Mason, C., McGahee-Kovac, M., Johnson, L., & Stillerman, S. (2002). Implementing student-led IEPs: Student participation and student and teacher reactions. *Career Development for Exceptional Individuals, 25*(2), 171–192.

Masters, K., Fuchs, D., & Fuchs, L. (2002). Using peer tutoring to prevent early reading failure. In J. S. Thousand, R. A. Villa, & A. I. Nevin (Eds.), *Creativity and collaborative learning: The practical guide to empowering students, teachers, and families* (2nd ed., pp. 235–246). Baltimore: Paul H. Brookes.

Mastropieri, M., Scruggs, T., Mohler, L., Beranek, M., Spencer, V., et al. (2002). Can middle school learners with serious reading difficulties help each other and learn anything? *Learning Disabilities Research & Practice, 16*(1), 18–27.

McGahee-Kovac, M. (2002). *A student's guide to the IEP* (2nd ed.). Retrieved November 16, 2009, http://www.nichcy.org/InformationResources/Documents/NICHCY%20PUBS/st1.pdf

McGreevy, K. (2005). School violence is under-reported. *School Reform News.* Retrieved November 16, 2009, from http://www.heartland.org/policybot/results/16680/School_Violence_Is_UnderReported.html

McIntosh, J. E., & Meacham, A. W. (1992). *Creative problem solving in the classroom.* Waco, TX: Prufrock Press.

McNeil, M. (1994). A peer tutoring spelling program for children with autism. In J. S. Thousand, R. A. Villa, & A. I. Nevin (Eds.), *Creativity and collaborative learning: A practical guide to empowering students and teachers* (pp. 243–259). Baltimore: Paul H. Brookes.

McNeil, M., & Hood, A. (2002). Partner learning: The power source for students, schools, and communities. In J. S. Thousand, R. A. Villa, & A. I. Nevin (Eds.), *Creativity and collaborative learning: The practical guide to empowering students, teachers, and families* (2nd ed., pp. 247–265). Baltimore: Paul H. Brookes.

Merriam-Websters collegiate dictionary (11th ed.). (2003). Springfield, MA: Merriam-Webster.

Mithaug, D. E. (2003). Identifying what we know about self-determination. In M. L. Wehmeyer, B. Avery, D. Mithaug, & R. Stancliffe (Eds.), *Theory in self-determination: Foundations for educational practice.* Springfield, IL: Charles C Thomas.

Murray, F. B. (2002). Why understanding the theoretical basis of cooperative learning enhances teaching success. In J. S. Thousand, R. A. Villa, & A. I. Nevin (Eds.), *Creativity and collaborative learning: The practical guide to empowering students, teachers, and families* (2nd ed., pp. 175–180). Baltimore: Paul H. Brookes.

Nazzal, A. (2002). Peer tutoring and at-risk students: An exploratory study. *Action in Teacher Education, 24*(1), 68–80.

Nevin, A. I. (with Stephen, Jamie, & Joanie). (2004). Managing educational supports: Advice from students with disabilities. In C. Bowman & P. Jaeger (Eds.), *A guide to high school success for students with disabilities* (pp. 98–107). Westport, CT: Greenwood Press.

Nevin, A. I., Thousand, J. S., & Villa, R. A. (2009). *A guide to co-teaching with paraeducators: Practical tips for K–12 educators.* Thousand Oaks, CA: Corwin.

Noddings, N. (1992). *The challenge to care in schools.* New York: Teachers College Press.

Noddings, N. (2005). Caring in education. *The encyclopedia of informal learning.* Retrieved July 20, 2009, from http://infed.org/biblio/noddings_caring_in_education.htm

Olweus Bullying Prevention Program. (2009). Retrieved November 16, 2009, from http://www.olweus.org

Olweus, D. (1993). *Bullying at school: What we know and what we can do.* Cambridge, MA: Blackwell.

Osborn, A. F. (1993). *Applied imagination: Principles and procedures of creative problem-solving* (3rd ed.). Amherst, MA: Creative Education Foundation Press. (First edition published 1953).

Palincsar, A. S., & Brown, A. L. (1984). Reciprocal teaching of comprehension: Fostering and monitoring activities. *Cognition and Instruction, 1*(2), 117–175.

Palincsar, A. S., & Brown, A. L. (1988). Advances in improving the cognitive performance of handicapped students. In M. Wang, M. Reynolds, & H. Walberg (Eds.), *Handbook of special education: Characteristics and adaptive education* (pp. 93–112). NY: Pergamon.

Parnes, S. J. (1992a). *Source book for creative problem-solving: A fifty year digest of proven innovation processes.* Amherst, MA: Creative Education Foundation Press.

Parnes, S. J. (1992b). *Visionizing: State-of-the-art processes for encouraging innovative excellence.* Amherst, MA: Creative Education Foundation Press.

Pauley, J. A., Bradley, D. F., & Pauley, J. F. (2002). *Here's how to reach me: Matching instruction to personality types in your classroom.* Baltimore: Paul H. Brookes.

Pearson, P. D., & Gallagher, G. (1983). The gradual release of responsibility model of instruction. *Contemporary Educational Psychology, 8,* 112–123.

Popham, W. J. (2008). The assessment-savvy student. *Educational Leadership, 66*(3), 80–82.

Prater, M., Serna, L., & Nakamura, K. (1999). Impact of peer teaching on the acquisition of social skills by adolescents with learning disabilities. *Journal of Learning Disabilities, 22,* 455–461.

Redl, F., & Wineman, D. (1952). *Controls from within: Techniques for the treatment of the aggressive child.* New York: Free Press.

Room 405 Website. (2005). *Problem summary statement.* Retrieved November 16, 2009, from http://www.projectcitizen405.com/Problem.htm

Roscoe, R. D., & Chi, M. T. H. (2007). Understanding tutor learning: Knowledge-building and knowledge-telling in peer tutors' explanations and questions. *Review of Educational Research, 77*(4), 534–574.

Rosenthal, S. (1994). Students as teachers: At-risk high school students teach science to fourth-graders. *Thrust for Educational Leadership, 23*(6), 36–38.

San Diego County Office of Education. (2009). *AVID.* Retrieved November 16, 2009, from http://www.sdcoe.net/lret/avid/

Sandomierski, T., Kincaid, D., & Algozzine, B. (2007). Response to Intervention and Positive Behavior Support: Brothers from different mothers or sisters with different misters? *BPIS Newsletter, 4*(2). Retrieved November 16, 2009, from http://www.pbis.org/pbis_newsletter/volume_4/issue2.aspx

Schrumpf, F., Crawford, D., & Bodine, R. (1997). *Peer mediation: Conflict resolution in schools* (Rev. ed.). Champaign, IL: Research Press.

Schrumpf, F., Crawford, D., & Usadel, C. (1991). *Peer mediation: Conflict resolution in the schools.* Champaign, IL: Research Press.

Schrumpf, F., & Janson, G. G. (2002). The role of students in resolving conflict. In J. S. Thousand, R. A. Villa, & A. I. Nevin (Eds.), *Creativity and collaborative learning: The practical guide to empowering students, teachers, and families* (2nd ed., pp. 283–302). Baltimore: Paul H. Brookes.

Schumaker, H. (2006). *The student-led Individual Education Program (IEP) process: An approach to increasing confidence and self-advocacy in 8th grade students with special learning needs.* Unpublished master's thesis, California State University—San Marcos.

Sears, J., Bishop, A., & Stevens, E. (1989). Teaching Miranda rights to students who have mental retardation. *Teaching Exceptional Children, 21*(3), 38–42.

Sennett, F. (2004). *400 quotable quotes from the world's leading educators.* Thousand Oaks, CA: Corwin.

Silverstein, S. (1981). *A light in the attic.* New York: Harper & Row.

Solomon, D., Battistich, V., Watson, M., Schaps, E., & Lewis, C. (2000). A six-district study of educational change: Direct and mediated effects of the child development project. *Social Psychology of Education, 4*(1), 3–51.

Steege, M. W., & Watson, T. S. (2009). *Conducting school-based functional behavioral assessments: A practical guide.* New York: Guilford Press.

Stevahn, L. (2004). Integrating conflict resolution training into the curriculum. *Theory Into Practice, 43*(1), 50–58.

Test, D. W., Browder, D. M., Karvonen, M., Wood, W., & Algozzine, B. (2002). Writing lesson plans for promoting self-determination. *Teaching Exceptional Children, 35*(1), 8, 10–14.

Thorpe, S. (2000). *How to think like Einstein: Simple ways to break the rules and discover your hidden genius.* New York: Sourcebooks.

Thousand, J. S., Villa, R. A., & Nevin, A. I. (2002). *Creativity and collaborative learning: The practical guide to empowering students, teachers, and families* (2nd ed.). Baltimore: Paul H. Brookes.

Thousand, J. S., Villa, R. A., & Nevin, A. I. (2007). *Differentiating instruction: Collaborative planning and teaching for universally designed learning.* Thousand Oaks, CA: Corwin.

Thurston, J. A. (1994). Art partners: A new focus on peer teaching. *School Arts, 94,* 41–42.

Trainor, A. (2005). Self-determination perceptions and behaviors of diverse students with LD during the transition planning process. *Journal of Learning Disabilities, 38*(3), 233–249.

Trainor, A. (2007). Person-centered planning in two culturally distinct communities: Responding to divergent needs and preferences. *Career Development for Exceptional Individuals, 30*(2), 92–103.

Treffinger, D. J. (2000). *Practice problems for creative problem solving* (3rd ed.). Waco, TX: Prufrock Press.

Treffinger, D. J., Isaksen, S. G., & Stead-Dorval, K. B. (2006). *Creative problem solving: An introduction* (4th ed.). Waco, TX: Prufrock Press.

Van Bockern, S., Brendtro, L., & Brokenleg, M. (2000). Reclaiming our youth. In R. A. Villa and J. S. Thousand (Eds.), *Restructuring for caring and effective education: Piecing the puzzle together* (2nd ed., pp. 56–76). Baltimore: Paul H. Brookes.

Van der Klift, E., & Kunc, N. (2002). Beyond benevolence: Supporting genuine friendships in inclusive schools. In J. S. Thousand, R. A. Villa, & A. I. Nevin (Eds.), *Creativity and collaborative learning: The practical guide to empowering students, teachers, and families* (2nd ed., pp. 21–29). Baltimore: Paul H. Brookes.

VanderVen, K., & Brendtro, L. (2009). From power to empowerment. *Reclaiming Children and Youth, 17*(4), 3.

Villa, R. A. (1991). *Collaborative planning: Transforming theory into practice* (35 minutes). Port Chester, NY: National Professional Resources. Retrieved July 20, 2009, from http://www.nprinc.com/inclusion/vcpct.htm

Villa, R. A. (2005). Voice of inclusion: Everything about Bob was cool, including the cookies. In R. A. Villa & J. S. Thousand (Eds.), *Creating an inclusive school* (2nd ed., pp. 125–135). Alexandria, VA: Association for Supervision and Curriculum Development.

Villa, R. A., & Thousand, J. S. (1992). Student collaboration: An essential for curriculum delivery in the 21st century. In S. Stainback & W. Stainback (Eds.), *Curriculum considerations in inclusive classrooms: Facilitating learning for all students* (pp. 117–142). Baltimore: Paul H. Brookes.

Villa, R. A., & Thousand, J. S. (2005). *Creating an inclusive school.* Alexandria, VA: Association for Supervision and Curriculum Development.

Villa, R. A., Thousand, J. S., & Nevin, A. I. (2008). *A guide to co-teaching: Practical strategies for facilitating student learning* (2nd ed.). Thousand Oaks, CA: Corwin.

Villa, R. A., Udis, J., & Thousand, J. S. (2002). Supporting students with troubling behavior. In J. S. Thousand, R. A. Villa, & A. I. Nevin (Eds.), *Creativity and collaborative learning: The practical guide to empowering students, teachers, and families* (2nd ed., pp. 56–76). Baltimore: Paul H. Brookes.

Villalobos, P., Eshilian, L., & Moyer, J. (2002). Empowering secondary students to take the lead: Training activities to promote advocacy, inclusion, and social justice. In J. S. Thousand, R. A. Villa, & A. I. Nevin (Eds.), *Creativity and collaborative learning: The practical guide to empowering students, teachers, and families* (2nd ed., pp. 431–464). Baltimore: Paul H. Brookes.

Villalobos, P., Tweit-Hull, D., & Wong, A. (2002). Creating and supporting peer tutor partnerships: Lesson plans. In J. S. Thousand, R. A. Villa, & A. I. Nevin (Eds.), *Creativity and collaborative learning: The practical guide to empowering students, teachers, and families* (2nd ed., pp. 405–430). Baltimore: Paul H. Brookes.

von Oech, R. (1986). *A kick in the seat of the pants: Using your explorer, artist, judge, and warrior to be more creative.* New York: Harper and Row.

von Oech, R. (1998). *A whack on the side of the head: How you can be more creative.* New York: Warner Books.

Vygotsky, L. (1987). *The collected works of L. S. Vygotsky* (R. W. Rieber & A. S. Carton, Trans.). New York: Plenum Press. (Original works published in 1934 and 1960)

Walter, T. (1998). *Amazing English!* New York: Addison-Wesley.

Webb, N. M. (1989). Peer interaction and learning in small groups. In N. M. Webb (Ed.), *Peer interaction, problem-solving and cognition: Multidisciplinary perspectives* (pp. 21–29). New York: Pergamon Press.

Wehmeyer, M. L. (2007). *Promoting self-determination in students with disabilities: What works for special-needs learners.* New York: Guilford Press.

Wehmeyer, M. L., Abery, B., Mithaug, D., & Stancliffe, R. (2003). *Theory in self-determination: Foundations for educational practice.* Springfield, IL: Charles C Thomas.

Wheldall, K., & Colmar, S. (1990). Peer tutoring for low-progress readers using "pause, prompt and praise." In H. C. Foot, M. J. Morgan, & R. H. Shute (Eds.), *Children helping children* (pp. 117–134). New York: John Wiley & Sons.

Wheldall, K., & Mettem, P. (1985). Behavioral peer tutoring: Training 16-year-old tutors to employ the "pause, prompt, and praise" method with 12-year-old remedial readers. *Educational Psychology, 5*(1), 27–44.

Wilde, J. (n.d.). Workshop 4: Teaching persuasive writing; Unit on persuasive writing. In *WRITE in the middle, a workshop for middle school teachers.* Retrieved November 16, 2009, from an Annenberg Media Web site: http://www.learner.org/work shops/middlewriting/prog4.html

Zins, J., Bloodworth, M., Weissberg, R., & Wahlberg, H. (2007). The scientific base linking social and emotional learning to school success. *Journal of Educational and Psychological Consultation, 17*(2/3), 121–210.

Index